Thank you so exceptionally much for your love, care, & support. Though there was a printing error, it's corrected.

The Sands of Yesterday

(The Second Three Fountains)

(November 2017 Release)

This batch will help show the Seed Fund idea

Robert James Koyich

& also earn reviews for Amazon to encourage future sales. Huge amounts of love & light & luck to you & Sandrago PLVRE! Robert

DEDICATION

To the process and development of all things past, present, and future.

Muddled between space and time.

Devoted beyond the understanding of this very moment.

Expanding into and from forever.

CONTENTS

Review Copy Introduction

The book that you have in your hands is a review copy, not the finalized version. The process I've committed to needs to be pushed further. With a main focus of the book, the Seed Fund, I know that we cannot earn money unless the books are sold. That will require a) readers, b) a book to sell, and c) readers that buy the book.

The copy you have in your hands is given to a promise to review the, all-be-it not entirely completed work and post on Amazon your honest opinion of what you'll read. The strategy with this is present the book to you and receive your posted review on Amazon to encourage sales of the book in the future.

I wanted to have the book available for sale by December 1st 2017, though the editing of the work is a grueling process that was taking a lot of time to complete. I felt urgency of how we need to have a book to sell, to earn money for the Seed Fund.

With these ideas in mind, I shall continue the editing process, and know that I need to do a lot more revision and work on this book before it is ready for mass consumption.

Thank you to Kyle McDonald, Mark Klassen, Bert Steur, Josh Hayden, Wesley MacLeod, and dear Opal Sprite (Shannon Nielen) for the $120 to buy the first batch of review copies.

It's a shared effort, network, and development of ideas we hold, so please dive deep into my exposition of thought presented in this work.

Peace, Love, Unity

The Respect part is something that I also must earn.

I shall.

Robert James Koyich – November 21st 2017

Seeds of Tomorrow

(The 4th Fountain)

Now to Then

(Part One in the series: *The Fountains of Faith*)

ROBERT KOYICH

INTRODUCTION TO THE 4th FOUNTAIN

Before Starting the Book (March 3rd, 2017)

Some would call her an angel, yet I call her my daughter. Her seeds of life shared by the Universe in the years that have passed. By the time she reads this book, she'll have lived for 10 years here on this planet. The ideas of her universal secrets and guidance have yet to unfold, yet told that the fragments of the stars hold her spirit. I can't tell her so clearly that her heart was formed of stone.

Some things repeated time and time again, some things mentioned only as a shard of instinct, and some linked by parameters not of this world. Her sister is one that holds the folds of time, though the rhymes course through the forces that are. There's still plenty for us to learn about her and how and who she is blended with eternity.

We evolve. We change. We always remember. Yet, though, forgetfulness hounds my memory.

I can't call her by name. She knows full well that would taint her being. Yet still known by the powers that have yet to unfold, the words were written on the psych ward wall.

I've been told to release the past, yet the faith of the *Seeds of Tomorrow* has yet to unfold. I told a bold lie to say that it was I that showed her how to cry. Though I still crave to complete the ideas of a lost soul, I cradle the depths of depravity that hold me down. Guarding us on Earth without needing to fly up to the heavens with wings of our own.

Silence holds a tone you still hear… The signals of the breath are something you may hold dear as a tear. The shoulsmen remember her gift, yet to lift up the wings of Dawn to show us of how some things must always carry on. Thanking too, my mother Sharon and my father Ron.

From the *Sands of Yesterday* the works flourish, and though the wish of delicate deceit's what holds the boat to the dock, there is talk to Spock to remind us the fact there's no other path to walk.

I stretch outwards to words for tomorrow. Not quite searching, yet gleaning every moment of time and thought and space at an unyielding pace. Who we are, cycling the card like a lost and stolen star, were held in the meld of the tar stopping the car before the measures from another bard's bar.

I can't yet fathom the explicit joy that creeps into the corners of her and my toes. The rows of text form one after the next share there's much held in the *Key to Me*. A lonely shifted path of one plus one math to remind us that the soul holds true. Just remember, dear Celest, that there are times you forgot about me too.

I share my heart with the world now. There *is* no other way. Adding to the prerogative to learn, love, live, thrive, create, play and pray, I still remember to earn for some things to extend into forever, even if only for a day.

Peace, Love, Unity, and an infinite layer of how some lovestones only want another solid and respectful partner and not a player.

CHAPTER ONE – A Grain of Sand

Though we've not met, the pets greet with a kind gesture. The idea of PLUR has been held in the weld, and though I don't know who you'll become, I remember I need to share the story of where you come from.

This book, Aeris, is for our family. Although I had thought of you, Celest, and Paradox even a decade before I wrote this, there are some grains of truth that extend back into my own youth. I had thought that I'd adopt, yet I know not if this is the case now.

I had not yet known your Mom, though I could see our home in my mind. The aquarium surrounding your bed is even held in my mind now. I see the windows of your room and the desktop upon which you work upon. Though I think you're three to five years away from when I wrote this, I sip in the cinematic and contialitic bliss while dreaming of the first kiss. Your Mom may not have yet known about me for a long time, yet I still hadn't a clue who she is to be. Maybe you are a grain of sand that already passed through the hourglass. I can't yet know for sure.

Your Grandpa is one that's taken great care of me. I hope they know that I want to shine out and through my own doubt about the plan. The thoughts of the plot are for the path of our story. I had wanted our home to be close to my Dad, though I've still not been clear about how we get to that point. One thing that I want to help teach you is how to dream. I hope you have a clarified vision of what you want, and then have the gumption and support to help yourself reach your dreams! I've thought about our home since 2011 or so, and the goal is to have the professional draft of our home set and made by September 5th, 2019.

I want to invest further time in designing our home. It may be a lost obsessive point, yet I also want to envision events, activities, and people in our home. You know it, though I still may have fear and a lack of faith. I have ideas about how you are brought up, and there are lessons that my parents have given me that I'll relay to you. I don't know yet if you'll have a brother or sister. I can't even imagine who YOU are to be, let alone know or believe that I meet your Mom. There still were so many pieces to the puzzle that needed to be found and placed. I tell you my stories, it just may be we need to be patient.

Your Grandma might like that our home be built in Canada. I have my own cares for her, and I think of the lessons I've been learning. I'm thankful that she's closer to me now than she had been through the years before, and I do hope you get to see her often. I think she holds my fear that we'll never meet because I may be too bold and fearful or meek and courageous. The balance isn't clear.

I'm wondering how we use this book for us too. I don't know what you would want to know of my past, and if the title is *Seeds of Tomorrow* when I wrote this, it's clear that you're one of the most important seeds that I tend. The Fountains books take about 3-5 months to write, though I think I could produce them faster. It does depend on life and my own understanding.

Since we don't yet know who your Mom is, there's the case I can write about the lovestones (women) I meet and have met. I had been given the advice to document the process, and that's partly what I'm doing. I too am thinking about how our garden is be a decade after being planted. There are some plants that only stay around for only a year, yet there also are some return year after year as we fall through the cycles of time. No matter where we live, I find a way to bring you to your grandparents once or twice a year and also invite them to our house too!

It's the case that the stars are far away. They align. Perchance I should think of the time closer to myself now instead of where you are when you get this. Perchance this book should not be just for you, Aeris. I need to let my imagination and heart twist through the Universe and bring it back to you. For now, though, I still need to search and seek for the lovestone that comes to honour, love, and protect you too. A grain of sand in the oyster of time. A delicate pearl that I ensure we unfurl.

I ask you to remain true to yourself. You find your heart revel in things and people that aren't there yet. I see the truth unfold from the first moments I hold. The ideas of the kitten's purr too finds the soft fur to nuzzle up and sup with the idea of a cup overflowing. We also show that, though I didn't know. The hope is still to bridge me to the points where we need to be. The words speak back to my heart, yet how can I know we arrive at our point of meeting?

How can we assure that the Universe does have my back? Maybe you *aren't* the will of God. Perchance my own foolish heart's clouded my being with the tears that're yet held in my soul.

I release control of the dream and write for those that'll team up to ensure you and I meet. The seeds are shared with some on the street and there are ideas that hold the beat to my being. While the fear of seeing deep into her eyes find I have no need to wear a disguise, the slight rise and fall of breath call out to her now. I can't concur that she knows yet either if it's for sure. The purification of my being finds that there are some who'll let us know where we come from.

What is taken to form the dream? The truth is held in the reams of text. What does it matter if another is next to you is to heed what I wrote? The sequence of the note shares that some who carry a wish pair her with the child when filed away into the night of the first day's light.

You can't tell me what to do for the next few years. You aren't yet able to speak to me, other than the intuition that comes from this. A certain curtain of bliss brings us up to sup. I hope you know that the pup is still to become a Shivan though I can't yet live in the same moment of intent that you've sent. The vents clear and clarify it's God, perchance, who'll tell us how and why.

I can tell you, though, that some of the gals that I've met in my life caught my heart. I wonder too of the people that you know and meet that aren't directly part of our family tree. There are some people that *are* part of our family, though, when you read this, that includes quite a few that I'd not known when this book was made. The combination of two lives into one through marriage melds quite a few different worlds, sometimes.

Will you have met the Haaves and the Wrys? They were the closest I had to brothers and sisters when I grew up. In the years before this book, I barely heard from any of them. That is partly since I've not made enough effort to contact them and there are many that I've not reached out to too. In the creation of these books, I had isolated myself a lot. It's not been a good feeling to do so, sometimes, though I've also thought that it's easier to be on my own. I wrote these books to learn and share my understanding and ideas about life. With some people, I have so much to say, and then there are others that I've left alone and have nothing to share.

Within the past six months, I've been held at home with my excuses and actions that have found me near alone. It's easier to be alone. There can be no one to hurt. There's no one to worry about having to care for. It's weird that I've cared so much for some I'm not allowed to be with, while forgetting about those that do love and care. Perchance some of them are afraid to reach out to *me*.

I want to tell you that we'll be okay. I want you to be there to ask all the questions you want answers to, and tell you my truth from my heart. I want to help you find your dreams. I also want to keep some things hidden from you to surprise you with love and joy when you think there's none in the world.

I fear to let you down. I fear that you won't want to be part of our family. I fear to lose you before you were even formed in the womb. I can and must resume with my life, though if I'm to meet you I'll need to not just live, though rather thrive! I'm terrified of thriving for I fear the hurt and betrayal that had hounded me in my past. I need to let go of so many things and wish that the rings of Saturn *do* orbit around my soul.

I pray well for our longevity and that we have more than enough for ourselves and our family. I also want to ensure that we allow our hearts to care. I fear the future from my own lack of faith that we *can* and *will* meet the ones that you grow up with. We honour, nurture, and nourish. We also provide.

The world isn't just our own selves.

I woke up early today. It was my intent earlier in the year to be up and out of bed each day before nine AM each morning. There were times when I worked at Wendy's in the past where I'd work closes and would be home near three or five in the morning and then sleep until the early afternoon. There also were times when I had no job that I'd stay up to 5-7 AM and sleep until the late afternoon. It's only in the past few months that I've stopped staying up late and instead have gone to bed at a reasonable hour. Even though I hadn't yet found my own solution, I still didn't want to abuse the fact that we can choose how we live. I wish not to abuse the freedoms that have been granted to me.

Our intent is a vital thing. When I've had intents to do some things, I've often lacked the resolve and commitment to follow through in what I've said I'll do. When we make commitments or promises it's sometimes easy to break those promises when they are made to our own selves. Those broken promises, though, can erode our own integrity. Accountability to other people can be easier and effective. Some other's lessons have taught this too... that we *won't* let down another when we've promised them. This is where I can strengthen my own actions and ethics; by making promises and keeping my word. I want to learn how to honour myself also, though.

I'm not clear, Aeris, if you and I have met some of the people that have been guiding and teaching us. There are some famous people that I like and have looked up to in the past few years, and although I won't push myself into their lives. I do, though, want to allow myself to earn the right to directly connect with some of them. This isn't just for the one gal that I had wanted to be your Mom, yet rather for some other people that I've been fortunate to learn from and have written to before. I again, though, need to clarify my intent.

With a previous book, I had wanted to share a copy with Lewis Howes, though I think I have been a bit pushy with him. I had been over-focused by pushing my own work. We need to think of what we do to help other's lives and processes. We also can't always think of our own benefit. I hope you find your heart and life and work to be for *other* people and not to be so much focused on what *you* gain; such as I have so often.

Fancifully, I wonder what the Internet will be like when YOU are a teenager! This takes my mind to tour our home again. I think of how of the windows of your room also have a visual/monitor type of projection on them. Younger people sometimes have a stronger link and understanding of technology. This makes me wonder how you'll be and what skills you'll learn.

My imagination, right now, seems to fantasize that you'll form your own network and community around your creative wants and wishes. I somehow intuit that you're be so much further into a life of integrated possibility than I was at your age. I've also had the fear of when you'll move away when you grow up. It's like I grieve you before you even have been formed in the womb. The points of time so much far further into the future. It's weird how I can't imagine meeting your Mom yet, yet also feel the sadness (and, yes, a layer of joy) that you'll grow your own life, and wings, and move into a future and life that'll be your own. You grow up into a young adult.

There's also a layer of edge and excitement at the boundaries of the skin on my arms as I type this to you. In the moment I write this, I feel the gladness of knowing we live in our home. One thing that I wish for in my life is a certainty. I've not grasped that feeling so often. I've so often shifted from full belief in an amazing future, to the fear that I'm just spinning my wheels. The faith, hope, and confidence I've sometimes held hadn't been so frequent. I pray, hope, and wish that you find contentment, peace, and you own assuredness that you'll be okay with your life. I'm a very accepting person. That's a good thing sometimes.

Being accepting, though, is another thing that I fear of myself. It's a fear of complacency; that I'll accept whatever happens and not push, work, and strive for what I want. I've sometimes thought of myself as lazy, yet also know that I've had some points of time where I've invested so much effort and work into life. This past winter there was a lot of snow, and I remember the excitement of having an 18-hour shift shoveling. I love the feeling of having worked or put in a great deal of effort, yet sometimes am terrified that I've accomplished nothing.

From an exercise from Lewis' book *The School of Greatness*, I set a goal of selling 15,000 books by August 1st, 2017. At the point of when I typed this, I hadn't sold a single book online during the first two and a half months of 2017. I'm scared of this. This is what I meant by how I put in a great deal of effort and wishes to have yet seen so few results. There are the wishes and hopes that my work is like a glacier, and just that the fragments of the books haven't yet reached the point of breaking off into the ocean. I also remind you that moments of déjà vu that you'll have are a kind reminder that you may be on the right track and path.

So, Aeris, this book, and series, *The Fountains of Faith*, started with you in mind. I've talked only a little bit about this with some people, yet I encourage you too to talk about your dreams, work, and projects. By talking about what we want and what we want to do with other people, we strengthen our faith. Though I have barely any accountability to other people directly, I fortify my own commitments by believing in our future and by working toward it. If I've had a lack of action and effort by committing to myself, then what shall I do for other people like yourself? Perchance I do more of the right things.

Though you were not yet even conceived in flesh at the point of me writing this, I thank you and apologize for using you in the way I have. I complete this and future works and though Celest may not be happy that I focused so much on you with this, I also had her birth in mind. It could be just you, your Mom, and myself as our core family, though the idea of having three kids in our nuclear family also is a notion for an only child.

Brad just messaged me about the rain today. It was raining earlier in the morning, which meant we were to not go work outside to trim hedges. The rain stopped, so we'll work today. I guess this means that this chapter was formed and that I need to head back out and go to work. I don't like landscaping. I'd prefer to work on my dreams. It doesn't feel good to have to be out in the cold, yet I also think of how some people don't even have a home. I still have work to do to make sure we help with the Seed Fund. I just would prefer the money for the seeds come from our books and not working outside in the rain.

As your grandpa would say; love you kiddo!!

CHAPTER TWO - In the Fields and Gardens

Some seeds are planted row on row, yet together the sunlight is needed to let them grow.

It was 11:49 PM on March 15th, 2017 when I typed the previous sentence. Part of my being wanted to go brew a pot of coffee and drain the words out from my being and into this book. Should I look into the fact that the days are where we also form the text? Do we need the sunlight to shine, or dare the night to be the soil in which I plant the design?

I often used to stay up all night and work on the computer. I'd get obsessive and spend hours on Facebook messaging people and reading the full news feed; not leaving a single post unread. Over the past few months I've barely been on Facebook. I've just used it as a way to push promote some things and I'm not clear that I had gained much in friendships with the use of the platform. I have even pushed away quite a few people by messaging obsessively and contacting them too often.

Since the previous year, I've been working and studying, yet I still think I've not been using the technology available to me to form friendships in creative ways. I think I've been too pushy.

"A seed that heeds from the wise through the vast disguise of Earth... Realizing that Heaven calls out for us to remain there and reveal its worth."

(11:54 PM March 16th, 2017)

Thank you again, Gary... You've fueled far more than I can comprehend.

I *have* been looking to impress others. I *am* wanting to reveal my faults. I *do* want to purge my secrets. I also, definitely, have been doing what I think I *should* do by the guideposts of others.

Lewis, you may not read this book, though you've given me many a seed through your book, work, emails, and podcast. I think I've been trying to plant *my* garden with *your* seeds, though. Your lessons have been taken in and they hold extraordinary value. I need to heed, though, that my garden of life is a different form. The practice of positive habits is crucial, though sometimes they've led to me doing some things that I've stifled myself with. The idea of being in bed by midnight and up earlier in the morning is being tossed aside tonight. I know that my addictions are NOT healthy (especially the ciggies) and tonight I throw out all of my #adulting and work on this book.

I've been a lot of talk for the past two months in saying that I've been writing books. I've released a few books and gotten *some* work done, though I've been posting myself up against time with things that aren't in line with who I am. Christy Whitman would say we need to set our intents in line with our being, and my being is one that seems to piss away the time working, seeding, and forcing the process. I use that word explicitly... *forcing* the process.

There are some things I've been doing that're going to be good for our long-term. I also know that by being 'responsible' and sleeping early and not putting in extra hours (like last night when I could have written, though chose to go to bed) that I've been stealing from myself. I want to write and create future books and not just rely on that already made. From the book *The School of Greatness*, I printed out a certificate of achievement that says "I've sold 15,000 books online and have earned enough seed money to house two people for the duration of one year." How's that going, Rob!?!?!

Well... to answer that... pretty f'ing awful!

I've not sold a single online copy of my books all of 2017 (On March 17th, 2017 I sold the first copy!). Some people have said that we need to invest in ourselves and our dreams, though if I'm not even able to buy books to sell, am I really just wasting my time?

I've talked so much nonsense through the years; Natalie this or 'book book' that. Music? PLUR? What have I really done? I think I've followed the advice of people with my own selfish interests toward finding my own path.

Seal would be disgusted at me for the lack of effort I've put into life, and though I loved Gabby's book *The Universe Has Your Back,* I haven't even, from my own self-judgment, am still far too judgmental.

I've made some commitments. I've also honoured them. I *do* want to sell books and haven't demonstrated strong sales skills yet. I know that I want to remove the conditional things in my life so that I *can* selfishly do whatever I want to do! I want my Freedom Solution; to do what I want to do, where I want to do it, when I want to do it, with whom I want to do it, and with full financial support.

I desire to have my own earned income from book and music earnings, and I've also not yet made the correct steps to do so. I have a negative view of push promotions. I see all sorts of tricks and tactics from other people (even those I like and admire) and if *I'm* to support myself with my creative work, then I *must* write, form the pages, and *also* sell them!

What about the books that are out up to now? I think some of them are good, though I also catch myself and my own marketing tactics and gimmicks. It trips me up a bit to think I'M being sneaky and sly!

With *Fragments of Intent,* my wish is to be able to order as many copies of the book as I want and give the books away to anyone I want to. I don't want to have to sell books or ask for sales. I have, oddly, some messed up inner idea that I *shouldn't* be pushing for sales. The idea of the Seed Fund is a money thing though.

My greed and want of earning money are too much and too little! I've told some people about the Seed Fund, yet I've been using the idea of the fund as a tactic. The idea of sharing money earned from book sales is what I *shall* do, though I think it's too sourced from an idea of my own prosperity.

I could tell you anything with this book. Maybe there're some things that I say and share that taint other's opinions of me. Aeris, I don't know how we'll get there. I have zero clues about your Mom and I don't even have a clue how deep down the rabbit-hole people find us tumbling, mumbling, and fumbling towards ecstasy with not even myself standing next to me! Then I think of the entrepreneur people. How much is money worth to you?

I send a wish and prayer out there. I wish that we always have enough money to help and share. I wish that we reach the future date of 2053 and still be alive with people we like, love, and know. I wish that we're able to find our own Freedom Solution, and that in the next three years we'll have done a great deal of good for the world. More than I yet comprehend.

Gary Vaynerchuk? Up to the point of now, I've not really had the full want to meet with you. You're a rad and amazing person and guide, yet I still seem to see you as one that would know I've been so lax, foolish, and lazy. I also know I'm not trying to form a business and that business is your full devotion, even if secondary to your family. The audio file that played before I wrote this chapter was *The Ultimate Advice for Every 22-Year-Old.* I want to purge my innards into this chapter like how you were shedding the layers of the Taylor who you spoke with.

I want to speak the truth. I know I can be quite deceptive and manipulative due to my own wants and fears. I also know that I've sadly invested a great deal of my being into the world by intent, and not by action. If I'm to be a writer, then WRITE!!! I can't just be adulating and adulting by going to bed early when I have work to do! I can't just expect the world to magically happen and grant me my wants, wishes, and dreams! I also know that I can't expect another to launch me forward into the Glass House. It must be EARNED!!! (Though what *value* do I have to convey?!)

I won't be so negative in the other chapters of this book, though, again, I want to shed some things. I also, then, wanted to slash again. Not by full action, though I know that I get far too poor me and pity party and that I'm not searching for sympathy either. I'm too concerned about what other people think!

Through the years I've learned and also been told so many things, and the fact of what I want to do also crosses some of my own ethical boundaries. I've gotten pissed off at other people and how they behave when I, myself, have some things that I do and think that're not fully good or cool!

The reason I want to shed all of my negative thought and emotion is for my own self. I'm exceptionally self-focused and, sometimes, aware. When I've been pushing away and/or have been mad at the very few that reach out to me, then I almost want to say "Forget them" and focus ENTIRELY on my own work. I'd prefer not to have to deal with other people's control dramas.

I'm in my garden. Not all the people that visit want to help grow and tend with me. Some want to take seeds or things that I've grown. I have a good garden, I have good soil, and I'll share my seeds with those who want to cultivate also. We plant in the fields and help grow the good things in other's gardens. I just need to protect myself from the others that want to take from us.

Our lives are delicate. I've been too accepting of some things and people. I'm one who helps others without, yet I also note that some without just want to plunder and take from me. I don't know what some people's intents are, and I also don't want to be used by people. I want to use myself, and my resources, to help some and note that when others have been trying to force themselves into my life, that not all those people *are* honourable. Again, though, I don't know people's intents. I must not make assumptions.

Dare I shed away every other asker and be a giver instead of one who is taken from? Is it *my* greed that I want the Seed Fund to grow? Are some of the people asking for help just *posing* as friends? Am I so lacking in truth that I can't even form my own cohesive defense as to who is true or not? I've scared all the birds away. My intuition, though, tells me a few many things that assure me I'm not to be used and deceived.

I need to clarify my intent. I need to guard against the ravens. I must not forget there *are* some that do care *and* want to help us come from a point of love. There also are some others that see *me* as the dove and still want to break its wings. I wish not to reveal other people's secrets.

There's a delicate line that nudges me to who is true, and away from who isn't. Sometimes the rhymes are a way to see through the ruse and deception of those in the plot. A knot tied up sure to ensure that the contialitic blur finds me to *know* who are the real friends, and who are just trying to keep me obscure.

On to the next chapter... I think I'm getting closer to ready.

CHAPTER THREE – An Overtone Seed

Google 'Yellow Overtone Seed' - the **www.astrodreamadvisor.com** link holds an explanation! We are guides to heed the need to disguise the rise and fall of Earth.

Though told that we hold the bold stare of the stars in bards of awkward measure, they remove the guise of her sacred treasure. Pleasures of the underground hear MindSound, yet each bound book looks into the text of one whose sects have held the cons and community. There are hidden lines of the infernal mutiny.

I bond, refuse, and choose to not evade paying dues. Instead, pray with the heart of how I'm a bundle of falsities that others wish to rip apart. The scolding start charts the galaxy in a teardrop to find her terrified I never stop.

Though you are in the thought of the plot of this story, there's a quarry found in the signals of meth from the breath of the ground. Though Beth was not bound to Katie and Matthew, the facts of what they tell her may be true. The fantasy is pulling all the cards to ensure the lad's words and prose are to find a sequence of time's shards to not be jumped like fences of time's tenses.

I must wait, even if there is an eternity before we even agree to the first date. I know too that the state of wellness finds the issues press the Latin influx of trucks into the dissected plucks. Ducks line up in the reservoir with a reservation of the nation to aid the condensation. A consecration avoids the constellation, yet a variation of even one small hooded sweater ensures the curses don't cross the letter.

Dot your J's and cross your F's as the staffs are what they believe I'm searching for. Though true that she's to resume the ways that the word's frays of text wind, threads find the next way I can't yet say "Forever and a Day". Another ought not to presume that she rides the loom. There's a midden bidding for me to be in the Sea to assure people keep the mule free of plume. The glee sometimes crosses face with voracious pace of text that shared the next idea. Respect and love to be something that ensure we connect.

I said I shouldn't reach out to you, and it's true. There are many others that have a clue, yet won't share that other cue. The *Deep Blue View* reminds me that we wind me up like a watch (or a bomb) to see if I'll freak out or stay calm. Though the fact that I abstain from the toss, I also note that if I'm going to church, why do I not leave my woes and fears upon the cross? I know that the loss of my intents have found you vent and be content with the addition of omission and how there's space to travel with the mission.

I found you. You never knew. I see your eyes. You forgot about mine too.

Though the years have shed the red fire and the sire, I do hope that you find the winding repetition found by my omission. I can't claim to know you, who you are, and what you do as a star. The other people also never seem to show the subtle unions that we used to know each other. While letting us flow, the mother shows the rose exposes the tender defender that rushes to the blushes. It brushes past each painter to shift the rift and gift the ideas of yesterday as she hushes me up.

I thank the sacred tether of tomorrow. I'm not wanting to be used as a horse to the source because of the feathers they wish to steal. It sometimes asks me to reveal that I've been linked to few that *are* true. I hope that timeframe passes and that I find some other great and amazing friends from the classes. I won't be negative or used, and though the elective has fused the idea of how some people read, I understand that I'm a Yellow Overtone Seed who knows some tones add clones for and from afar for those in the zones that need.

I thank all of the stars might for allowing me to be honest, true, and right. By my own internal plight, I keep this with what I made in the nights I refused to sleep. I can't yet share how much they've fused to have what I keep, yet I also make steep accusations of how we aid and nourish many nations by not diving deep into sleep.

I'll write much about the Seed Fund and hope that people don't use or abuse. Though some have gained a ruse, there's a selected path we make to assure you too choose. I wish not to confuse, and I also wish not to use deception. A creation of intents shares the interjection like contents of a mystical instant mention.

I mustn't lend or borrow for the *Seeds of Tomorrow*. Each friend makes amend with reparations for the variations of my own mistakes. Though knowing some of the reals become fakes, there's also the reverse. Some wish to steal what I disperse and converse to share the seeds like a dandelion. Ms. Bernstein, let me glean insight into when I'm doing things right. It's like a social curse to be like "Heellllooo nurse!!"

The owl takes flight while the dragonfly holds the sign and sight of the mantis as this is in an involution from another world's contribution. The distribution of the bread and body aren't always just. I must understand the depths of the land and find us unify the heavens with the dispersal of seven elevens. One grain of sand held in the oyster juice finds Bill to conduct and conduce a drink of how I'm sometimes the one who seems think obtuse when they try to put it in the caboose.

From other people who've moved the knot be tied, I've vied for the chance to dance in the waters that enhance the web of the True Cyber Ebb. I receive the fateful weave of how they wish cleave. Truth adds and multiplies from the unity of youth. Though I'm to be held in the booth, the tooth isn't removed as others have reproved. You've removed the spin of kin and share the tin with those who ARE truly part of the heart within. We win and find a clear missed intent of how they know full well they aren't to ship the ideas into a tent.

I thank the Universe and God for the fact they teach and reach a pact. This allows the plows to dig deep into the sands of sleep and assure we reap a harvest of full yield. Though my own pull of greed has been revealed, I still wield the way we say 'Forever and a day'. I've feared to pray and note that my own actions have shed those led to the goat.

I still lie too often. It should be never. We've been told to be surreal and not clever. It severs from how they seem to deem the teams are ever clear in the ear when we choose not to hear. I thank my dreams of yesteryear to be held with my future dear. You've helped me rear up our child to have found our angst filed away into she smiled the first day. I wish and pray we may find each way to say that there are billions on *this* planet that teleport us to *That Day*.

My addictions and vices cross through all the devices, and though the prices to keep are steep, they also are what my heart yearns for too deep. I can't, and must not, weep for you any longer. I hadn't for years. I mustn't claim that my love becomes stronger, it might deepen your fears. I can't claim I know you too, for the facts are painted in a violet hue that there are many thousands of people that also shed your tears askew.

It's like I'm almost always near the beginning. It sometimes feels like the end. My friends are ones who've been pinning, which makes me want to believe they pretend, yet I've continued to make assumptions about others and their motives. The gives and takes find the waves in cakes that want to ensure Dave takes each letter and the effect that every one of them makes.

I'm far too poetic sometimes. I also know the devotion to the rhymes till some seeds of how this needs to be written in lines. Cos sines of English only a fraction of what's been put to the page as different alphabets and tones shift characters from the stage. I can't see through your eyes. I have an idea that you've seen through mine and every one of my lies. Some people say life is short. I don't agree. It's like I've been around forever, yet can't even see the moment of when and why you would be close, let alone sitting across from me to never sever.

From the ocean to the sea. In the devotion a notion of how to be. Erosion of every key into the shivering quiver of who we deliver. Please take in a deep breath and reset yourself to how you are naturally free.

I cast an arrow across the stone. Though some things have already happened and aren't to be known. I wish for the fish find the repetition of the tone to have clearly shown that it's our soul I've come to have shown. I still live in fear. I've been terrified of the safest things. The terror of being wealthy is one thing that pings my own concern. It's the fact that I've had decades to learn. Perchance I did not pay attention to the blatant signs you forced me to mention, and perchance it is I, rather, I know, it is I, who betrayed YOU time and time and time again.

I've not been respectful sometimes. There are some points where I've been goaded to violent thoughts. I've been honourable to some, though the idea is that I've focused dislike upon a few reminds me to keep away from the anger, rage, arrogance, deceit, (lust), and greed that I seem to sense. I was to type 'I show', yet I also believe I also weave away from the creation of negative seeds to sow. I, maybe, say it far too often, yet it's love and luck that we've had.

My patterns are clear. This should be a concern. I'm predictable and one that they could smite at any minute. That idea is what causes me a fear of one who is completely infinite. I told you I'm afraid I'm just sitting here on my crystal seat in the sky. I told you I can't run the marathon merely to find the heavens accept me for *any* reason why. I doubt, and almost refuse to even think, about Heaven and Hell. Dreams tell me the memories of these lots of life I've cast. She's never been in my future because I never seem to last.

I'll start a project, plan, or habit and then grab it away from my own heart. I've stolen every moment of my future because I've wished for us to start. My own depravity and filth may be magnified, yet I'd prefer it be shared. I wish to have *nothing* to hide.

My past was tainted with decades of lost hope. I also wish to break away from the paths that others would wish for me to only cope. I cannot, and must not, follow what the world tells me to do. Yet that *is* what I've sometimes done. It's like I can't speak the truth, and yet I want to delude myself by assuring no lie is told. Is that why I should shut my mouth and engage not with any thought?

Paradox! I've not forgotten! Celest? Would it be the case the son is unbegotten? My dear lovestone, the phone is something I'd love for you to use! Yet in the suits of spades and hearts we dig deeper into their, and my own, infernal ruse!

For those who are reading this, I feel I've stolen from you too. You don't know the depths of what I've been through, though I also know not how we'll reach the point of seeing the fields bloom. Though a multitude of claims has been made, we must trust that some things have yet to occur. When I was writing this chapter, the book was nowhere near done. By the time you read this, it hopefully will be years after the point of my own gal making the effort to find and abide with me. The points and seeds of the past fuel the memories of the future you are yet to see. I can, though, type a wish for you; dare it even be a prayer for your own self to say.

"Let our hearts always be pure, even if tomorrow will eternally be yesterday for the lies of which they pray."

CHAPTER FOUR – Who Should I Tell?

Bri Severn, THANK YOU! Bri bought the first online copy of *Fragments of Intent* yesterday! It dearly gladdened my heart! A happy-light-foolish and gleeful smile! I've been at the bookwork for two to three years now. I've not, so much, been working on promotion. It was 2016 when I used CreateSpace to form my first book *Finding Natalie*. I had some loving support from Ali and Josh early on to get printed copies of the books and am on my journey.

From Lewis' work and book *The School of Greatness*, the advice was given to write a certificate of achievement for a major goal that made me feel a bit nervous and fearful. I chose 15,000 books to be sold AND to have used the sales to house two people for a full year by August 15th, 2017. The Seed Fund has been talked about in some of my books, though I know not how much of my work you've read. I want to cover some of the Seed Fund idea.

The Seed Fund is a vision and commitment I've made. 30% of all money earned from my online earning (both books and music) is meant for the fund. The big hairy audacious goal of the Seed Fund is to house 250,000 people and give them homes so they need not live on the street. I've estimated that the cost of housing a person $850 for rent per month in our local community, though I also want to help further. For each person that's to be helped with a Full Seed, an allocation of $13,328 per year is needed. This means that when books sell we're able to help people in need.

For right now, as only the very first book has sold, it seems like a great distance from the point of housing the first person. 15% of my snow shoveling, eBay profits, and landscaping earnings have gone to the Seed Fund. Up to now (March 18th, 2017), I've been using this money to buy gift cards to different stores and sharing them with people. At the point of when I typed this section we had $74.76 in the fund and $58 in gift cards. I wonder how future allocations and gifts shall be given. That clarifies as this evolves.

I also read some about homelessness in the town I live. There was a report made for Chilliwack's Social Research and Planning Council that allowed me insight into the situation. Though the report is about two years old, there was some good information. The night I read the report, I started the document file for the Seed Fund to track ideas for how it's used now and for the future. I have some concerns about how some might respond if a person receives help from the fund, and another hasn't. I have faith, though, that we'll be able to work and form a dialogue, discussion, and solution to arising issues. One person I've talked about the idea with knows quite a few people and has knowledge about what it's like to live without a home.

With my responsibility for the Seed Fund, I need to ask and garner support. Sales of the books and music help bring money into the fund itself, yet I have an idea to ask other companies, individuals, and organizations about helping with the fund too. Another friend told me that they think it may be best to just give money to a different and already existing organization in town since logistics are a concern. My thoughts on this idea shift into super-long-term ideas; that the Seed Fund idea is to expand outside our local community.

From Jack Canfield and Lewis Howes' advice (the idea of writing 30 things we want to do, 30 things we want to have, and 30 things we want to be), I had written 'To earn enough money with my creative work to house 1,000 people' and 'to be the founder of a charity that provides homes for 250,000 people'. We know this isn't something I'll be able to do on my own, though I have faith that as we gather enough heart, care, and love, that we're to work to accomplish these objectives.

I then for some reason thought forward to a different personal goal I have that scares me a bit too: The Glass House. I've written about the Glass House in *The First Three Fountains* and want to devote a full chapter to describing it in the future, even if not this book.

I have a concern of audacity about having these seemingly irrational goals. The online lessons from the personal development field recommend having huge goals that seem far out of our reach. I agree with the advice. I have a belief that if we *do* set massive goals for the future, then those wishes and hopes become guideposts that we use to direct ourselves, and others, into a positive future. There are some, though, that don't have wishes, hopes, or goals. That then makes me recall how some people just want a place to sleep.

There's a vast difference in the lives that each of us humans live here on Earth. Even in our local communities, there's a drastic difference between people and how they live. When people have a stable home and enough to eat and drink, their attitudes can also be drastically different.

With some friends, I see that they're just scraping by and are in the trap of *having* to work. There are some that *are* okay with their lives, yet I think of how they're just maintaining. Some people don't have drive and aspirations and are okay with keeping their lives the same. I must remember that success *is* entirely different for each person.

One friend that I've been quite critical of recently gave me some insight and shifted my heart a bit. From my judgmental viewpoint, I was a bit pissed off and frustrated that they were doing so little from my perspective. This same friend, though, reminded me of some things that I had neglected to note about them. They have a home to live in. They've stayed drug-free. They've kept themselves out of the psych ward and are engaged in life. They also do have ideas and plans for the future, even if not so extravagant as my own. The individual has some of the battles with addiction that I've also had, and they *have* made great progress. I had gotten biased and critical of them because they were not having the same magnitude of aspirations as myself.

I also note that even though I have all these huge and expansive goals and hopes and wants, I am a bit inward too. I've said in the past that I want to help some people and work with them to build their lives, yet I, in my own situation, have lacked stepping up and actually helping sometimes. I've not yet had the successful business, the amazing and wonderful relationship, or, even now, have kids or pets. If the Glass House is meant to be a place for people to gather and build lives, then we'll need to gather these skillsets.

One argument is that if the Glass House is to be built in 2025 and that I have the next eight years to gain and earn and learn more about those things. I also, now, creative-wise, have a curiosity. I'm often tangential and I don't stay on topic well. I'm random and have formed scrabbled nattering even with what I write. What happens if it trips people up or even upset them? Is it even kind of weird and pleasing for some people to read as we tumble down the rabbit hole? Who am I telling this to?

The stream of the past two/three pages makes me believe my work is like an Emerald Tapestry. When I type some sentences, I have a few other ideas in my mind that I want to share. Issues confuse my concern about the repetition of topics. I'm not wanting to mention the same ideas or people too much, and also, when in rhyme mode, use the same fragments and sequences of words. I note with the editing of *Fragments of Intent*, that I make many references to my own work. I'm way too self-focused. Additionally added, I also am aware that my mind is like a bit of a gnarled mesh of wires. It fused with different pathways that lead to foundational work. "All the random makes sense!"

Then, regarding the topic of success, I think I'm both far too obsessed and slack. I'm exceptionally neurotic and mental, yet I also sometimes have zero clues as to where I should focus my energy. I push for success, and also don't want to force the process or use too much push promotion. I've been wishing, and not working, for my Freedom Solution. I've been so lax about hustling and actually doing things. I look up to Gary Vaynerchuk and some other online people, though the amount of effort I've put into life is tiny in comparison.

The Ultimate Advice for Every 22-Year-Old audio file reminds we should not compare our lives to others. Gary also teaches that we need to know about ourselves (self-awareness). Many others, including Gary, push 'hustle hustle hustle!!' yet I find I'm just coasting. If I want to have substantial success and fuel the Seed Fund with enough to actually pay for people to have homes, then maybe that'll motivate me to work harder and actually *earn* the privilege to be one to help house people!

Just as success is different for each person, so is motivation! My self-awareness recently is that I have a super strong desire to talk about my ideas and discuss substantial futures, goals, visions, and dreams, yet with whom am I meant to talk with about them? This is something I need and I want to find a solution to. I have found some answers. If you're one to have already read what I write, then you already know that I go throughout a bunch of ideas and that I use my books to help me sort out my own inner world.

Like, for this chapter, I thought I'd gone so far away from the title: *Who Shall I Tell This To*, though I spun back to the previous paragraph saying how *these books* are the channel I use to share. Those who read my books, including myself, are 'who' I'm telling. There are many people that won't read these books, I must find other ways and channels to talk and process these ideas. I need to level up.

I don't want to abuse attention. I have the idea also (yes, a Vaynerchuk one too) to learn to listen and let others be the ones to teach and share. We learn exceptional amounts of life from people if we give them the chance to speak! It may, now, be a rare commodity for us to have people talk to us. As I've been growing up, I note that I've sometimes gotten sick and tired of hearing my own self-speak! I also probably have pushed away so many people by talking so much about my own 'stuff' and wonder if restoration is formed.

I'm thinking that the medium of printed text is the best channel and thing that I can use. I can write ANYTHING I want to, people don't HAVE to read it if they don't want to, AND that those that want to read it have full access to an extensive amount of the random crap that runs through my mind. There also are far fewer interruptions to what I'm saying when I type. The benefits of having the ability to type ideas and books are amazing. Though they rely on the words having value, that's where this experimental exposition helps me learn and share.

I'd like to talk with some people in person. I don't have a strong *need* of being in the company of people, though some do. Maybe it's because I'm not so much searching for people, or maybe I've gotten used to my comfort zone of just reading, studying, and writing without being around others. If I've cut off some friends from mooching from me, I've also lost some of the conversations with them that I would have had if they did come over for cigarettes. There's also a layer of how I also 'lost' my car friends by going without a car since June 2016. A weird thing for me, though, is that I can often see opposite sides of ideas and situations.

One friend a few days ago was alluding that they were out of cigarettes, and I projected that they were reaching out wanting me to offer them smokes without them having to ask. It seemed like they were fishing. Three things about that… One) I don't want to be used by people just for resources. Two) It was in my capacity to help them. Three) I also didn't want to form an unhealthy dependency or expectation. This seems to contradict my statements of intending to be a giver and helping people. The main issue was their fishing; they didn't want to ask.

I like it when people are direct with their wants. If you want something, please just ask. Also, accept if the answer is 'no'. I think this is an idea of conditional friendship that I really don't like. If a person is using another for resources, that really is a pretty aggravating thing unless both people agree to it. Guilt tripping another into offering isn't a call to compassion. True too that sometimes people might not offer help, even when they know it's needed.

With the Seed Fund, there may be quite a few people asking for help, and I need to be ready for that too. There's an idea to have a $50 buffer boundary for people. What I mean by that is that, when we have enough in the fund, that people can borrow a bit, though that there be a limit. It's similar as a $50 overdraft for people. I've been a bit restrictive with money up to now. I've been reluctant to sharing money with some people that have a home as the fund is meant more so for those that're homeless. The buffer idea would allow access to money for those that're in need.

My Dad and Grandpa often have/had given the advice of "Never lend.

Never borrow." Within life, I also know that scarcity and lack *is* a thing. Putting a $50 buffer allows some help to be given, though with defined boundaries. If we use the buffer idea with the Seed Fund, then anyone could borrow, though only up to $50. I know I'm not a bank, yet I still think this a good idea to help people in need.

I've also mathed (yes, I know that's not a verb, though like using it as one) some other ideas out. I'll explain some of the math. For the individual Fountain books, I've set a price point of $9.95US on CreateSpace. The minimum royalty that's received for us selling a copy of a book through Amazon is $3.82. 30% of $3.82 is $1.15. Even though other books may earn more than $1.15 each, the financial principle I use is to assume the lesser of the possibilities. With that premise, I use the $1.15 per book as my number for calculations and allow a greater earning to be made.

For the per person amount for the Full Seed, I wrote initially $15,000 per person. After mathing (again, not a verb) the actual amount is $13,328 per person per year. This amount covers one full year of rent ($850/mo), $50 per week for groceries, and a monthly bus pass. I also told you I want to seek others to help the Seed Fund, yet by presuming no monetary donations are given to the fund, any donations or earnings are extra support. At a $1.15 minimum royalty per book, the yearly Seed Fund need of $13,328 per person holds a concern. We'll need to sell up to 11,590 books per year just to house one person.

Another lesson is how overthinking and obsessing about things can compound and bring us back to fear and lack. From a hopeful point of view of selling books and sharing money with people, my over-processing tripped me up. When written, I was taken to a point where I had a lack of faith that we'll even house one person, let alone the personal goal of 1,000, from my own personal, book, and music and earnings.

When I reach a point of falling to lack, concern, and fear, I then just stop myself there and carry to the next moment. When I'm writing, there actually is an additional layer that I notice where I can't only process my thoughts, though focus in and dissect the minute moments into a longer explanation. This is why I think that people should write to figure out their own ideas and also to explicate them to someone!

When you have a lot on your mind and you want to find some solutions and have no one to process with, I recommend getting onto the computer or writing in a journal. Typing on the computer is *a lot* faster and allows for others to read your words more clearly than handwriting, though handwriting is preferred by some. You may, or may not, want another to read what you wrote, though, still, I think that having space and time to write out our ideas is an exceptionally valuable thing. Some people process verbally, some people just need to meditate and think about their situations. Some people may not yet understand the power of putting their mind, heart, and ideas onto paper or screen.

What I do is use my books as a way to discuss, process, and share some of the ideas that flux through my being. I know that even if no one reads my books that I still have gained. My weird bit of self, though, then also thinks that some of the ideas I have *should* be shared. Information and knowledge should be shared, not hoarded. The challenge and issue we've had with these books, though, is that I do lack structure, sometimes. There's a truth how I've said the Fountain books are my 'process' books as they give me have a place to process and do my 'messy' work. They also are seeds to share.

If I'm to drop one idea into your hand, right now, I give you the challenge to write something for another person. Get on the computer, and write two thousand words to someone telling them anything or everything you'd like to tell them. It may not be easy for some to write 2,000 words, though I bet you'll find some pretty interesting things coming out of your own self by doing so. The recommendation is for and from others to try something new!

The process evolves and shifts, yet I also want to remind people we each have much to say. The step into sharing our hearts with people is one that'll also allow us to learn about others and not just ourselves. Something, I deem, an exceptionally valuable and worthwhile thing.

What'll you write about? (And to whom?)

CHAPTER FIVE – A Glimmering Illusion...

(This Chapter was inspired by Jack Canfield and Principle 12: Act as If. It's a message to myself from my five-year future self.)

About five years ago, you read something in Jack's book *The Success Principles*. It was your second reading of the book and the idea of a "Come As You'll Be" party hadn't yet inspired you to the action of throwing a party of sorts. Now, you've experienced many of these parties in actual living life... though not as an actor. This IS your life.

You found access to the vision for the blueprints of the Glass House, and thought you were meant to have built the home in 2025, it seems that it happened just a bit sooner! Even if she's not the one that we came to settle down with and build the home she's a great friend. Thank Lewis for the introduction! You knew that you were on the right path. You also knew that you've been off course a bit by pushing the process. You also knew the key nights to stay awake at the plow to create the fields of tomorrow.

Thank you for investing your entire, even though flawed, being into the world. I'm grateful about the work you let us do in Chilliwack. The Seed Fund *was* just a seed of its own, and you've found many of the initial seeds grow to maturity. Getting the first five people housed was a difficult process, though you learned how to transfer the program to other communities too. You were terrified of your work, you did lack a lot of faith, though thank you also greatly for staying course and maintaining your promises. Gary was right, the word as the bond is crucial and I thank you for staying true to yourself too!

Though you had only just sold the first copy of *Fragments of Intent*, thank you for sharing that book with the world! It's now a crucial note in your Victory Journal. I thank you for planting that seed for us so that we can live here. Aeris is still just a young one, though you've given her a great home! I also think you chose a pretty cute gal for her Mom! Good choice in lovestones have you!

Thank you also for enduring and keeping faith in yourself and your dreams. The extreme lack of support you had was part of the incubation process. You needed to clean your insides and dredge out all the gunk that was stuck in your being. Thank you for letting me also have gotten through the past five years without having a toke. You also break the chain of addiction to cigarettes. Also, remember that your Dad is 75 years old now. You have 15 years to plan the party and I hope you also see how much surreal and true love you *give* now!

I also thank you for learning so much! The 2018 trip to Italy was a huge step out of your comfort zone and you made it home safely!! 45 bonus points for ensuring you learned the country's language before going there! I also should tell you we've studied some Russian and we've delayed the Saint Petersburg trip until Aeris is 15 years old. I'd like to teach her to speak too!

Also note, I think that your idea of having a passing window between Aeris' room and the second work desk is a good idea. It may have minimized the amount of aquarium space on the western wall of her bed, yet now she can talk to me or her Mom much more easily when we're working there. If Aeris gets too chatty, we just make sure that one of us breaks from our work and are wholly present for her. You had the idea of her to be an only child and not have Paradox and Celest and I think that was a good choice. You've helped create an amazing human with limitless energy!!

I also am wondering about how you gave up on Natalie. I know that you had thought of her for near two decades, though knowing how she lives now, it's a good thing your and her worlds didn't have to combine in marriage. She's so much further out there and adventurous than you, and I really just like being at home and going for one or two major adventures per year. You also didn't know yet that actually living with someone is much different than the idea of who you thought they really would be.

Five years is a lot of time. I think you kind of get that. You had some friends that were not future sighted people, and taking steps toward our prosperity (like going to Toastmasters to learn how to speak) were vital steps that you made for us. Thank you!!! Now, I'm allowed to carry the messages you tended to years ago to a global audience. Your work was not monetarily rewarded yet, though your foundational work now allows ourselves and our family to bring people to our home to work on other projects that have a dramatic impact.

I'm also really glad that you made the island in the kitchen. The island allows us to have guests over and mingle in the kitchen area. The kitchen you designed also allows us to have a few other people help prepare our larger meals without it being too crowded. The idea of having a sleeping area over the master bathroom also was a good idea. Though we don't use it too often, it does give us the chance to have groups of three visit our home instead of just one couple or one pair of business partners.

Even if you've seemed greedy for wanting the Glass House, I'm glad you kept to your income commitment of 50% Seed after $10k a month. Since 25% of your income was for the Freedom Fund, and 10% still goes to Victory Church, you did need to keep what you were earning to *actually* pay for the house. I say you may have needed to keep more for yourself, though as of now, this home is amazing! Thank you for earning it!

I also should let you know that the decision of getting a car back on the road super quick was a good idea. I'm glad you kept a bus pass and actually engaged and interacted with people. I know you were afraid of having more than other people (the fear of envy) and also were not comfortable with being so close to your Freedom Solution. The fact that others *don't* have things pissed you off just enough to make sure we could provide for them too. The added challenge of not only finding your own Freedom Solution, though also wanting to help others find *theirs* is and was the correct choice. Five years later we're loving the fact you made the decision.

I can't tell you if we're living in Australia or Chilliwack though. I have to keep some secrets from you so that you'll squiggle with delight later! The conversation with Natalie wasn't as much of a surprise as it was meant to be, though thank you for letting go of her sooner than you wanted too. Your own gal is so aptly suited to the life we're now leading and, I tell you again, I'm okay with this. She's amazing... You love her... And more importantly, she loves you more than you comprehend. Thank you for making the correct choices!

Thank you also for letting go of your control issues as time progressed. Your faith and trust in the Universe helped us and our family get to where we are. We did work exceptionally hard to get where we are, though if you had known the ability to relax, breathe, and remember that the Universe (and God!) had your (and our) plans in heart, mind, and intent, you would've been much more at peace and not so scared and 'pushy' with your process. Even if neither of us is one of the three corners of The Holy Trinity, They've cared so dearly well for your past, present, and our protected future.

I also let you know that, even five years later, I still think that the trip to Tuscany may have been a good idea. I've no idea how you could've paid for it, though. You had been too hooked up and playing the poor me card. Your fear of prosperity was hindering you in so many ways. You had conscribed to your parents telling of "Robert, you can't afford that" far too much. You parents *did* help you out so much (even back to when you were in your twenties) and I let you know that, even against your own faith, you broke past the boundaries of needing to rely on them for support. They also know now too that you love them amazingly well, and that they didn't need to give you money or buy you things to let you know they love and are loved!

Thank you also for waiting until we moved into our new home to get another cat! The life you were living was in that smoke ridden apartment and, even though great for you at that point in life, you knew not getting a pet allowed you to focusing on building the life you've allowed me and our family to now love and cherish. You did need two or three years to really gain traction, though it's also really cool the amount of REAL love and support you earned. Thank you too for that, Robert!

I've not told you about your books, though, or your music. Though people still had told you that you should be a rapper, I'm thankful we found our path through writing while still working our lyrical craft. You were right about having a message, an earned message through years of dedication and failure, to be able to inspire others. We also have a couple visiting our home in three days to work on their lives. Life isn't always business and money. It also is some people that need healing of the heart and fortification of their own beings, hope, and relationships. Thankfully you learned that.

Dare I even tell you some of the things of now that include people you had known? Dare I tell you about who *really* is a friend and here five years later helping you with our work? The names of some of those people might surprise you. They may not have been active in your life when we wrote this, yet four years ago is one year from now. Take note of that when you're four years away from me (March 30th, 2018). You may have feared some people were just using you for their own gain, yet I'm here to tell you that they *actually* believed in your dreams.

What advice would I give you from now to where you were five years ago? I'm not sure... I'm thankful enough to have trusted you, God, and many others to allow our community to thrive. I thank you for making the December 14th, 2016 commitment, and for compounding it with the advice from Anthony. What you learned of your own life with his guidance hadn't settled immediately, though is good. You had taken from yourself, though your regaining of ground, your honouring of our life (and your devotion to commitments to more than just yourself and the Seed Fund) were vital for the life I'm allowed to share and give now. I send you a hug from the one I now love more than you have your Dad so that you can feel the sadness in her arms too. She hadn't known you yet, though the tears in the corner of her soul keep forever as something we're still helping her to learn, cherish, and heal.

Chilliwack was a place for you to be. You did great work there, and you know the journeys you seeded there are for others too. Some of your friends did want to break away and from. You can let them. You don't *need* to find Natalie or search for tomorrow… You are here, now, with the life you love. The inspirations and guideposts that you traveled to get where I am now are something I want you to remember. Your chains were not held to another. They were held against yourself.

You were terrified to let go and fall into the arms of the world that would hold you like a grain of sand. You were one node in the Contialis we live within. I'm here to tell you that a true gem was formed. You even knew in the moment I wrote this to you that you're not a Jet. You're not a Sapphire. You definitely aren't a Mox Diamond either, though they've continued to help us to develop our shared unification of life.

The future I've painted won't be tainted by a slight. The darkness of the past our rite develop depths of decay and despair cast away like your sin. An eternal life is, again, something that we spin within the kin.

You made *A Distant Glimmer* a *Fountains of Faith* book. Your idea to share that series was a correct choice and though that book was the first major income earner for Chilliwack and the Seed Fund, you had finally put your heart in the correct garden. The second part of the book wasn't yet formed yet (pun), though I want to reread the book that cues help for Pencils of Promise.

Being kinder finds her to renew her vows on our 10th anniversary. I want you to carry her down the aisle like a file stolen from the text. Though we're now in the years of prosperity, you knew it's not always been that way.

I want to tell you how you hoped and wished and prayed for the path to be clear and laid out for you. It still is. There was anxiety that you felt; that depraved knowing and bundled up feeling in your stomach from thinking it was all (as Mike said) "for naught". You already had one from 'the one better than zero'. You did see the number 258 sooner than you thought. You just needed to get in correct alignment.

Remember I carry a lot of the memories that you've yet to have. There's so much life to live and cherish between when you can look me in the eye in the mirror. The sandstone nourishing my bare feet while the water cascades down my spine and into the drain. The fact that you've nothing to fear here in your own home and also that you can visit your Dad on an hour's notice is amazing. Even if you followed Seal's advice and did urge myself to get actual bulletproof glass for the main windows, I'm happy we did and won't need to test them. I've had a long day too... The difference between now, and when you wrote this from me, is that now we get to enjoy the rewards of your devotion.

Even if just a slight nudge, please recall *Fields of Formation* was put in the correct garden. Thank you for tending to *their* home and *their* dream, even if they hadn't faith in the process. Our work continues to evolve and develop. We're nowhere near done. Like you felt, five years before, we *are* almost always near the point of the beginning. That's okay. I continue to till new ideas and projects and relationships. Recall the Contialitic Advice document: *"Be glad for all, and keep an eye out for newness to refresh your soul."* The advice I share with others carries twenty years after we wrote it. We need to remember we too help teach others to be catalysts for monumental change.

You were exhausted... You needed sleep... You also remembered that by keeping at the plow that this is the life we keep. Even though it's only been five years, you should see the wonders that others have helped us build. I won't forget about you. I won't betray you. You keep the *Sands of Tomorrow* hidden from the eyes of yesterday. Three points of blue, and, now that we have a Sol Ring, please use the extra point for another Vault.

Halt not the plan and plot. It's together that this is. Love is brought. It's not "for naught" and though the lands fuel the duals of things you think I forgot young jewel, the plot's deeper than the plan no matter how far away from tomorrow you think I've ran.

Give yourself some rest Rob... I need tomorrow too.

CHAPTER SIX – The Splice of Advice

I was on a car trip to Surrey a few days ago. I was given a great deal of advice and feedback from a friend that gave me some perspective. They seem to think I didn't glean what they were trying to tell me, though I *did* take in a lot of what they shared. They had told me some things about what I've been doing with my books and Facebook posts, and I agree with some of their points. I should not be using Seed Fund ideas as marketing leverage to earn money and sales for myself. If I'm going to give back, I must earn sales advocate for distribution of the books.

The friend's advice gave me some insight into how I know I've been quite pushy and money focused. By 'trying' to be transparent, I was actually being a bit scummy. When I've been saying that I'm not creating for money though want to earn with what I've created, there's a contradiction. If I'm going to work to earn money, then I should maybe explicitly make the focus of sales pronounced. I also wonder what would happen if I shift to becoming money focused for my own sake and keep my charitable work secret as they suggested.

I had made a post on Facebook two days ago asking for financial support to order books. The friend that gave me the bundle of advice told me that they thought I didn't listen to anything they said. I know, again, that I *did* take a lot away from the conversation, just maybe not what *they* wanted me to take away. They think that my ordering books is a waste and that I should just get my own bookbinding equipment and print at home.

Their conversation's advice also reminded me that for someone to actually give money for a book, let alone the time commitment to read it, is in some cases asking for too much from someone. They think that I shouldn't be pushing book sales since it's asking for too much. From this conversation, in retrospect, I also think to not let another dominate the conversation and to actually speak up my own points too. I said barely a word because I wanted to hear what they were saying, though maybe I should have let them know more of my own opinions instead of passively taking in everything they were saying.

In a different conversation with the same friend a few days before, they said they think I should post often on a blog and monetize by posting ads on the page. I don't like this idea, though, maybe, I should have been direct with them and say that I really don't like it. Earning pennies on ads, and also having ads on my blog isn't something I think could be effective as I barely have any followers on my blog. I note I'm a bit stubborn adapting to others input.

There's also the idea of how so many people tell us what *they* think we should do, though we must keep true to ourselves. Using my blog to share ideas in snippets, a two to five minute read compared to an entire book, may be a good idea. If I do write often and garner higher viewership, that might help with the books and music. The idea of people passively supporting with a banner ad click or a like or share would expand our reach, though I personally am not clear if it's an idea I'll use.

There's a great worth in hearing other people's ideas, feedback, and opinions of our work or activities. I now know that some people think I'm sleazy for pushing books and money ideas out there to the world. Maybe I was not being true enough to myself. Maybe I was deluding myself about my own intent. I like hearing other people's input about my process and work as it helps me adjust and restructure what I'm doing. It also crucially reminds me *how* and *why* I'm doing what I do.

I also must stay true to myself and my own prerogatives.

I've not been productive at selling books. The feedback given on the Surrey trip was that I was preaching what I was doing as having altruistic motives. I've been telling people about the Seed Fund, and I also know I had an edgy feeling that I was being manipulative by pushing the idea. I kept my commitment made from my Intents of Income declaration, though I may need to be withheld about sharing my intents. Maybe it's true that people are accepting me pushing for book sales even if I could claim the earnings as personal gain. What is done with the money charitably? Is it more palatable to push for my own personal gain than to work for a cause? I'm not clear on this.

There also have been some key people and supports that have encouraged me to continue doing what I do. The post that I made two nights ago (and some additional messages) has found three people that are okay to put $50 each for ordering copies of the books! This allows 15-17x books to be brought into Chilliwack! I have ideas as to why I want books; to put some in a local store, to bring the *Fragments of Intent* book to Coles for review, and to bring *Fragments of Intent* and *Shared Node* further forward by sharing them.

I also wonder if my intents are different than some that that's why some people don't understand what I'm doing and why. Even if we know our own true and honest intents, we must also accept that we may be viewed through the lens of another's perspective. This is where I think books are the way to go! If readers *do* buy a book and actually read it, those who write their own can share a fantastic amount of information. They also may more clearly clarify their own truths and reasoning.

My audience is an extremely narrow group of people up to now. I personally believe in the power of a small few to do the great work of many. If you are reading this book, you've given a great deal more than just the purchase of a book. You've given us a chance to learn, grow, develop, and share ideas that some others too are given a chance to be heard. You've done this by letting me write for you.

I'm still not a big fan of push promotion advertising. I don't know what the tipping point was for you buying this book. I hope it was because you wanted to and not because you thought you we obliged to. There are a few people that did chip in $ to buy books from me that, then, didn't read the books that they bought. It's nice to have made a sale, yet there's the case that sometimes the gain I'm searching for is to be read, and not just to have received money. The differentiation of how there are some people I really want to share the books with, even at my own cost.

Knowing our own intents is vital!! We need to know *why* we're doing things so that we can act ethically to and with our own prerogatives. I want to work and share my process. I also want to find my own prosperity and self-sufficiency. Knowing *what* we want also should be supported with *how* we gain those things. I think the Surrey friend was right in that some of my intents were out of line. I was pushing ideas to generate sales. Maybe the Seed Fund idea should be a byproduct of what I do. If I assure my own prosperity, then I can share, instead of saying I'll share so that people will buy my books.

Jack Canfield's idea of E+R=O might want to add the variable of 'I' for intent. The 'E' event and our 'R' response (I think) should be coupled with 'I' intent to get the 'O' outcome. We may have the right intent, though if our response is off, it doesn't guarantee the wanted outcome. If our Intent is off, then we also can be doing the right things, just not achieving the outcome we want. We need to be in line with our own values to act in the ways that're right for *us* to find the personal results (outcomes) that we want.

The right things, at the right time, for the right *reasons*!

The part about the right *people* is also part of it. When I have doubts about people and their honest intents, then I can be put off from welcoming them into my life. If I know that someone is working with correct and proper intent, I also note I'll give more grace and *want* to help them, even if there are other issues. As a note, for right now, I'm not clear or knowing what the Surrey friends intent was. I should give them a call.

They think that ordering books is a waste of money and that if I'm running a marathon that I'm shooting myself in the foot before I run. I'll come back to this tomorrow...

April 3rd, 2017 @ 11:54 PM. Italian lessons not done yet, though my hour of reading, and a play of Eric Thomas on Lewis' podcast, are complete. I focus. I hone. I develop. I craft.

Some people believe strongly in waking up early and getting to work right away. This is a great way to live, though I'm not one of those people. I'm a person that extends and pushes myself within boundaries of ability. I think that I've not been accomplishing much recently, though the night fuels me to stay up late and work. I'd prefer to keep at the plow and work to earn our future, tap myself out, and then recover.

This 'tapping out' is a Magic: The Gathering term of when a player is out of available mana. There are few things that can be done without mana in the game. Mana is used to fuel spells and abilities though I use Magic as a metaphor of how I've tapped out often with my finances. I've often overextended myself and then hope to recover later in the future. I don't always like this feast and famine attitude. It's more of a behaviour, not an attitude, though it does cross over to how I work. Going to sleep early is to me sometimes almost like quitting. I'd prefer to tap out and use all my energy, and then miss parts of the next day. Some Magic players would also note though that I don't want to pass my turn.

I have a strange and weird belief that if I keep pushing myself and my process there *can* and *will* be positive results. I know I'm productive at night and that fact has been with me for many years. I *know* it's not healthy to stay up late every night, though I also know that I really want to get my work done. I don't know the answer to the dilemma, though is it not a great idea to really dig into my work and form my ideas when actually inspired? Is it better to work at night instead of just passively doing what the world thinks

I should do?

I've been digging into Jack Canfield's book *The Success Principles* again. The principles he teaches are really crunching into my own belief, heart, and intent. While the Surrey friend's opinion is that it's asking too much for people to actually pay for a book AND read it, couple Jack's opinion of the principles of *"Ask! Ask! Ask!"* and *"Reject Rejection"*. This fuels me and reminds me that there are *billions* of people on this planet and that my work *shall* help. They may be amazingly good for many people. I know I'm open to criticism and guidance, though I also know I won't give up and I'm willing to pay the price.

I know that I want to get to the point I've told so many about. Since I've gotten so little advice up to now, I'd like to reach the point of giving others feedback. I'd like to add some valuable advice and information that people can use to improve *their* lives. Going back to how some people don't think I should be pushing my work and books at people, I also know that. As the books develop and progress, they help purge many of the bits that're still twanged in my being, though I must get to the point of giving back.

For *your* life, the advice I've heard and read is that we need to get ourselves sorted out first before we can help others. I know that my first few books will probably not generate lots of money and there are so few that have read what I've written. I've only been writing for a short few years and there's so much to write and form. I know and accept that I've not yet earned my audience yet. I again acknowledge the Fountains books *are* a selfish and self-focused part of my own healing process. (Then remember too, Rob, how many friends have said you should create for yourself and not others or money!).

Anyhow, there's a wish that a few people I've learned from that I also wish; that we become more self-aware. This's been the case with me. I'm at the point now where I know a lot about myself and *why* I do what I do. I've clarified my intent and though it took forming five books to get to the point of actually finding my knowledge, clarity, and faith, I have some ideas and care that help others. I'm also a bit impatient about developing my work.

I want to carry my intents, process, and follow-through with my creative work. This book is meant to direct a secret guidance through a sense of knowing that I had been a muddle. I've sometimes been too accepting to form a rebuttal. I'm honestly so clearly lost about the cost of what's bossed around the heart that I clearly again tell we're always before the next certain start. Though the curtains may cart the second act away, it's on the third part of the play that we find how you too learn, love, live, thrive, create, play and pray.

Maybe it's my fault for not caring enough for others. My intents and declarations give me something to work for, though there's a fact that some want to close the door on me for what I've committed to. It also reminds me of something. It reminds me that there are some people that *do* assure we help other people live lives. We can, do, and shall love that that allows us to be free.

You may not believe I heard or listened, yet perchance too you seem not to know that my heart soaked in more than you intended me to know. The facts of my own pacts, though, may blend in some of your ideas into how we know the fields grow.

CHAPTER SEVEN – Rebuttal to the Process

I may be heeding the misleading and planting some of the future fields, though some yields are made to help support the four of spades. Some conveyed before we've laid out tracks and believe the CPU's core. A door opens the lens of how half-speed greed could find the need to graph the tweed to bass. It's like Mr. Garrison's spoken speech to find Glacius reach back to the track to find the smokes in a pack, though we don't lack Correct Diction, an affliction of rhyme, or a pact of true addiction. We help keep the slime away from where we'll come from to climb and pray.

Relevate!

Please put the Pearl into the curl of keeping away from my love. The Sapphires above find the mana to fuel the dove, and like a glove, there are five things to till with two different words shared with Bill. Oyster juice! Though some may wish a noose around my neck, there are others who merely wish to deck the halls with some severed calls. The technology does work in your favor, yet I savor the track of putting drinks on the stack. I was a raver without a pack, and though the wolf's generating card was bought from Domri, we see that the net abets as Gary knows he gets the Jets.

Carry the vet to help the elephants across the river. Though Cupid hit my heart with the entire quiver, the one that sang Shiver isn't the one that has our children to deliver. She instead must trough her own offer to Rube for the fact that decades of love are still packed within the tube. Use lube is she starts smoking, yet Ryan T Wilson reminds us that if she's dry, you're doing in the wrong way. Maybe not, though, about how the spout turns the drought into a place where OUR love may become real. It then is to proceed into space as a fortified tree from a sprout of grace.

Though thrown out, you had known about me for decades according to how The Spirit wades in the keys. Capital letters of the fourth neglected setters in the G.A.C.'s. These past few ideas hounded and surrounded the grounded currents of the thought stream telling me that I'm still far too arrogant. Dreams think that teams find the kind relevance to sense how I slink into a drink of trust. A link to bind kindness to future events where intents must have said: "Bizarrely I am a guide." We reside in a tide of DNA and think of the lost the key of Rae.

I speak and soak clearly in the water. We grow old and wise and share with my daughter. Though not a son, a potter makes sure we know there is a bit of fizz from the memory of Rizz. Holding my work in the plan finds life is my vocation. Yet you are in far off and distant nation, yet each consecration shows how some notation is held in the meld of now. How, still, we weld back the track to show the subtle union of the flow hidden in that you show.

You're not my lovestone. I barely even have a shard or shred of truth to the things I've said and led from my youth. My own notations are known to put askew the many few who've shown others want to assure you meet me too. Three points of blue and a ciggie. No mana further than that be we need. It did take four turns, though, to remind me that each land drop is True.

Why should I sleep? Why can't I share the fathomless reaches of the worlds we wish you keep? Do your fans seem to be like Rawkus with the suspicion of an Introversial mission? Does fishing the eaves find the links to Sindel and how she also knows full well about your lines that also straighten spines? Will you share and show to your fans that you have absolutely nothing to owe? Will the sacred doe find the roe that popped like bubbles of love? Even though not a Don, does the Chirashi remind you of how you played me like a pawn? Do you recall the garage and who was also one to assure that my Starbucks card is like a tainted camouflage?

92 Dodge Shadow ES!!! (Electric blue none the less!)

I'm not meant to press my music onto discs or vinyl. I know that the evolution of my lyrics is for my own personal clicks and never final. I know they sever the trial links to Winks and how Minou too was alive at the point of the crew when I first encountered you. This applies to a select few who knew exactly what to do.

I hold the cue to speak with three points up for the leak. Should I only keep one swamp untapped and make sure it also counts as an Island to ensure that none are capped? Is it a Sunken Hollow, a Watery Grave, or dare we even remind that Amonkhet helps show others to learn to save and cycle the flow of that tapped debt?

I feel like I'm both chained to nothing and trapped in a cell. I don't know if that means something, though I wonder about you as well. It must be love, not lust. I think chapter seven of the first book told us also that it's myself I don't trust. Lust isn't enough to live with until dust. There must be ever more to the brew between two. I recall that you love me too. She is an amazing friend, yet I don't' think it's her heart I could mend.

The Universe does have my back... And sometimes I think it tracks me well when I'm alone. If there's no one there, then may I find the fact that my fears of some things. The rings, tears, and years we've lacked? Twenty years is a long time, Dad. I don't think you comprehend that forgiving and living for another may be things easily cast aside. I know that she resides near the tides of now; even as the sands of sleep remind the kind bird that there are some crumbs that tell me, when I wrote, there were near zero sums.

In the moment of then, I wanted to remind how, now, we find the rare and solemn hen. Her men I don't know, and though there are some other gals that're groovy cazh and nifty pals, the fact of this is that there was a cross tainted across my chest. I wish so dearly to stress the love and vest of how the nest is built without feeling a test of guilt.

There's much of which I've asked for. I also hear the calls of the Ravens and how they've watched out for me before. I don't know if you'll come to show me my stone is adorned with love, even if I've never known that I'm the one she holds over the torn wings of a forgotten dove.

I don't shed tears anymore. I've come to peace with being one who never seems to push so much for having fun. The door does remain closed, for now, yet then when again the pen and pad of the lad find the ten to make the quivering Len. I dare not provoke the fumes of Smoke, yet Emerald did remind the entire country that there was some magic to invoke.

I thank you too, Dad. You've been so gracious and giving and helping with the living that I'm allowed to do. Though I've thought you also are keeping secrets from me, I know that she can't tell you that she knows me either. I've lied and cheated and stolen my life to be my own. It's like no one else on this planet has my own love shared or correctly shown. I'm a rock, not a stone. The flocks of spiders cast nets of static into how I'm also a cowardly preset clone. I drone on and on and forget how the acrobatics of the swan's wings folded around me to hold me for, and from, the sacred Dawn.

Many aren't in the MK code. They needn't battle for their position. Some people that are (or become) ultra-successful at what they do compete with only one person, themselves. Me too. I accept that there are many few that want to flaunt the things they do, yet others also share the view that we do more for others too. I invite you to renew and find the spirits wind through how we know you're also sacred and kind. You promised, "Till death do we part" and then were given the gift of a broken heart. It's kind of strange to impart that mine, instead, was shattered from the start.

I too hide some of what makes me sad. You may have to ask me a few many questions to get to the middle of the riddle. I do play poor me with a broken fiddle, yet still no toking in the sun or spittle of rain are also what I must continue to maintain. The cross isn't something I call from Ingraine. You alone can't be are the only stone I cherish, even if found deep within the sanc. An emotional pain does call at my heart, yet I've built up legions of walls to keep my sleep from being something another gal is to reap. Some other stones just want to ride all the bones, while some other women too just want to drag their man up to the tabernacle and sit on their thrones. I know not what your preference is.

Though I'm rich in time and knowing I'm poor in the biz, I thank the showing of devotion to remind me exactly for whom some of this is. I yet still have clues as to who is to sip the smile struggle potion from the message they use.

Carry yourself up to the mountaintop from the ocean, we may not know who's floating down to with the notion to stop. I have a few clues from the ruse that there *is* a voice to choose, yet still wish and wonder how I share a moo with the one you fuse an op. "The news's not always great about what we create", yet the gates of fate's love have always been open for you to pass. It's the case, young lass, which you never made the choice to peer through the windows of my heat's soul like panes of shattered and stained glass.

Maybe it's my fault for not inviting you. I seemed to fear you'd reject me too. If I let you know that my heart is guarded against you, and that if you do choose to meet and greet, we find that it was worth the isolation and sitting in my seat.

I wonder now how this caries. My rhymes are like a cryptic dismissal for those gals that want to float in. I still have the bits of tackle stuck on my innards. Some lines *are* still attached, and though I'm open to conversation and relationships with some gals, my chains still hold. I mustn't claim to be positive and bold, though getting old we are as the third rock orbits the seed to call the star. Don't forget that the lines crossed also connect exactly who you think you are. You may not know me, yet there's a slight intuition that you know some things are to be, True, even if I'm not the one for you through the cue of a blue McGoo.

Thank you for reading this book. Creating it made me look at some different things that tell me that I'm one who's in mediocrity when formed and not wanting to be God or one of the Kings. The rings did hold the two of you together. This I know clearly as something that may have given you layers of distrust and disdain. I also know that when the tears are shed in the rain, that it's joy to be your own faith and hope we maintain.

I'm still just one person. So are you. I also learn to understand how to make amends for the many times and rhymes I betrayed. Some things aren't forgivable, yet still, you are alive and not forgotten. How could I even think to allude that it was okay? I know isn't and wasn't. I've been chained to a tree of self. It's myself who holds all the barriers and brambles and fears that keep me from you. And though the black shifts to blue, I ask you too to renew your vows to yourself too. I can't always view or paint anew the things that you and I do. I also wish not to rhyme. It's an exhausting process, and maybe that's a sign that you're either a) fully worth the effort, b) that you are NOT someone I should search for, or c) that my own intuition tells me that I'm in the correct field of tears, even if it takes another couple of years.

Live well lovestone. I hope you read The *First Three Fountains* too. They'll tell you of a few things that I've yet to find or remember. I stop short of this chapter. Sometimes it's best not to say too much.

CHAPTER EIGHT – Repentance is Futile

I've written a chapter to God in the 2nd and 3rd Fountains. This chapter is in line with some of those ideas, and also the blend of my heart. Religion is a crux for many people on this planet. I have no idea of the stats, though I'd bet clearly that most of the world that believes in one religion or another. It almost seems a universal idea. I use this chapter to discuss some of my thoughts about the world in which we live, and my own active component of organized religion.

Though it was near midnight the night before Easter, I spun in a cup of cold coffee and sat at the computer. There's the fact that I could still get to bed early and aim to be at church tomorrow, though my own lack of faith, in a dearly true sense of the word, is lacking. I still may be far too self-focused by thinking there's merit in what I write.

I may go to church tomorrow. The feeling of the cool, calm, and solemn air in the Italian cathedrals and churches call my heart too. There is, and should be, an extreme reverence for Christ, and I pay homage to Him in ways too. I just don't have, as some North American churches may wish people to have, an understood personal relationship with Christ. I don't have a full comprehension of Him, yet still have prayed outwards to God many times and in many ways. I drink my coffee like it's alcohol.

There is, as I write this, a heavy layer of energy on my shoulders and the back of my neck. I intuit strangely that it's the forces of God. When I wrote *Searching for Tomorrow*, I wrote about how I thought God was angry with me. I now want to send this out to Him in that He knows I do have extreme feelings of devotion to Him, yet have asserted my own lack of ethics by wanting to write instead of getting to bed early. I also don't want to speak or write negative things about the church and have a daft inversion of how I may be projecting my own beliefs.

The world(s) that cross over and unite through the spiritual realm are something I've had some guidance, experience, and intuition about. I do again call for the first R of Global PLUR; Respect for every religion. I assert that that's a crucial component of how we on Earth are to help resolve, fuse, and cultivate an earned understanding and compassion. My own fears of not believing strongly enough in the same way as other Christians do also draw me to not be at church tomorrow. When I'm in church, I've had inklings that all the others are so deep in their own beliefs and homage to God and Jesus, while I've been riddled with doubt and disbelief.

With books I've read and have been reading, the idea of people using the terms Source, The Creator, or the Universe is an alternate term for God. Collective consciousness filters in. I think too of how faith in oneself is also something that many promote. My argument is that if I don't have a full belief in Christ and that I've not been preaching Jesus that I should not consider myself a Christian. The additional layer of how the church's pastor said the church isn't a social club also calls to me.

I believe that relationships with people, spirits, and other entities are amazing things and valuable for our hearts and souls. I have a layer of not wanting to taint *any* church with my own muddle and lack of correct acuity also. I believe that God and the Universe use me in many ways, and I believe that I have a cosmological role to help by supporting them too. I also then selfishly fall into my own wants and such of asserting that I wish not to proclaim things I don't *know*. I seem to think that belief is like a theory and not something as fortified as fact. I've held my own waffling awareness.

There *is* an amazing guidance from a higher power and I know that I'm not that force. I'm a mere human on this planet. Though I've gone to church often, I feel like I'm a total false because I don't believe strongly enough to call myself a Christian. I believe in respect for every religion and I don't condone acts of violence stemmed from when those beliefs differ. I believe in self-responsibility and I have reverence for the force and ideas of God and Christ. I lack, though, a committed resolve to push for the church, though, from my own skepticism. Is it because I can't yet fathom what it is to believe in Jesus from the point of one who's given their entire life over to Him?

I believe too cognitively about the saving power of the name of Jesus too. Not even from a spiritual or redemptive viewpoint, though from the point of that if one calls and proclaims Christ as Lord, that they could be given grace by other Christians. I wish not for protection from just from the people of the world, though from all the powers of life that include all things. I also fear human condemnation for not preaching and proclaiming Christ. The balance of maintaining I don't proclaim I know by claiming so, when I know clearly I don't.

My Dad's not a religious man. Neither is my mother a religious woman. My Mom went to the convent for high-school, though I've not heard her speak much of her viewpoints on Jesus and the church. I'm kind of curious about that conversation, yet it's 12:53 AM and not a time I can call her to ask.

I also submit that I have zero sovereignty in this world of Earth. I've often called myself a vassal and that, if the world is a chess board, I don't even want to have to be a piece. I don't want to be controlled and manipulated by people for their religious or other agendas. I've held the belief that some may be pushing or painting me to be one I'm not.

Then, add layers of Magic and how I've drawn signs from that. A current set of the card game rewound back to the Egyptian ideas. We find how the layers of religion back deep from the past into modern day. From other mythology and religion, we also could think about Athena or Zeus. I understand some of the premises about my own lack of intuition and guidance. It's from the overwhelming notion that I'm still too self-focused and selfish.

I split across the landscape of thinking I *should* do things because of being told to, and also the edge of doing what *I* want to do from following my own intuition and inner guidance. God, I won't be at church tomorrow as far as I'm yet aware. It may be that I do wake up near 9 AM and get a lift to church to be there, though I also have a belief that You (and the Universe) are telling me through my own perception that to write this part of the book *is* the right choice for now. I'm not clear on why, though it feels right to do so.

Another book I want to write (forgetting not of *Fractured Formation*) is *Built from Within*. That book's idea started as being about the bridges between spirituality, religion, chemicals, communication, language, and psychosis. I have some experiences and ideas that I'd like to share and explain. The intent is to bridge people with ideas and concepts from different viewpoints. It may be, partly, that I've understood a great many things through my life that're held in different worlds of thought. What I'd like to do with *Built from Within* is to develop and help people understand their own *and* others viewpoints with a new thought.

I also want to read texts of other religions. I have an obscure belief in God and Christianity, though I'd like to learn and incorporate other ideas to help bridge between people. Some Christians have *always* been part of a church.

I've not. My involvement with religion has also shifted and changed, and I'm not clear that going to church is the right choice for me. I send homage and respect to God, though as the chapter is titled, I also have a layer of fear that repentance can't clean, cleanse, or clear my being. That seems kind of weird; that I fear God's judgment. Some say that's the most crucial thing to fear.

I still want to be a catalyst for improvement on this planet. Not necessarily change, for there are some things that should *not* be changed. With the Seed Fund, a financial viewpoint and attitude are held, though I also want to help people in a social, spiritual, emotional, and mental level. The one component I left out of the six parts of life is physical (health). I want to help people be part of life with social inclusion, communication, and openness. I want to help people solidify and clarify (again, not needingly change) their spiritual beliefs, religious or otherwise. I want to ensure that we're okay and responsible for our emotions and reactions including, even, healthy expressions of anger or sadness.

About an hour ago, I'd have projected that I'd feel more guilt, shame, or condemnation for choosing to write instead of going to bed. I must, though, heed my inner guidance. I may be dancing on the edges of what is good for myself. I also wonder what the effect on others is by sharing what I've written. There have been layers of fear about sharing too much, and there's also the case that, sometimes, I think I should have said or written far more.

If this book was started with Aeris in mind, and I said she'll read it when she's ten years old or older, I really wonder where my heart, mind, and spirit will be then!

Aeris, when you read this it'll be a decade plus since I wrote it. You may still be too young to understand all that happens in this world. I'm not clear if you'll be able to understand this or my other books yet, though I send you some ideas and wishes. Please be sure to trust your inner guidance system. I still didn't know when I wrote this who your Mom's to be, though I also really hope we visit your Grandpa again soon. A lot of the lessons I'll have taught you had yet to have been learned. I know you'll bring a great deal of joy to him and your Grandma too!

One thing that I'd yet to learn for myself was to ask my parents more personal questions. My Mom and Dad still (when I was 38 years old) had me talking all about my own life. I wonder how you, Aeris, will be with your Mom and me when you grow up. One thing that I put on my list of things to do and be is to be the father of the bride and host 100-150 people for your wedding. That may seem like a foolish dream to you, though we'll see how you feel about that later in life.

And then back to the others that read this? We still haven't a clue how much of this formed.

It's said that we each form our lives by choice. My choices have often been ones that have been formed by impulse and intuition. The advice of 'ready, fire, aim!' makes sense to me in how I've acted. We move forward and take some action, and then correct and adjust to ensure there's improvement the next time. With not going to church sometimes, I still don't want to push that my actions are correct or not. The argument made from opposite sides, though the most crucial components of our own choices are our own selves.

I may always be an exceptionally self-focused person. I may not come clear to the moments of time that often meet the signs along the way. I may say a many few things that ping into the spines of people in ways that resonate with the abyss of our minds, yet still, I know that forward motion has been made like looms and mental winds.

I like that I don't have to rest or rely on pushing for sales with them. My financial situation (when I wrote) was one where I was still impoverished with my actions and situation. Where some may think I should have been pushing book sales for myself and not even just for the Seed Fund, I was instead giving free copies to people to read. My value systems and ethics are far different than most, and even if I'm okay with that, the spin is the judgment of others upon myself.

With the notion of how I also fear condemnation for not preaching Jesus (the church's mission *is* evangelism), I'll also speak the truth and not proclaim things I don't have full faith in. It may be best that I *don't* go to church so often for I also wish not to separate the seams and fabric of the church with my tainted self. If the church *is* like a bucket of pure and good water, then I also wish not to be that drop of oil in its weekly bucket that could contaminate the spirit(s) of those who are there and *do* believe.

I think, though, of something that one of the people at church said that I agree with. Not in exact words, though they said that as long as we're doing what is right in the eyes of the Lord, then we need not worry. The idea of being 'Good with God' could carry over and far into the fact that following our own inner guidance. Since we each have a different relationship with God by being different people, it may be the key that some people have yet to comprehend.

I want to write more. I'd like to share my creative ideas with the world. I'd like to help people develop and fortify their own beliefs in self and develop further spiritual faith. We also ensure that some learn and develop new parts of themselves that they don't know. I want to solidify my own ability to provide so that I assure others find their own freedoms.

What can I do to atone? What may I find that has *true* kindness shown? Where can I hone my own intents if not part of something that I have full faith in? If the church is a family, then does this mean that I'm to make myself an estranged child again? Is it my own faith or foolishness that's led me through the gnarled tapestry of insight? Will it almost always be assured to me that 'it's alright'?

Dear God, I ask that You help and continue to reveal the paths of which I'm to travel with people, and not just alone. Please allow each of us to know that what's shown for and from ourselves isn't only for You, yet for others like ourselves too. Thank You for being one to guide us internally; by giving us guideposts and signs like those You use with me from the rhymes and lines. Please let us continue our journey, and thank You for the fact that even if I'm alone so often, that it's for good reasons that we'll come to know. Please allow us to have connection, worth, and purpose *with* and *for* other people *and* also our own lives.

I thank You for allowing me to write and create, and I also thank You for nudging me along and having me sometimes stay up late. I can't do this on my own, and You know that. I thank You for the grace and guidance You've given me, and though I haven't even a bare understanding of some of what happens in and for my own life, I ask that some of the visions put in my mind to seep into view. Our heart and soul are exactly where the future is to start, from You.

Amen.

For those that read this book, *thank you too!!!* Even if I have zero clues about who you are specifically as I construct this, I hope that we learn to hone my craft to help renew. Please forgive me for being overly focused on my own process and journey, and please let me know what I can do with and for your guidance and support too. It may be the case that you were given this book for free as a gift from myself, yet then again, maybe you are one of the people that actually gave money to read this work. I *do* want to sell books and music to earn my income, though even here in the 4th Fountain, I still have a sacred blend of not knowing *who'll* invest in my dreams and my work. The absolute faith, though, is that I'll always have more than enough to help and/or share. It's confirmed by the tingles in my feet.

Please keep the conversations you have with others open to possibility and wonder. If you have ideas you want to turn into dreams, or dreams that have called your soul to make a vision or declaration, please engage in activating your wishes!

If you are a friend who wants to help, you already have. If you want *my* help, then please be open to asking about my future too. We'll help and support some people in some many ways, though the reciprocation of knowing we matter to you too is more than just money and resources. It's something we're glad to know.

"For the doors to the mind find the thread find and weave the loom. Some things left alone on Earth won't just resume, yet rather bloom"

CHAPTER NINE – Back to the Plough

I really do recommend people use their own ability to write. There are so many benefits to opening up a page on a computer and just letting the keys spill out your mind and heart. Some people find using a notebook to journal is helpful. I advocate for future people to create. There are many amazing gains and internal work and learning by putting words on a page, yet each person has a story. We've heard that before, though I hope that no one disagrees with it. What I also want people to know, and learn, is that we have to share is more than just our story.

On April 20th this year (2017) I made my first speech at Toastmasters. The first speech at Toastmasters is called 'The Icebreaker' and is used as the introductory speech to let fellow toastmasters know about the speaker. When I started writing my speech, it was first a recounting of my history; where I've lived and what I had done in my past. I had started with the idea of writing about my past. I shifted from that though. I seem to think that what I *have* done isn't as relevant as to who I am *now* and what I *will* do.

In April 2018, there's a TEDx gathering that I'd like to speak at. The idea of a speech to form around the ideas of metaphors between people and technology. The 2018 gathering is based on the topic 'Time to Reboot' and I think of how the church was involved in a talk of 'Reset'. The keywords *reboot* and *reset* made me think of how going to bed or having a nap is like restarting a computer. All of the data is kept (the storage of our memories and ideas) and the reboot is a way to restart.

The computer metaphor of the reset also carries how when our computers shut down or reset when we don't want them to. We may lose what we working on or connected to. I don't want to lose what I'm working on! The fact that I don't want to turn off my system for the night (going to bed) is because I also know that work may be done before shutting the computer off. I wonder, though, if the desire to convey something valuable is still something trapped up in my mind that find my neurosis to carry obsolete ideas; ideas of how I should write and also be in the fields tending the soil.

There's a patient thought, though. The idea of a seed is a great one to use metaphorically. My issue of the quality of my projects (the quality of the seeds) and the idea of needing to give a seed time to grow (germination period) add a double layer of my own fear. Am I waiting for seeds to grow when I've really planted Cheerio's?? The Cheerios reference is from grade one and how I was given 'magic Cheerios' (yes the cereal) to plant. They told me that they would grow! Even if I have faith in my seeds, what is there to guarantee that the seeds are good? (hint: their source!)

This is why we need to be clear about what we're intending to reap, and not just sowing random idea. If we're clear in what we want to grow, then we may gather the correct seeds that need to be planted and tended to in our gardens (our personal lives), the fields (our communities), and also, in some cases, the planets and cosmos itself (the Universe).

I've mentioned in my books some people that have given me seeds and ideas to sow. Jack Canfield, Lewis Howes, Gary Vaynerchuk, Christy Whitman, Gabrielle Bernstein, and also Anthony Robbins and Grant Cardone. When I spoke to SnowPeaks (the Thursday Toastmasters group) I diverted away from my intended talk because of the garden I was in. It was recalled that each person also has his or her own garden to sow. Ideas may be considered seeds, though I also may have been planting in gardens that aren't my own to tend. I may not be welcome in some people's gardens.

Then, and some may agree, worse yet, I could turn into a dandelion. The idea of my thoughts being strewn and carried over the world prolifically and, as some may say, infecting the fields and gardens of others too is a thing. Sometimes the weeds may not let other things grow and use the resources of the soil. I love dandelions, though many people DON'T. From Gabby Bernstein's *The Universe Has Your Back*, the dandelion was revealed as being a sign for me from the Universe that all is well. I just hope *I'm* not treated like a dandelion!

The notion of the sunflower is also one that spans across the fields. I'd like to attune myself to be guided *by* the dandelions, though to *be* a sunflower. When you get the chance to see a full field of sunflowers in real life (which is a rare sight for some) they fascinate the mind! I saw fields in Italy, and I think of how I love and wonder of that vision (thank you internal visual recall!). I'd prefer to be a sunflower for a few reasons, though the main one is the way they are used in different ways. Some of their seeds may be used to plant another sunflower, they may be made into oil and they also may be used for nourishment (and not just the humans!). Also, when we see the fields of Sunflowers, they all are aligned in direction with each other. There's a danger, though, of being chopped off at the legs.

We may take signs even from things that we don't like or aren't good for others or ourselves. We should take note often of what we like or love. The law of attraction has been prevalent in a lot of success and life building work, and I do scribe to that too. Where I've not yet been able to open to myself to abundance, I still would like to keep full faith and belief in the law of sufficiency. I always have enough for myself.

My want for abundance may need a clear intent, something of which I've yet to articulate. I've talked about the Seed Fund as being a channel for what to do *with* abundance, yet there still is the mystery and challenge of how to achieve that grace. There's some nervousness about this with my frequent lack of faith. I've yet to fortify and secure my own won faith in the Universe and worlds to grant us more than we need.

I need to regather. Ideas cast to the wind like the dandelion may produce and propagate well, though may make plants that people dislike. The dandelion wine, I'm told, is wonderful as is a dandelion salad. The online influencers or famous authors also are like the sunflowers in how they've provided. They help form fields of sunflowers with a consistency that are a well-organized row on row to then produce their own bundles of future growth!

If I carry the idea of myself being a sunflower, then what happens with our yield? Will the seeds be roasted up, salted, and put in a bag? Will we find that some of my seeds are be saved, tended to, and then planted in a group to grow future sunflowers? Will those future sunflowers then share *their* seeds of ideas and heart? Or, shall the seeds from my books be used to form oil to help smooth out some things of this world.

If we each are seed bearers, then we too should be cautious and bold to ensure that what we grow is tended to properly and not destroyed or hindered. Each of us is a garden producing that of which we sow.

A theme I've been hearing and reading recently also is that we should limit our involvement with some people. The ideas that I hold too include inclusion and tolerance. Knowing of my own lack of consistency (not just work, yet also my attitude and openness) reminds me that I vacillate with my behaviour around some people. I agree that there are some people I'd prefer to never have to interact with, yet there also are some that I've gotten upset at and do like to interact with sometimes. Perchance it's an idea to write a chapter about my personal preferences and ideas about communication between my friends and myself?

Also in the fields of this chapter should be the idea I had for *Seeds of Tomorrow* and *The Fountains of Faith.* For the three books in this series, I'm using the full amount of earnings from their sales for charitable work. With the advice from the Mox Diamond (the Surrey trip friend), they had said I shouldn't use the Seed Fund as a marketing ploy to sell my books. This is a true point from my view too. I'm not clear if I should push the fund as a reason for someone to buy my books. A question then stands as "What if *all* the earnings from the book were going to the Seed Fund?"

For *this* book, 100% of all earnings are going to go to the Seed Fund. The idea of having different buckets or jars for our money is one I like, and as I write books (even the smaller 60-70 page individual ones and not just the three book compilations) we can attribute and allocate the earnings into separate funds. Pencils of Promise is a cause I learned about through Lewis, and is one that I'd like to donate to in the future.

This rewinds back to where this chapter started I still want to urge people to write. Pick up a pen, or open up a blank document, and put a bunch of ideas onto paper or into text! I've been lax with the *Fractured Formation* project (the psych ward book) though an idea I wrote in that book is the idea of journaling. I believe that journaling gives people a great advantage by understanding and tracking their own life.

Writing down what we've done and what we were dealing with, the diary type journaling, is helpful for becoming self-aware about our thoughts, life development, and patterns. Daily journaling may include other things, though, what we read later in the future reminds us of vital things in our life. Stealing two ideas from Jack and Lewis is to write down our victories of the day, and also things that we're grateful for. Some people may make separate books for these; a Victory journal and a Gratitude journal. Having a notebook or computer file to track and plan your work, projects, and goals is also amazingly helpful.

There's the thought of how when people recommend ideas there can be resistance to heeding the recommendation. As I get deeper into learning from others by reading and or other media, I realize these bits of advice and knowledge are seeds. When the seeds grow to maturity, they may cross-pollinate deeply valuable ideas and share a combined benefit. I'd like to blend the idea of those that read a lot, and then share what they've learned. The bees that help many different plants propagate carrying the pollen of knowledge.

Be cautious in other people's gardens though. This may be a rerun, though too much water, too much sun, or too much fertilizer can ruin plants. If what we speak is blue mana, water from the Magic code, then speaking too much and overwatering may drown out a plant. I've overwatered many a person and it's known I used to talk way too much causing people to be pissed off. Conversely, when we shut down or don't say enough, we also may have the other 'dry out'.

There's also the fertilizer part. Is that the interesting bits that help vitalize the conversation? The sun also links to how some plants open up and direct themselves to the sun to gain some light. Too much light could also burn a plant. Some plants thirst and need a lot of sunlight, while some others prefer the shade. I know one friend that I overwatered and also torched by giving them too much light. It's not easy to tend to plants. They, like humans, can be delicate and fickle. Some friendships teeter or being that fragile stone flower; and some others still stand strong and true in blazing heat and also be averse to being touched (alluding to the cacti).

Remembering again of other people's gardens; they're other people's gardens!! Don't trespass!!!

I talk about my garden, yet how does that benefit you? I'd prefer to keep the blade of the plow in the earth to plant fields for combined yields. Each of my books is a different type of crop. If we plant the fields with these seeds, then what's planted may sprout and grow (to be read). I think of how if different fields are planted with different books, then some of these fields may be attuned to different people based on preference or interest. They also must be tended differently because of what's needed for them to thrive.

It's not easy being a farmer sometimes. Real farmers have experience and knowledge from years, and even decades, of cycles of time and how their crops grow in their fields. They have other friends that farm and know how to grow and tend them. Some farmers also know that by sharing their best seed, that the cross-pollination between fields grows better crops for all those involved. I've not been in the fields a long time. I've learned some good things from some decent farmers and they've given me good ideas to sow. I should not just be hobby farming. I should get to work in the fields and find some others to help us grow so that we can provide.

I also, though, should not forget my own garden. Maybe I like crows! They're not all bad. Why should there be a scarecrow to push away? Is it better to be alone and have a garden without anything sprouting, or should I leave my own garden well alone and slave in the fields? I'd like to have a garden; it may be good for my soul! I don't want just anyone to puddle into the dirt, and I think that maybe it's like some people are that scarecrow keeping the crows away. Crows are amazing animals! Though true, maybe, the garden would like some more flowers. What if the crows pick and choose and eat the seeds for themselves without giving them a chance to germinate and grow?

We may just need some seeds. What seeds do you give to share?

CHAPTER TEN – One Page Later

First and idea

Then a word

Then a chapter

Then a book

Then a series.

Somewhere in that time, there's also a greeting;

A romance

A dance

A marriage

A child

A life…

We develop our own lives with the help of God and the Universe.

I'd like to invite you on this journey, though you've already followed some of the precarious steps that I've made. I put a book out to the world with the idea to get my dream girl a copy to read. I wrote the first book, and even at the point of release, it was meant merely for her to learn of me and come find me. Then there was *Searching for Tomorrow*.

I thought that Natalie and I would meet on Christmas Day and that I could lure myself into her sight to find she had known me already for a near eternity before. We may not find a meeting, and I still twinge with the curled involution of her being in my innards. A lost and torn hope, dream, and obsession. I thought I could not live without her. Poetically, it's that I must.

I had betrayed her time and time again. I had tossed so much of myself away and off from the shelf where there's no chance a depraved and salacious soul like myself could be worthy. I find forever, even if not with her.

As the work I've formed up to now has been 'all about me', there's also the case of the Sea and how the process brings my lovestone to me. I know that the *Key to Me* is the devotion to be free, and it's rad to know the union of the flow isn't always what I need to show.

Though I had tattered and scattered my own faults, the thing I seem to urge is that the vaults of my future have yet to be opened. They are for many and not merely for one devotedly chosen gal to open.

My heart is for the world. I share that. As we evolve and turn the pages, I must also repent. I had sent myself toward a multitude, and through each and every one other than her was *not* True, ironically, I trust myself to know exactly what to do.

This thing pings the Sonar memory and how the first CD shared caused me to think of the circled 'C'. Not the shoe... Not her... Not you... It's just the fact that my own Freedom Solution includes many in our worlds and not just a few. I thank for helping us with this; each of you.

The process of sprouting into a new life is scary and vital. I know that what I've written up to now may not be what people wish to have in their own gardens of their mind. I also know that if you've wound this far into my work, that you sense there's something that's definite to defend. A star-crossed lover... A diligent soul... An obtuse and loyal friend...

Even if I've been told my work has no value as marketable material, I still note the call to another's dreams and imagination finds many a few hearts to renew. They let the sands of time settle into the hourglass as each does, and doesn't, pass. The theory is I'm a noble gas. I hold my form by what I'm contained within. I have some solid theories about who I am, and though I may not be a solid adult at this point, I note that may be an advantage.

As I allow myself to trust our process *does* hold some shards and fragments of worth, we nourish another's hope. I wish to sew some wishes in the fabric of our core. To know that, when we're only one, that adding anyone or anything else is more.

The doors of my mind and heart are open to many. I choose to allow people to delve and dive deep into my mind and spirit to find those inklings of truth they may not think another understands or believes. You too may weave your truths into the world and find them to nourish the precipice of death that we never fall into or from. There are some people that wish not to live. Those people clearly may not have a willingness to read what I've written. What value do I hold for them? Why would one who has the wish to pass from the mortal realm into the unknowns of the afterlife care to take a leisurely stroll through the fields of text I've formed to share?

Because some people are afraid to close their own lives, we may bring them into our hearts. We may remind them of their brilliance and beauty, even if they believe it a myth. We find some people who'll see your kind smile, or hear your subtle song of the heart. If we consider each kind, good, and lifting action like a speck of glitter, think of how some may see and experience the world if we do these good things for all others too.

The fact of being good is dangerous. "Only the good die young." I'm inclined to think and wish, though, that some of the good are also eternal beings that're guarding us and nudging us along into a future that astonishes us with the amount of love, luck, fortune, and care that's there. We land. I recalled wanting to die also. Decades later I'm so thankful that I made the choice that I didn't and that I'm still alive now.

I almost have a devious wish that those that *do* want to die instead have a complete shift of life, situation, and heart and find themselves (as I had) decades later in the wonder of how magnificent the world we live in is!

If each person's act of kindness is a speck of glitter, let it be the case. I heard that glitter is 'the herpes of the craft world'. If kindness becomes so infectious and pervasive in our lives, then it also might be that we share those bits of kindness in other people's lives and pass forward happiness and gladness!

"Amongst the crowd in a cloud of smoke/There's no money in my pockets but it doesn't mean I'm broke"

The focus about having the money or things is one I've succumbed to too often. We know I've pushed away a lot of friends by wanting to sell books. I know that being sales focused actually has inhibited me from earning love, which is deeply valuable. A lesson I've also found is that when I focus on my needs and wants, or rather the lack of them, I can turn into a twister of inner turmoil and fear. Instead, and this is only recently, I choose to follow wonder and gladness. I choose to keep my attitude light and thankful and also attuned to the things that I like, love, and want.

Seek your dreams. Cherish grace. Honour integrity. Strengthen your understanding. Cultivate compassion. Intuit your soul. Yearn for faith.

This was written after *Fragments of Intent*. Few have sipped from *The Fountains of Yesterday*, yet this book is part of *The Fountains of Faith*. Like the first series, they track my process and evolution as I find my own Freedom Solution. You find yours too, and I think that people need to start with their own heart. Natalie *was* my heart, and I found I needed to put my faith in something else.

This book and series are aptly titled with the metaphors I use. If you read them, you may come to know who I am. I've wanted to share as a Yellow Overtone Seed, and I also know that the Universe is kind and working in my favour. I know I'm not the only person who thinks of this inverse paranoia, as we prepare to sow and reap the *Seeds of Tomorrow*. We reach the *Fields of Formation*, and after some additional fields are tilled, we find *A Distant Glimmer*.

Some people may think they'll never see kindness. Maybe they should read what's written. As we expand and gather our beings into the works and worlds that form, we also find I know I'm not the only one to form this process. I *am* only one. Add another, we have two. Add some more, we are a few. Many are fused in our unity.

Considering how many different lessons I've been taught, and my own blend of how I share, it's a process that needs time to grow. My Mom told me that she thinks my life and mind is like a snow globe. She suggested that each person is like a snowflake in my mind. When I wake up in the morning, all is calm, and the snow settled on the ground. Then the globe is shaken up when all the ideas and people mix up and start swirling.

It's only in recent moments of time and thought that I've understood that writing at the end of my day lets snowflakes (my words) settle on the page for others to see. The metaphor, though, extends. If I break out of the snow globe (my mind, life, and work) maybe we can find something substantial that my words and ideas form. We may turn it into a glacier!

If each layer of snow is the ideas and fragments from my own and others days to land upon the ground, then each wave of snow slowly accumulates on the ground through a lengthened course of time. As the layers of snow settle and rest, slowly a glacier is formed through the years. Dare I even allude to decades and centuries (or even millennia) of the human generational forces? Many may not know or have been alive to be there when the snow first fell, yet it's clearly the fact that we know a glacier holds much substance, mass, and form.

As we carry forward with this process and work, it may be an exceptional few know about my own work. A *Glacial Structure* formed that's hidden and separate from the other points of nature. Still, it's absolutely part of the environment. What happens if all the snow melts? What happens to those people that learn of and discover the glacier and then want to explore? I'll give you a hint… If you're reading this book, you are one to climb the glacier of this project!

Keep dear and true, though, and know as you are one climbing the solidified version of this work, there may be faults and danger. You'll need to care for yourself and your wishes and dreams too. A glacier is as it is, it can't always preserve or protect you. The jib in this, though, this glacier, like all things, has been guided to develop faith and belief. My words are guided by the interest in line with Their accord. Your belief in anything could assure you everything. Yet a belief in everything could leave you with nothing.

I may be getting a bit divergent and poetic, yet please be sure to put your faith in more than just yourself. Believing in ourselves is vital, important, and valuable, yet when you believe that you, your work, and your resources are being used for something far greater than yourself, you may become a conduit for monumental consecration.

I repent that I've been too self-focused and thinking of my own, even if peripheral, benefit from what I do. I shift from that. My purpose is to have a purpose and not to force my own or other another's journey. I must remain open to guidance, I must clarify my own truths, I too must share those truths, and I must remember that, like a snowflake, each of us is different. Though we all comprise the glacier nestled in the valley, this landscape is assuredly not just humans. *Built from Within* covers different ideas that may valuable, yet as some of the water has seeped from the glacier and back into the ground, so comes the water for the rivers and fountains.

I want to advise, tend, and teach. I also note that writing only about my own ideas is almost like a breach of being one to preach. I must find, like my advice to you, my own truths and *also* share their sources. We're not alone on our journey. I may be alone often as I form what I write, though it's because some other glaciers (people and their works) have been teaching me how to navigate the other worlds of life. I climb these mountains and also, later, dive deep in some seas. The irony of *my* life is that I'm also to share the ideas in the mental breeze.

Let your dreams unfold. Trust your inner guidance, no matter what you wish to label it. Keep in communication with other people about what your wants and wishes are… *many* help you. Remember to stop sometimes, to look inward (or outward) for ideas and truths to guide you, and develop trust into something more than just an idea… develop it into faith.

Plant a seed. Nourish it. Give it time to grow.

Heed others need or greed. Take note. You may need to remember.

Allow yourself to be known. Believe. It'll be clear when to do so.

Honour your *and* others lives. Seek to understand. Your truth is shown.

So, yeah… We have two more chapters in this book. I had the idea to close it with a chapter to my Mom. When I wrote this, I was not clear what chapter eleven's to be. I thought to write about the Glass House and describe it, yet there's another idea that lingers from JJ Virgin from what I heard on *The School of Greatness* today. I've not been studying the podcast too much recently, though an idea she referred is to write a full exposition of what we want!

This exposition may include materialistic wants, emotional or mental wants (or perceived needs), or even socially desired things. I think to include what I wish for the Seed Fund to do if allowed full expansion. The idea to write out our full wants, dreams, and wishes is an idea *is* a great one, though I have a fear I'll be viewed as greedy or irrational. Thing is, a wish list *is* a *wish* list. Many buy into the dream of winning the $50 million LottoMax. Consider the next chapter as what I'd like to do.

CHAPTER ELEVEN – My Ultimate Wishlist

(This section is a wish and prayer for my wants, including materialism)

Please let me have a 2010 or newer vehicle with 30k km or less. Let us find the first five Full Seeds to be in place so that people have a home to live in during the winter. Please allow the Glass House to be built by September 5th, 2025 and allow my books and music to be used as a channel for providing for the Seed Fund and my own personal life. I don't want to rely on governmental or parental support to live. My wish is to be self-sufficient from and with my creative work.

Please let me find my next girlfriend soon too, please. Let there be random, magical, and miracle meetings with some dear, groovy, and sweet gals that keep our hearts light and full of joy. Please let me meet Aeris by the point of January 2022 and by January 2019, please let my mortgage for my current apartment be completely paid for. Also, please let us fuel a great income for the Seed, Freedom, and Dream Funds.

Please let the Seed Fund find additional financiers beyond my own self. Let us support, be supported, and extend outwards from Chilliwack while keeping the heart and its central operations here in this town. Let us find ways of supporting other causes too so that we may synergize with other caring, kind, and compassionate people to help other communities, even internationally.

Let PLUR be a guiding motive and action. Allow my own duplicities become less so that I'm walking the talk I speak, and that I fortify and strengthen my own integrity even when none are there to witness. Please help me live ethically and in line with and for the greater good of many, and not just those that I personally know. Allow us each to find our Freedom Solution and be open to a future better than any that we yet imagine.

Please keep people safe, guarded, and protected and that our needs be abundantly provided for. Thank You too for the grace You've given me through the years, and thank You for letting my attitude and emotions have become positive. I'm glad that passions help sustain my soul, and I thank You for the blessings You've allowed me so that I may work for many others, and not just individual people and companies.

Thank You for allowing me sufficiency and not being one to ever need. I thank You for the fact that I have a home, food, drink, and even tobacco. I thank You for allowing me to have maintained my commitment to not smoking dope. I hope too that I can be healthier with my future choices. Thank You for the connections and contacts that You've put in our life, and thank You for distancing myself from some that aren't good for me also.

Please let me continue to learn and share the ideas and concepts that I learn from others. I share my knowledge and resources and ask we may have more than enough for each of us. Thank You also for the access to The Spirit that You've granted. I know I'm a mere child in some regards, though the fact that I also feel the years of wisdom and insight that I ask to develop and fortify further to provide more than just shelter for others.

Please allow all people food and water. Let us find a way of truly supporting a multitude of people without them conscribing to hate, fear, or lack. I know that the world in which we live is one that isn't a place where we should think just for our own benefit. I repent of my self-seeking behaviour, and I thank You too for the intuitions given. These intuitions bring me back on course when I may have strayed.

I wish for longevity as well as prosperity. I wish that my wife and I are alive in the year 2053 supporting and developing ideas and lives to bridge people between conflicting viewpoints. Let us work and strive to improve a shared understanding and kindness. Please let us use our work as a channel to assist people to find their own truths and how they affect, and are affected, by links to other worldviews.

Please let our work be a catalyst for those who are feeling depressed or hopeless. Let us find others to also uplift and restore the hearts and minds of those who've been trodden on. Let PLUR grow, develop, thrive, and redeem those who may not have thought themselves to have a chance to live.

Thank You for letting Earth continue to exist for millennia and eons further with our species allowed to live, love, and thrive. Thank You for visionaries like Elon Musk who are contributing to the longevity of the species while also finding future outlets for the human race to expand. Thank You for the people of the world that want to be part of the solution and actively seek out others for whom to ally and work with. I know that when people join forces, a lot may be done than each only working solo as an individual. I selfishly ask that I may be a person who's included as an active part of healing and support.

Let there be an expansion of our intuition, understanding, and love. Let our hearts rule the faculties of our soul to be in alignment with what is right, true, and beneficial for many. Please keep us each safe while allowing us to reach out from our own self-imposed limits and confines of action and pass our own fears. Allow our faith and trust to be strengthened and justly placed in those who'll honour and cultivate the process of life. Let my future be one that understands her and my partnership is to be a working and evolving journey that we commit to fully. Please allow our partnership be founded upon a shared and expanded set of values and integrity to further strengthen our bond for decades.

Thank You for allowing me to have contact with other people and that there are many to learn and glean from. Let these connections add to our resources, our knowledge, and our skill sets. Let our creative works shift to being works that relay insight and wisdom to others. Let the works and ideas be shared, relayed, and helpful for many people's lives. Please let people be given a spark of hope or idea to create future leaders and guides that attune their own hearts, minds, and actions that support and improve lives.

Thank You for allowing me my past hardships and experiences so that, even if I'm not in the same situation now, I can have empathy and understand how to correctly support and guide people to cultivate lives that they'll love, cherish, and honour. Let people be acknowledged for the things that they've done to assist other's journeys, even those whose paths may not cross in locative life.

Thank You for dreams, signs, and wonders that allow us more often have open hearts and minds. Let us share new ideas and people and be thankful for the blessings and abilities that have been granted. Let us also be thankful and aware of the technology and logistics systems that allow the future to expand outwards, even exponentially. Please let us be true and kept true to others and our own prerogatives. Let us be authentically aligned and in harmony with generate and sustain goodness. Let us also be allowed to revel in pure wonder and fascination.

Please allow me on the path of abundance. I had struggled for years with barely having enough. I wish to have more than enough for others and myself so that we may share. Having $2,500 per month for myself *after* fueling money to the Seed Fund and Freedom Fund assures my own Freedom Solution. As I'm allowed my own, let me too tend to others to help them find theirs. I've been told that I need to take care of my own needs first, and true as that is, I also thank You for letting me help others.

Let the interest in the books I form increase. Let books sell online to people all around the world with the ideas, heart, and interest to expand and take root in the gardens and communal fields. Please let me be a person that uplifts and inspires others to develop their points of being. Let us add our instinct and intents to spurn us to allow others to prosper and share too. Let each good seed find a place to grow and flourish and be tended too by others and myself. I ask we may grow a magnificent world and journey to be shared by many.

Thank You for Your grace. Thank You, and others, for their kindness and generosity. Thank You for letting me catch myself when I have to limit thoughts or beliefs and please put my mind back in gratitude and gladness for that we have and will have. Deepen and strengthen my faith while allowing my mind to be nimble and aware. Dare I need to be cautious and avoid the pitfalls that may be found or set, let me overcome adversity and learn lessons that I may share with others. Let us be kept safe and upon solid ground.

Even if Natalie's not the focus that she once was, please let her and I have a conversation to discuss life. I know that I don't need her to complete my life and that we should not meld; yet I do still want to talk with her. I hope her and my meeting helps finish the shedding of my latent psychosis.

Please let us have loved and trustworthy friends. Let them feel free to share their honest opinions without fear of judgment, and let their feedback and advice help us hone and focus the journeys that we're on. Let us give and receive hospitality. I ask the Glass House be a place where people gather as I wish our homes be kept safe, secure, warm, and welcoming.

I ask and wish that all four of my parents are alive and well twenty-five years from now. Let me host their 90th birthday parties in the Glass House and have them present at the events. Please let them meet their grandchildren and be loved by them. The idea of having only one child is still an idea, yet there's also the second calling for the idea of having three children and then tying the tubes.

Let people be motivated from within and that they crystallize their positive habits into gems that they may share with others too. As we earn and develop the seeds of life, let each also be a seed bearer to share their ideas, wisdom, advice, and love. Let people's self-directed and shared intents and ideas be a guiding force and intuition for us to do the right things, at the right times, for the right people, and for the right reasons. Let the seasons pass and amass each to be a class act to refract a combination of forward motion with a substantial positive effect.

Some people pray for change. I think we should pray also for the good things and what *is* working right. I thank You for the internal guidance system that You've given us and for incepting crucial pieces of text into the awareness of readers. Please do this so that we too may be guides, teachers, and providers. Let us unite and assure that there's no need to run or fight.

Thank You for the friends and family that we recall, even in their own unique ways, as the nights and days phase us into and from the maze.

Holds the folds of rhyme in place. Though told time and space assist our climb back down to grace, the melancholy pace of the seconds given to trace her are a delicate treble cleft left to lace. Strong and true hugs, and not because we're told to or trying to push for plugs of deep resonant drum and bass.

Let us continue to shape and mould that we hold dear. Let the tears also be shed once in a while to remember the streaming smiles that had started years before the files. Let the cross be honoured true, and let the moss grow well and old on the stone that's foretold by You.

We are in a garden of life. I thank the forces that be for allowing me to key the words we've yet to see. Thank You to You and also from me. Thank her for turning the sacred key. Thank He for the ideas of the Sea, and I also ask we move forward and reveal what comes to be.

This world is held in the *Course of Fate* and *Destiny in the Key of E.* Amen.

I didn't divulge all of my wants and wishes in this chapter, yet one more still lingers that I must share. With my Freedom Solution, the ground base of Chilliwack and the Glass House is primary. The other key is that I wish to travel! I still would like to go to Italy again for a month-long trip traveling from city to city on a solo mission of adventure and self-reflection. I'd like to go in September of 2018 and it'll require being fluent in the language by then. It'll be a huge step out of my comfort zone, though there are amazing worlds to see far beyond that point also. It's a life-altering adventure that's focal for my heart as I sometimes think we need to be strangers in a foreign land.

So for the last chapter of this book, I wanted to write to my Mom. I also had the chance to visit with my Mom this past weekend. The day that passed the night I wrote this part was May 2nd, my 39th birthday. I feel so much younger in attitude and decades older in the soul. I'm also inclined to write about some of my drug trips and experiences, though that may be for a different book. I've not yet a clarified scope for what *Fields of Formation* is to be, though note there's still much to share.

CHAPTER TWELVE - A Primary Notion

Decades of devotion have yet to unfurl. What curls in my heart is almost like a personal ID badge.

Planet: Earth.

Profession: Life.

Vocation: Contialitic Shoulsman.

Perchance I should stretch out the lines of thought and stitch the next falsity into the webs of deceit? Am I writing these books for myself, and/or am I using them as a way to insight shards of intent? There's an inclination that the basis of the words is from a tainted heart bitter and never worn by the one who was chained to me. The tenses of future events hold fences that carry a century into a mere thread that was clipped short and pulled out like the stitches on my left wrist.

I had slashed my wrist in the tub. I was convinced that those who claimed to be a friend were actually filled with hate and were plotting my demise. I could not look them clearly in the eyes. I was not true and know full well I deserved to be sent to Hell. I had corrupted my mind and am shocked I was not shattered like the stone I threw from the balcony.

The laser sights I imagined following me across the streets from the building tops found my shadow alluding that I was a Sith. I know that not to be true. I may be self-focused and boastful, yet still I know my being to be on the side of light. I used to ask people what was their deepest fear and darkest desire. I used to try to absorb the energies of which I wanted to change and transmute to good, yet I was overcome.

Drugs severely damaged my soul and mind. In the beginning, I had thought drugs divine and remember one gal's spirit streaming through my own as if my joy was her own secret insight. The delight of knowing her smile cleaved me to the idea that she was my soulmate. Maybe the connection did die. Maybe there would have been a meeting or chance to meet, yet I tossed her off and away so many times from climbing into the internet or into my own imagination.

There was no consecration that could tell me what the fact is, not even when I wrote this. It's like I pissed all over the fires of love and turned them into a stinking puddle of filth.

I have much to repent. To whom though may I make reparations? The *Fragments of Intent* share how it was only for Natalie my heart had been, yet we also know I alluded to how I couldn't be faithful both to her and my own life. The two lives separate and distinct. Still, though, she may not have been interested in my petty excuses. This mental entanglement kept her out of my heart. She thinks it black and empty. Why would anyone want to delve into the swamp and get mucked up? We know clearly who I can't be, True.

Yet then, we send across the circles and cycles of rhyme. We climb back on the track and understand that those many years stack as what we've known as lack. I've been told that it matters not who I am, yet rather who others think I am. This may be why I distort my behaviour and actions to glean favour. I've tampered with the division and it's the case that many others wish not to tolerate me either. I've been pushing for purpose and value from my own self when I should recall it matters what I *do*, and not what I *say* I'll do.

Though some gals may roar up with their own intents, I must abstain from soaking in some of their cloaked desires. I've been entangled in the facet of my own understanding. I need and wish too to step out of my own perspective and not push my own truths. My truths matter not if another refuses to believe. A dear lack of mention about how some wish me to be free to see and be one to have them spun into the tapestry. It's a web of delicate deceit.

Though mastery of our own beings is a goal for some, I also must plumb the wishes into how the fishes find their home on the reef. I must remain away and apart from some. I can't behave like I came from a place similar to that they wish for me. If I'm to earn and live free, then I too insist I must correct my own choices, behaviours, and attitudes. If I'm to be true and honourable in action, thought, word, and deed, my work must also heed that the need is something to guard indeed.

I wish not to manipulate the gate of Heaven or the doors to my future. Paradox's notions catch latent issues of lost potions sipped from their control. I fit not into only one role. One who's to fuse the dues and wisely choose how, what, and with whom to share the sacred blues, claims my own fortified clues. I can't tell you exactly what's the result, I know, though, that I must catapult some things out over the walls of my life. Some boundaries have been breached, yet still taught well on the inner sides of Shell. There are a few people that I'd prefer to teleport, and though purport that there are many that wish to abort. Some wish for the life to bloom, and for those that do, I should resume.

I presume lots of what I write won't make sense to people. I accept that. I repeat again that I'm a rare form of a muddle. It may take work to read through that that I've written, yet it urge us to remember we're still far away from the moments we greet. It's often always near the start of the next moment of time we have yet to meet.

I may not have much to relay, yet the way I've done so up to now is based on faith. My faith is that I put trust in God and the Universe to allow corrections to my own directions and instruction. The function of my books is to share new ways of thinking and instill parts of the Contialis that may be sporadically random into a solidified and permanent linear form of text. I say so little to some, yet then there are others that I divulge almost anything to. How do those who have zero references to who I am and how I act view these books? Even those that do know me and read these books may find some confusion.

I know that it's strange to think that the links of text cross the oceans to some that want to know my story and where I come from. My wishes to expand and extend our ideas blend far past my current network of contact and friend. With the metaphor of these books as being brought into other people's gardens of mind, I really don't know how they'll grow when tended to properly. There's also an odd idea that even if not watered or given good light that they still may flourish. "What you wish on me on thee in three."

As we wind up the thread, the spools of thought have been brought out for you to weave into the loom. Even if precise and exact from my view, the shreds of idea and thoughts are to be wound up and helped to form a new and unique cohesive way of thinking in your awareness. The purpose isn't something that I often understand. That, again, is where I put my faith in the Universe, world, and process. The sense of truth is made and given as we follow my wandering, pondering, and stumbling through mumbling jumbles of text.

What you need to know is made known to you. What I need to share naturally becomes shown and known by those that need the information. I mustn't push or force my purpose; that too is beyond my own won understanding or control. What I do is put my trust and faith into those that hold my fate in their heart. That's where I'd prefer to keep them too. My crack thoughts keep some secrets safe, yet I wish also to not have secrets. I want to (as punny as it is to say as an author) be an open book. If I do things that I wish others not to know that I do, then it may just be best not to do those things.

"Lead by example, even when there's no one to witness." - A random kid on Earth.

I've also been so focused on saying what I want for *my* life. As my heart learns, grows, and develops, I hope to find myself making wishes and intents for other people. I know that a substantial part of our journey is to cleanse myself and shed sin. I know, and many others know clearly too, that many of my faults, errors, and transgressions are clear. They are the past. The question to ask is: "How will we act moving forward?"

Grace and forgiveness are something that other people also need. They are things that I wish to not need so much of in the future. I can't control other people, though my own choices help provide opportunities for myself to adjust and, although a tricky word, recalculate what I'm doing, for who, and how. My penance is delicate and my own self-awareness and intent to share resolve strengthens. My understanding and illusions also find some mirages to be clearer than facts that the world's held as absolute truth. Not all things *are* static. As each of us grows, evolves, and changes, the facts of our own selves shift, thereby causing different causational reactions between others; those too whose truths may adjust the core of our being.

Please have faith in yourself. As I make the choice to put things out to the world that could be misdirected or construed incorrectly (or even exactly correct, showing my own weaknesses) I also put faith in readers, the world, God, and the Universe. My trust is be a pinnacle part of who I'm becoming, and my prerogatives and values guide me to act according to my own truths. I intuit that many of my solitary ramblings aren't so isolated as I had initially believed. A pervasive notion and bundle of ideas have been shared with you and you may do with them what you wish. The hope though is that you use them with your own talents and awareness to work for all of Earth.

There are few people that have yet read what's formed. Those people hold and radiate their own interpretations and perchance you should confer with some of them? I don't know how my books yet help others, yet my obsessive nature and intuition tells me that each row of text carries some notions of interest and worth. I need to heed a cohesive future for Full Seed to be revealed.

I thank you for carrying this book and its seeds and snowflakes up across the mountains of rhyme. I'm thankful that this book is almost complete. There must be trust that what we're tending does have worth. I kind of say

THE SANDS OF YESTERDAY

that to myself. Up to now there's been little earned from the written materials I've formed. This book's earnings go to the Seed Fund. I set that intent a while ago, and I do think it a manipulation of turning my works into something good for others.

I almost feel that writing more in this book is a waste. I've shared my wishes and intent, I've come back at myself from where I'll be five years into the future to now, and I've definitely displayed my own lack of clarity into the keys. Though, trusting that there still is much to form, maybe it's time to move into *Fields of Formation*.

I close this with some explicit requests of you.

Please clarify what your wants are. Write them down on paper and DON'T limit yourself. Create a full list of what you want and tuck the page away somewhere. Consider your page of wants as a wish and prayer outwards to boomerang back to you with blessings.

Clearly define what your own truths are. If you have doubt about your beliefs, talk with a trusted friend and tell them what your beliefs are. You, by speaking, may find out what your own truths are and learn new things about yourself. Having self-awareness allows you to more clearly tell others your wishes and wants. This then opens a channel for those wishes and wants to be more easily met as you let people know how to help you.

Develop and compound your awareness of the things that you like and love. Put your focus on these things you are glad or grateful for. The notion of these ideas compound and shift awareness as we gather comprehension.

Think of what you would do with your life if you had *zero* restrictions. Think of what you would do if you didn't have any time commitments and also what you would do if you were given a billion dollars. If you could go anywhere on the planet, or do anything you want to, what would you do and where would you love to go? Also add to these things, the question *"with whom* will you love to do these things with?"

Start envisioning and designing your dream home. I mentioned my home a few times in this book, though I didn't describe it to you and write a full chapter about it. I'll heed that as an idea for a future book. When you envision your home, you can imagine ANYTHING you want. Some people may think of a huge multi-story mansion, while others dream home may be an apartment or even a tiny home.

The last thing that I request in this book is to find your wishes, to find your dreams. Choose three to five things that are your ultimate wishes. Make those wishes known to people and keep them clear in your heart and mind as you carry through your life. I know that my wishes and dreams have shifted through time, though having a few key dreams brings us through as a guiding light and idea.

I may be both open and subvert with my goals, hopes, ambitions, visions, and dreams. As I do so, I hope and wish they increase the chance of them coming to fruition. The more people know what we want and wish for, the higher chance there is of people helping us attain those things and also coming alongside us. Perchance I've *written* a lot, though I hope to also *speak* my wants.

Seeds of Tomorrow is complete for now. I pray well that we may set the next book into the world in line with it being as the second Fountain of Faith. I still have much dreaming and forming to clarify why and how we travel along this journey, though I thank you for delving into my words. I send a wish out the Universe that you may find *your* Freedom Solution bring heart amongst the birds.

ROBERT KOYICH

Fields of Formation

(The 5th Fountain)

Developed from Yesterday

(Part Two in the series: *The Fountains of Faith*)

INTRODUCTION TO THE 5th FOUNTAIN

I've been digging in the dirt a bit, while also keeping my being in the clouds. This book is one that formed succinctly with my path of life. That's a good thing, as the Fountains books are meant to track my progress and ideas of life.

When I closed the 4th Fountain, I was Seed focused. This book started with ideas of the Seed Fund too, though, I also was called to heed different energies and people through the formation of the book. Though the individual Fountains are short books on their own, they'll be used in three-part compilations. We should not build our houses on sand.

The process of my own life has been tracked and traced, and though the timelines have been spaced out and apart, there's the truth that you and I hold the very same heart. We have been the same people we are in physical form since the point of our own lives inception. The changes to our values, meanings, and beings are part of the meld, and I hope that we continue with our lives, even when we may not be where we want to be.

The book *Fields of Formation* covers a span of three to four months where my own instincts and appreciations shifted and were lodged in some ways. A return to the base level of how we're fully integrated sometimes also hold away and apart from many people and ideas. Some things aren't yet things we should know. I'm surprised to have made it this far on the journey to releasing this book, and I hope it sits well in your being too.

 Though I still am not clear about many regarding the plan and the plot or community and consect affiliations, the process reminds me of the classic saying "Let the good flow with the bad."

Keep your own dreams and love open to chance. There's a dangerous and delicate dance of fortified protection and safety. I know not how deep the rabbit hole goes, and may it be best I don't find out. Perchance, though, we'll remember that the Earth is what defends the sprout.

The lives on Earth may be focal and local, yet we must remember too that there are some that're universal and not just global in this mission

CHAPTER ONE – It's Not All about You!

You're right, Mom, it's not. It's about (and for) all of us!

(May 11th, 2017 12:11 AM)

We have started the journey of the Seed. It's a long arduous process, though as we develop, the clarity of my heart and mind solidify.

Tonight I found a crucial variable for the Seed Fund's work in Chilliwack. Chilliwack has a population of 90,000 people. From a March 2017 count, there were 221 people who were counted as homeless, up from 73 people counted as homeless in 2014. If, as discussed in *Seeds of Tomorrow*, a Full Seed is $13.4k per year for one person to have an apartment, $50/week food, and also a bus pass each month, so let's math some ideas.

In the 2011 Census, it was the case that 30,135 people were employed in Chilliwack at that point including part-time employees. Taking the $4.02 million required for 300 Full Seeds divided by 30,135 employed people, that's $134 per person per year, yet if we make the numbers kinder, that's $11.17 per month. One hour of employed earnings, at almost minimum wage, is just enough to literally shelter, feed, and allow transportation for 300 people currently without a home and in need.

Karen is right, though, some people *choose* to be homeless. Some value the freedom of obligation and the luxury of not being fixed to a specific place. Some others, though, may wish to have a home and food and don't have that at this point. The work of the Seed Fund is to help those who do need *and* want help. If we're to 'solve' the situation it requires a unified effort. To do so it requires a great many people to 'fix' what some are concerned and complain about.

Many people may not understand poverty. I'm not clear that I completely understand either. At the point of writing this book, I was on PWD, a disability income. Being on welfare or disability is a gracious blessing and gift that allow some people a chance to live, even if not at a super prosperous level. Some people have a strong anger that their tax dollars are given as welfare or disability to people that "don't' want to work". I also have a strong intuition that there are many facts those in poverty or lack that many others don't know.

For the regulations of welfare (*not* PWD) in British Columbia, it's the case (as of May 2017) that the support rate for an individual is $235 per month plus a potential shelter portion of $375. I don't know how much rent costs in your community, though think of this shelter portion quickly... Where can a person live by paying only $375 per month to rent? This isn't quite rational.

Even if the support portion of $235 is combined with the shelter portion of

$375 and a person *can* find a place to live for $610 per month, where will the money for food or anything else come from? If shelter and food are covered, which rationally can't *both* be done with $610 a month, what of *anything* else that a person would like to have? Basic toiletries? Bus fare? Clothing? This $610 a month isn't enough for a person to live on.

Seeds of Tomorrow is where I shared my vision about the Seed Fund, yet the idea is compounding further in my awareness. It's not rational at this point to think that we'll house and feed all the people in the local community, let alone expand outwards and help others on Earth too. My faith and fear blend as I think the Seed Fund is a great thing, yet at this point I can't imagine how to perform well with the program for many on my own. My royalty earnings from books at this point are $42.70.

One hour per month from each employed person in our local community *can* literally house *every* current homeless person in our town, yet there are many that would laugh at this idea. I support the ideas of universal care, though I'm not foolish or naïve enough to believe everyone does. It almost seems sometimes like an exceptionally rare few do.

I know that I was not born in this town. I was removed from Vancouver in 2002 because of my drug use and a lot of unforgivable actions. I went through psychosis and rehabilitation and a decade and a half after being ejected and landing here, I'm still wary of my placement in this town. I was *not* born here, and sometimes I get apprehensive about my projected fears of not being welcome in this town too. It's not my town, though I still hope and wish that I am granted continued grace to help this community.

I've had concerns that some people and friends are angry with me for being too ambitious. This makes sense to me with some of how I've been pushing my works and living free when some of them have to work jobs they hate. I have an extreme aversion to structured employment both mentally and emotionally and I've demonstrated a running history of not lasting more than 6-9 months at a job before getting fired or quitting before I get fired. I may be a bit too 'wild and free' because I feel like a caged animal when I'm trapped or locked up in a job. My own value of freedom is exceptionally high, perhaps a bit too high.

We track and journal the process of my Freedom Solution. The books are one of the most crucial tools I use for my work and our journey. They are strongly centered and stemmed from my own self-obsessive viewpoint, and though there's not a vast readership yet, I have faith the vital contacts are made.

I have lots of ideas I'd like to share, quite a few people I'd like to write to, and I also want to evolve the books to be something that people *want* to track and read. I still, though, am only near the start of my writing process. What I've written has yet to be soaked up by people. I'm a sapling right now… maybe even a sprout.

There's a strong social component from what I write in these books. I've found through the printed copies of the first few books that I want to share my heart, story, and messages with some people. There are some that I really want to read the books for free, and I've also found myself overtly money focused while not entirely wanting to push for sales. I love having resources and not just those I share. My own materialistic wants are grand. I want to build a home that'll cost a great deal of money and have a car again, yet I still think the truth is I assure my own prosperity by providing for others.

My ideal personal expenses require only $2,500 a month, though as I set aside my wants and let myself work for others, I note there's an idea we earn a lot beyond that. I've heard from quite a few online people (and agree by faith and experience) that when we focus on *other* people's needs and wants, we often find joy, freedom, and prosperity by not focusing on our own needs, wants, and issues.

Although not the topic of this chapter, I recommend people finding their pathways to remember the wealth they have in different parts of their life; time, connection, and ability. These things should be focused on, shared, and appreciated to shift away from fear or lack.

Also wondered now, is what I share with you that read this book something that benefits *your* lives? Are you open to learning new ideas, concepts, and practices? Are you reading this because you're interested in the process? Did you contribute to the overlying cause of this book and *not* for reading it through? Was it recommended to you? Was it a gift to you? Have you read any other of my books? Or, is it because you too are one who has ideas and wants to develop *your* plan of how to help the world?

What if the books have evolved to the point that each preceding one focuses in on the failure and future of my own focal wants? What if writing these books causes a wave or movement that shapes our future to invert upon itself? What if they bring us each, even, a singular dream to finding our own soulmates; those of whom we build the future with? Should each book be different and catered to for the specific audience of all, some, one, or none? Is this just one kid and entirely unrealistic dreams? I know not. That's part of the journey.

I rest on an unnerving edge of what I write. I wonder if to fuel the book with my plans and dreams and if I'll wander into giving advice or recommendations. Some people like my rhymes; shall I write to entertain for those few too? I've not specifically targeted an audience with the Fountains. That's how they're like a fountain. Fountains are streams of life that hope to universally help those that sip from them.

Up to now, the books have formed in ways that're strewn and unfocused. They've followed pathways of natural formation. They also have honed in on many different and unique ideas from some varied perspectives. I want each chapter to be (partly) able to stand on their own as a crafted piece, yet I also admit my own 'one-take wonder' sort of writing. I'm not quite a professional writer, though I also think that parts of what I write carry their own value and increase in skill level.

With *Finding Natalie*, the cup of my heart was poured out *sul pavimento*. It was not something for just anyone to consume. I also really wonder if I was a cup of poison to the one person that book was intended for. Not all water is safe to drink. We know this as humans, though, that that *is* pure and clean to drink could be tainted by another. I've had the concern about this in my own mind and worlds of thought. My objective is to create things and works that *are* good and clean and that they remain that way. I'm not the only source of water though.

From TheWaterProject.org, it's said that one *billion* people don't have access to clean safe drinking water. One million people being granted clean and safe drinking water is only 0.1% of the total solution. That, to me, doesn't seem an adequate goal to set. I want there to be a *full* solution. I had set a big hairy audacious goal of the Seed Fund to be a foundation that provides clean and safe water to one million people. I don't see that as a large enough objective. I also, now, wonder of how we'll join forces to work for these larger objectives.

One thing I value and focus on is to read other people's books. The book I was reading when I started this book was authored by a person another thinks is only out for money. I completely disagree. My opinion is that there are many issues and challenges in the world that need funding, and that an effective organization needs to ask for and receive money. There's a lot to be done to help solve these larger global and international issues. The book *Giving: How Each of Us Can Change the World* was written by Bill Clinton. The book shares many different programs and initiatives and also shares how and what individuals can do to give to the world.

We know that people give time or money to causes, and that's even a bit easier than some other ways we help. Additionally, the gifts of skills and knowledge may be added, and they are valuable. Skills and knowledge may be taught and multiplied. If a person has $100 to give, only $100 may be relayed. The gift of teaching someone something, like *how* to earn $100, is then be passed on and forward across borders, and even generations, we may compound and provide much more.

Ideas are a powerful thing. The propagation of ideas is like the dandelions I've mentioned in previous books. Ideas may spread prolifically with mixed opinions; some people may not like how I scatter my ideas to the wind, yet some people do like dandelions. I don't want to be a weed. I'd prefer to be one to tend the fields and share good seed. If we have a good seed and tend it well, it may well be fruitful and produce crops that provide, share, and produce seeds for other people's fields and gardens.

I know it's not all about me, yet at the point when I wrote this, I was the only one contributing to the Seed Fund. If the fund is to expand and garner support, it'll require a lot more than just me plugging away at the keyboard typing words that none have seen. I need to focus too on *how* to get these ideas out to people. As much as I don't like marketing and pushing my works, it's necessary at this point. There aren't too many people yet helping the expansion of these projects as far as I'm yet aware.

I need to quit scattering my ideas and thoughts to the wind and actually get my hands and heart deep in the dirt. Please let me start making things grow! As I'm the one that's started this process, it's my commitment and action to allow it to flourish. I'll need to marshal astonishing support; both through book sales and also partnerships with communities, individuals, and organizations. The Seed Fund may reach a point of full prosperity, and although my own fear and faith tell me I'm on the right track, we'll need to garner massive amounts of love, luck, and support.

As the Mox Diamond said, asking a person for money for a book AND the time commitment to read is a big ask for quite a few of people. The idea of providing *is* a good one, though it matters not if people don't believe in it too. Math and numbers are easy to form, though the *activation of achieving those goals* is one thing I've had a great difficulty to meet. If the fields are our communities and the gardens are our own individual lives and groups, though nothing grows if nothing's planted.

I do ask and request your help. There are quite a few things that people could do to help, and not all of it is money or the purchase of a book. You could share *your* ideas, feedback, and opinion. If you're a friend, you could invite another out for coffee to talk about *your* lives and *your* dreams. You also may ask for people's advice or recommendations. As you start thinking about what *you* could like to do for the world and others if you were unlimited by any means, you also may find what you *shall* do to be part of the solution on a personal, local, national, and/or even global level.

If you have your own ideas and dreams, please share them with someone! I've heard a bit recently the words *micro* and *macro*. Some people dream big. I like that. There are some people that're committed, driven, and passionate to work for large-scale ideas. I must remind myself that I'm in an exceptionally fortunate and blessed position to have the luxury of being able to dream. That's where the macro shifts to micro… some people aren't large scale.

Remember that some people aren't clear on if they want to live, if they'll have their next meal, or if they'll ever have a home. Even some that do have a home to live in may not have the inspiration to form wishes, dreams, and plans to form a future they'll love. I know that it's difficult, sometimes, to have hopes and visions for the future, though it's a lot easier when one's basic needs are met. I commit to the process. This work is to provide. I also commit to jostling some hearts back into the reminder that many of us *do* have amazing hearts and lives, and that we should not hoard them to ourselves.

The key reminders from this chapter are to please remember that we're not alone on this planet, that there *are* people in need, and that they can use your support. There's so much that we may give to another even if we don't have money and resources; a greeting, a prayer, a gift to uplift their dignity. Another kind soul may need reminding that they are worthwhile and loved. I've not shown that clearly, and that too is where I need to learn and grow.

I need to develop my own heart and slow down. I also should remember that some people don't want things or money or substances. Some people, like me, also may need to be given a bit of truth, kindness, connection, and love. There are many ways to give; be creative!

CHAPTER TWO – A Brief Trickle of Insight

As many of us have lived on this planet for more than ten to twenty years, it also doesn't mean that we've not lived only one life. This chapter is a streaming chapter. It stems from the advice of tonight to "Do what you love, and love what you do"-Josie Savoie. I like to write, and though I may meander like a stream, I recently have read and been given the advice to share more of my heart.

I open myself up to the Universe in a call for faith. I ask for the insight, guidance, blessings, and protection of what is right and good for many and not just myself. I ask the Universe to clearly place each letter and sequence and moment of time to assist the fact I know that these books are each a pact made.

Though we wade in the water of what we hear and say, the senses blend and find the Pearl to come astray. I feel the full union of the soul in the moment of how we know that maybe I'm in the field, and that the world *is* planting the seeds through me as the plow. I won't be too poetic, yet I also must heed my own intuition of the saxophone reed. Mr. Clinton, I may call on you for help. Please don't turn a cold heart or response toward me. I've repeated this a lot and shall continue to do so.

"We are all on the same planet."-Leslie Park.

The quote was given to me on a DMT trip. I makes me remember that the world is unified in its state of being in similar ways. Every life is separate and distinct, yet this links us all. If we're human and are, or have been, alive, we each know the same one thing: Life. My often unfocused ideas have been upon the human condition, though I acknowledge also the forces of Heaven and Earth and must trust in the other animal signs and guides too. Some people don't like crows. I do. Crows have guided me with the inner workings of my soul and life of reciprocity.

An idea for a book is to have each chapter to be a word from the extended PLUR credo and philosophy, the PLUR term I use. We know that philosophy is valuable; especially when we want to know what our own values, morals, and ideas are. My Freedom Solution includes making what I want to make and for whom I want to make it; my creative freedoms. I also note from Randy Pausch (RIP: 2008) that freedoms come with responsibility.

Bizarrely, I don't even have a full comprehension or belief that I have an entitlement to my own rights. I still consider myself to be an exceptional example of a mysterious and wonderful grace that's allowed me to do what I do and have what I have. I hold an eternal gratitude for the fact I'm allowed to live, be, and exist. I'm baffled by the fact that I'm still alive.

I've wanted that other people also have their lives tended to and supported. I have a deep thankfulness for my life being taken care of. I *have* been loved, cared for, and tended to. I want that for others also.

I learn more about others and the value of what they've done for us. I learn and appreciate this through my own awareness of the awesome grace and blessings that I've been given. Even if not always conscious of it, I'm eternally afraid that my gratitude isn't of a magnitude great enough to assure that I continue to be able to live the life I have. My want of others to thrive is so that we *all* have lives we'll cultivate and love to share.

It doesn't make sense to me why I'm so fortunate. The online gurus and coaches would say that we create the lives we live. They tell us to focus on gratitude and to hone in on the things we like and love to produce more of that. I also recall a message to a friend I wrote that said: "It's okay to want things." I still believe this.

As I wrote this, I found a deep fear of losing my own position of life. I value my creative freedom to write what I want, though I also have a resonant fear in my soul of others wanting to end my life because I've been so free. My fear of envy and others wanting the life that I have draws a neurotic twist. I want others to have an amazing life too so that others also have lives they love. This awareness is different.

I need to perform more inner work. I need to shed falsities and resentments. I need to find my own faults, expose them, and burn them clear from my own being. Is that why I smoke? There's for me a great audacity to do what I do. I don't claim sovereignty over another person, place, or thing. I accept entire responsibility for what I do, have done, and shall do. Again, this brings fear to me. My determination of some of the 'R's of the extended PLUR credo help me stabilize myself.

PLUR is explained in the other books, though if this is the first time you've encountered the word/term, the base is Peace, Love, Unity, and Respect.

The '8' that I've written in my version of PLU8R is added as infinity and also many other 'R' words. An example is my Responsibility to tend and create.

Representation, Reciprocity, and Reciprocation also are R words. I've been given an exceptional amount of grace and I wish that it be granted to others too. I believe in equality, and my own fear of the scales having been tipped so far in my own favour, have me fearing another R; Retribution. I note that Retribution *isn't* an R of PLU8R, though Restoration and Redemption are. Relevation (to thoroughly enjoy something) and Revelation also are PLU8R words, and as a human with a mind, part of our work is to make sense of others and ourselves, which leads to Rationalization.

Recognition is a PLU8R word. I recognize, for the accord, and myself, that I must abide by PLU8R in full regard. It's a co-requisite of me being part of life as I also know that the streams and waters of life flow as they shall.

I must be a vassal and servant of Peace. I must develop and learn and cultivate my own understanding of Love. I must strive to work for, and not against, Unity. I also must foster, cultivate, and share mutual Respect. My own Responsibility to create and tend is vital to and for this. I also must remember that Repentance and Reparations are also part of PLU8R. I must atone for my mistakes and acknowledge my faults. I don't want to rely on grace or special treatment to allow myself to live.

It may be grace and not a right to life that keeps me alive at this point. If some believe that I *do* have a right to life, please let that be something to assist. I'm not clear on what my own *actual* rights are. What allows them to be so? My appreciation for having what I have is something that continues to grow and amplify through time, though I hope I may be given and keep a right to life.

I hope others also want to share the things they appreciate. There's a strong component that I want others to have lives they're thankful for. For those that don't have lives they love, I want to help them find their way into a future where they also may be grateful for the lives they have. My focus and access to resources have been an overtly known topic. The positive spiritual and soulful feelings and appreciations also are something I'd like others to experience.

It's the case that every person on Earth is explicitly in his or her own shell of a body. I try to articulate with words what my thoughts are, yet the feeling of who we are and how we are in the world are often explicitly our own to know. I added the word 'often' because of my own psychosis.

During my psychotic episodes and some of my drug trips I had found myself transforming entirely into different people and felt as if I was them, and not myself. This may still have been purely imaginary, yet my experiences of 'becoming' other people are clear in memory. Even if it was me imagining what other people were like, it's the closest I've ever been to 'being' another person.

We can hear what a person says. What they say may not be what they feel. We sometimes may think, or even know, that what another person is saying *isn't* the truth. Many people do lie and use deception and I hope many of these deceits may be revealed. There's also the point, sometimes, when a person tells us the truth and we don't believe them. Still yet, another key point of truth is that sometimes what is true in one moment of time may not be true at another point. What is fact may change, just as we, as people, change, evolve, and shift.

Another strange point to consider about us is how we change and evolve in the future. We also may have changed some of our truths from the past. The wild and wonderful notion too is that *you* have been in the exact same body from birth until now in the life you are currently living. I've played with these ideas in a semi-random question I ask of some people: "Who are you today?"

I was born as Robert. I still am Robert. Who Robert is in nodal physical form is the same human that was born 39 years ago. The many different people that have encountered him on Earth may each have a different concept of who he is. A lot of what they believe or knew may have been fact at that point, and a lot of what some have believed or claimed may have been false. The vast array of who we are and what people think of us doesn't change the fact of *who* we are. I'm myself, just as you are yourself.

What was true or viewed a decade ago is still bundled with beliefs, memories, and opinions of what *was*. Regarding ourselves, there are parts of us that haven't yet surfaced. We may dig deep and find truths about ourselves and the process through self-reflection to aid us in learning about our own selves. Other's feedback tells us things we may not know about ourselves, and as our opinions and truths shift, we may change in how we act with those new beliefs.

Just as we may change who we are and what we believe in, other parts of our lives may change. With the advice I was given, that we can change our commitments with our own intents and ideals, I revised my Income Declaration. I use capital letters for that term, Income Declaration, similar to the ideas of Seed Fund and Freedom Solution. The ideas are vital to myself and how I act and behave. They are components of my financial situation here on Earth.

The need to revise my own Income Declaration from December 14th, 2016 came from the fact that I know I'm in a transitory financial situation of my own lack. I also know I know how when I made the initial income declaration *Seeds of Tomorrow* was not yet formed or part of the agreement. I didn't know I'd use 100% of the earnings for the Seed Fund. Why do I do this?

I wish that others too could work with their abilities and skills to generate an income from their own creative efforts. I also wish that my works be used as a conduit to provide. Though sometimes the boat may not need the end of the river, maybe the rains fall to wash away the leaves.

We shall see how this evolves.

PLU8R!

CHAPTER THREE – Dive a Bit Deeper

(Delving into who others think I am, and some confirmations by myself)

The previous section really meandered off course from its start. I've often liked psychoanalyzing myself when I talk to some people. I've not quite done it in the written form though. The premise of this chapter, for me, is to dive a bit further into the core of who I am, why I do what I do, and also to increase my own self-honesty.

I've told you I'm fearful. It's true. I also am in the process of opening up myself like a can of worms. Comments in the previous books spoke about how I have a lot of internal wreckage and my own want of further exposition and exploration unites. Before delving into my projected viewpoints of what I think others think about me, if we even get there, is to let you know some more about me that goes pre-Chilliwack (2002).

From my raver days, one of my best friends was Dave. Dave and I had a bunch of drug trips and associations (ecstasy and mushrooms). We were friends in high school and also during my first two years at SFU. Dave was a friend who reminded me that I was exceptionally all about the drugs and that I neglected people as people. I mention Dave, though, from the way he introduced me to some new people one time: "This guy swears like a motherf@$ker!"

It trips me up a bit still that this was how Dave introduced me like a great selling point; that I swore a lot. For the first printing of *Finding Natalie*, my angst had drawn out a 30x F'bombs in that book alone, though I adjusted and edited most of them out for *Fragments of Intent*. I've sometimes caught myself when I'm about to swear. There's a layer of a perchance more common thing that I know of; not doing things because of the fear of how we'll be judged. Not swearing with some people is a respect thing (my cousin has a preference I don't when we talk) and it also is that I don't want any swears I write or say to dissuade another from reading what I've formed.

So, in the past my vulgarity was a selling point? I don't want to market that.

The second point of my past; I also used to lie A LOT. I recall that lots of my lies were over-exaggeration to impress. I also know I'd hide the truth. I still hide truth sometimes, though in some cases this may be a good thing if my paranoid delusions are true (I'll discuss later). I also note I have a want of keeping other people's secrets, though my mind is easily hacked. I can't hide my own secrets quite well, I think, yet when there's confidential information, I fear a mental leak.

Exaggerations to impress lead to the next part. I've so often, and still sometimes do, focus on making a good impression, or, phrased more-so with my recent attempts, to 'make people like me.' I've been over-focused on being seen in a positive light, and from my own perceptions, I've not done so well with my own habitual failure and recovery. There're only a rare few people that, from what I tell, that actually like me for who I am. The strange part is *I'm* not always clear on who I am. My own duplicity of what I say, what I mean, what I want, and what is true are far too often mixed up and interchanged. I wish to shed my own behaviour of acting to impress. It's going to be tough, though, as I sometimes fear who I really am.

I'd like to change that further. I'd like to clear my unknown self into my own mind and then not be so fearful about speaking what is true about myself. Speaking truth is vital, though I'll also respect what is confidential information about others and am tactful.

I have a mental urge to purge and repent the things I've been learning about myself that I don't like. A word I've used quite frequently is 'intent' and I've been finding many places where I'm off. The underlying layer should not be *what* I intend on doing, though rather *why* am I doing things. After I cleanse my intents to *be* the right reasons (and not what I *think* are the right reason) maybe I'll learn how to *actually* be a decent person.

Many people know about the Seed Fund and what I want to do with it, though I think I've been fooling my own self. I could present you all the theories, though I also don't want to type them if they are false. It'll require some clarity and self-analysis, yet I do need to self-investigate myself. I also recall some divulged information that I've heard in conversation allows me to know some of my own secret truths.

I know what I'm going to do and my commitments are made. I also know that I've repeated and rehashed and told many others what the Seed Fund is to do. I don't like how much focus I've put to Seed to have yet done so little. My belief is that I'm trying to force the process of books for my own benefit, though I don't want acclamation for what I'm doing. I do, though, want there to be a cause that *we* (not just me) work with and for. I'm trying to gather people together, sometimes, though I've not done it well. I admit additionally with the financial part of the Seed Fund is that I know full well if we *do* generate Full Seed that my own financial situation shall easily cared for.

Let's go back to some fears, though. I think that I'm also drawing a lot of negative attention from pushing the Seed Fund. I have a lingering concern that I've been making too many promises and declarations that may call people to be angry with me. Some people would say 'you can't please everyone', yet I also know that by pushing my books, music, and ideas have put many away and off about me. Some lines from Lauryn Hill's song *Forgive Them Father* call out to me:

"They say all the right things, to gain their position
Then use your kindness as their ammunition
To shoot you down in the name of ambition"- Lauryn Hill

These lines shift in and out from the different perspectives. The key part is how I've been preaching and proclaiming ideas for prosperity that I think people are upset with me for wanting to accomplish so much. The notion of people playing me like a pawn, take all they can from me, and then get rid of me. I have the honest concern I've wished for too much and that even if I earn for the Seed Fund, that I'll be considered greedy and smote.

My own fear felt then calls back two other ideas: 1) If your dreams and visions for life don't scare you, they're not big enough, and 2) Even if we do succeed with Full Seed, would people still get jealous and want to remove me? The advice from the Diamond Mox (not revealing their real name) seemed to have told me that they think I've been greedy and asking for too much. There's also an alluded concern that if the books are formed and gain traction, then why would I be needed to be kept alive if they're already formed?

Then Gabrielle's advice calms me... The Holy Instant. The Universe has my back. I must trust that what is being done, what's been done, and what is done is for the best interest of all. My latent Christian concern, though, is that I don't have knowledge of God's plan for me, and I have a fear he is using me too as a fool or martyr of whom I wish not to be.

Other people have relayed the notion: "You know dead rappers get better promotion"- Jadakiss

Good thing I don't consider myself a rapper. What if others do though?

There've been a few people that have told me that artists don't become famous until after they die. A note to place and share; I don't want to be famous that way. I'm not seeking post humus acclaim or fame. What it boils down to is that I want to be free to do whatever I want to do and should be wise about how I act. Some people admire those that have the 'whatever it takes attitude'. Some people are honoured and lifted up and encouraged to do what they want to do. I've not yet seemed to have understood that I may be garnering that type of support.

The fact I've *not yet* found my solution to freedom I take as a sign that my intents and alignment are off. If I *am* doing the right things for the right reasons, would I not be generating the right results? I think I'm far too self-interested in my work. Am I trying to fool myself? NO! I think I *have* fooled myself.

I've had the belief that if I was working for a cause that's valuable, that I could enlist support for that cause. When I presented a speech to Toastmasters last week, my call to action was: "Be part of the solution." Radical honesty? I wish that I could abandon the *promotion* of the Seed Fund and just put my full committed earnings into it. I'd like finance people, not just those homeless, without the need to enlist the support of others. I feel like a daft fool making proclamations of "provide shelter for 250,000 people" or "provide clean water to a million people" or even putting up posts asking people to help the cause when, up to when I wrote this, few have cared enough to even talk about it with me. Maybe I need to start the conversation more often.

Though if we want to have a conversation, with whom?

I'm quite skilled at spinning my own wheels on my own personal journey. Why should I broadcast as a fool when no one else is willing to help share the ideas? Ideas such as each person having their basic needs of food, shelter, and water met *at a minimum*. The solution of near one hour's wages per month from each employed person, $11.17 a month, would provide so much for the homeless in this town! It does find me with astonishment that people would argue the idea. Then again, that's why I think I'm a fool. Why would anyone care about my wishes? Think of the basic human decency! I now know I have a mix of sheer disappointment and anger sometimes; I can't make people care... that's clear... How do we find people to work together for the benefit of many?

It starts with a seed.

Well... I guess I went off course. This chapter (when I started) was meant to dig at myself and my faults. Should I recap them? I'm too self-focused. I try to impress people. I push my own agenda a lot. I don't keep people's secrets well. I'm sometimes money focused. I've not tended or cultivated friendships with people. I've been irresponsible and haven't found a way to support myself. I've squandered away decades without starting my own family. I gave up on holding a full-time job. I've spammed my friends by marketing books and push promotion. I've sent too many messages to some when not wanted. I've not *actually* found my own profession or vocation (unless it's these books (which seems pretty unlikely from the results up to now)).

Though as the chapter says, let's dive a bit deeper.

I've relied on support from others to sustain my own irresponsible life. I've not fully honoured my mother or father. I've evaded some people because I've gotten into the routine of giving them things. I've inadvertently sought to help ensure I don't get removed by making the choice to help others. There are some friends I've avoided because I don't like interacting with them. In many conversations I've focused on my ideas, issues, or projects instead of valuing and having interest in the other person. I've acted like a coward and have lived in fear. And, my own ethical faults still are held behind walls from the text of this document.

I've sought my own monetary gain by forming books and attempting to gain interest in my work and myself. I've withheld my concerns and advice from people because I'm afraid they'll not like me. I've not given to some because of my own scarcity mentality and, in some cases, due to my own judgmental nature.

I've complained about things and have spoken harshly of some. It doesn't matter why, it's the fact that I have. I've used gimmicky marketing tactics. I'm had pity parties and have played the poor me card often to solicit sympathy. The issue of checking out gals is one that still hounded me. I've not taken a genuine interest in other people's concerns, issues, or situations. I've put faith in the world. I've lacked faith in myself. I've lacked faith in Jesus. I've relied on my faith in the Universe and God to cover my needs. I've abashedly revealed a great many of my own secrets to the world and still have asserted that it's a trust issue to have faith in the process.

I try to pull back some of my layers of deception and manipulation to try to gain favor and trust from others while still crafting my words to hide the deeper layers. My intents of the heart are still chained to a tree that should be free of myself by now. My greed shines brightly by wanting to have enough money to build the Glass House. I've plotted and planned to own buildings in the future to rent out to others (potentially Seed recipients) so that I'll be able to afford my future life.

I've explicitly not stepped up to help some people from my own cowardice and also neglect. I've clearly, even if only known to my own self, have analyzed things and shifted my viewpoint on them to focus and work for my own benefit and good. I even noticed how I typed 'I've' so often (which is I-have (implying my own semi-conscious wish to have even more)).

The fact that I have my own place and luxuries of food, smoke, and drink, when there are many that don't have a home? The truth that there are some people that I'll not let into my home as a guest, yet still talk with them and be their friend. The fact that I'm still paranoid that people would try to break into my home and harm me and/or take my things. The idea that others should be able to have all the luxuries that I have, even if they are given for free with zero expectation of reciprocation. The idea that I've said that I'll do all sorts of things, yet they've been promises for things that I've

THE SANDS OF YESTERDAY

yet to provide.

To me, it seems like a losing battle. My wishes, declarations, and even prayers for hope and support are like I'm trying to barter with God and Earth. I have a daft ability of not knowing what it's like to actually BE a friend instead of trying to gather friends like Pokemon. My wish and hope to be a socialpreneur or run a visionary enterprise have had me pushing my works and ideas so much that I actually have alienated myself and lost much true friendship and connection with so many people. I've not even been able to *actually* sell things! Add that I've lived so freely and without restrictions when some people slave 50+ hours a week and *still* can't yet cover their own family's basic needs. And the final point, still sitting pretty on my crystal seat with a laptop to type on and sparking a cigarette (when some don't even have bread)!

It seems it doesn't matter what I wish. It seems it doesn't matter what I dream. The facts of life are here.

I AM living a blessed life, I AM in my own situation that's nowhere near the poverty of which many have. I DO have my creative and living freedoms (that others may be jealous of) and I also have my wishes. I want to guide you to chapter eleven that I wrote in *Seeds of Tomorrow*: *My Ultimate Wishlist*. Even if I mean every word that I wrote in that chapter, it's a high probability that it doesn't matter to almost all people on Earth.

In *Fields of Formation*, it seems the shift is too great. I do have my creative freedoms (my books, my work, and my words) yet I know I can't bribe you, God, or the Universe with my wishes.

Following what I said in this chapter, it twists back to what *is* right and true. My wishes are given to the Universe, and also to you. Even if my own words are trite, self-focused, and unfocused, maybe there are some wishes you too have that you can post out to the world. Through reading what I wrote, yet still a note may float up upon the shoreline.

CHAPTER FOUR – A Need to Reveal

Does each person have a need to share his or her heart? Is the soul that I feel my own isolated point of energy that no one else can perceive or experience? Or, are we all connected to life without choice? Does my work even matter? My answers? I find I wish to share my heart, I know my soul has often been plundered and exposed, and I'm thankful we made the choice to live. For the last question, even if my work matters to no one else, I have gratitude that it's formed.

I think I've been too problematic with my proclamations and audacious wishes. I need to curl back up with myself and reset and ground. Even if I repent or have made wishes to the Universe and God for things way out of my current realm of ability, I must trust they are known and delve back into myself and what is and what's not in my control.

A lesson from PD Seminars; Breathe, Aware, Acknowledge, Accept, Action, Appreciate, and Humour.

I must breathe and bring life into my own body. As I remember to breathe and relax and go inwards, I become aware of things; ideas, feelings, memories, and thoughts. I then must acknowledge them; to myself and/or another. As I become aware of things, both new and old, and then tell them to another, or myself. I then shift to the third A; accept.

Acceptance is vital. We may be aware of many things of ourselves that haven't been acknowledged. Our own secrets or traits that we know of ourselves may be things that we're conscious of, though, as I sometimes do with my writing, they must be noted and shared. As I acknowledge my own faults, and also positive points, my acceptance of them being the truth is not always easy. I'm aware I'm self-focused and dream. I let you and others know that. As on this personal journey, I realize *and accept* that that's part of who I am.

The fourth 'A', action is the next part. What am I going to do about it?

I've made the choice to continue with my work. I may not be successful with sales and distribution, though I know that I do gain much from the forming of these books, even if I've not yet earned an audience to help share my ideas. Lori Christine (a fellow Toastmaster) shares often with her talks. Her talks include crucial lessons, ideas and concepts. One of the first lesson I heard from her was talking about how to overcome fear and that carries into this text.

I have to release my fear(s) and I do. I first must be aware of them, acknowledge them, accept them, and then make the choice of what I'll do. I may be afraid I won't earn my own income from my written work, and my choice is to accept that and still move forward. Kevin's advice about doing what I do for myself, and not others, is one bit of advice I had pushed away from. I thought I needed to do more for the world and not for my own benefit.

Solemnly, I'm okay at the moment of now. My income choices have been made, and I honour them. I also, though, must release my need to achieve them. I need to be okay with what is and not all that I wish for. I must be okay with my current situation and not be stressed out by not having not yet reached my audacious goals. I have to accept that the world may not need what I create. I must be okay and accept (and be gracious for) the few people that *do* care and love and support. I must quit wanting more and appreciate what *is*.

That said, the idea to shift back to gratitude. I thank God and the Universe and the forces of life for allowing me to be. This journey and process holds facts of what *is* and what I think needs to be. There's a bit of pressure and self-imposed stress for not yet reaching my goals *and* a nudge for a bit of self-compassion instead of self-condemnation.

What would happen if I shed my want of money? What would happen if I shed my believed need to provide for others? What would happen if I released full control of my spirit into the Universe to use me as *it* wants me to be used? What would happen if I realize that it doesn't matter what *I* want? What would happen if I learned to appreciate and allow myself love? I know I've put far too much focus and projected importance on myself. I also know that I've not released full control of my own words.

Our divinity is kinds of Id that fuse the kid's rhymes as a way to lift the lid and dues of what they choose. I allow the plow to be held another way and stay true to the fact that my work is learning how to thrive and play, and not how to act today. The pacts of the grave save me to be free to see that it doesn't matter what I am or want to be; that each turn of the key allows thee to understand. I still learn and land in trusted hands to unhand the reigns I never hold. I'm far too young to consider myself to not be told the plot isn't bold.

Thank you. I'm calm now. Even though you've no idea what I've written, I thank you for allowing me to be. A tentative inversion of how when I release and resist not the plan of the plot that You bring me back to what you think I'm not.

I'm not a savior. I may not be, as much as I thought, a fool. I'm not as vital as I wished to be, and there may be safety in that. If I release my preconceived wishes, ideas, and ideals, we'll find the thread to wind back about the spool. We *are* held together here on Earth and I should remember that some others too wish to push their agendas as I have. I can't understand, yet, what it's like to be a Dad, though I also note I'll find more of myself when I get to be grand.

Thank You again for the reminder. Thank You again for the hope. Thank You again for the fact that I learn to help myself thrive and not just cope. Gabby too, thank you for reminding me that if I've sent a wish or prayer out to not hound it for completion. I'm part of the Universe, my wishes are known and have been made, yet I also must allow time to hold the form of what truly is to be relayed.

Maybe this work should shift back to the form of writing that's written to specific people. Perchance it's the case that I should stop, sit back, and think. Although I'm not the vital link that I was attempting to wish myself to be, there may be more for YOU to share that keeps the ideas free to float in the wind, skies, oceans, land, seas, and air.

I don't want to slip back into rhyme mode right now. For myself, I've said enough in this super-short chapter. Extreme gladness to know I release the reigns and allow this to carry on into a new field. For today, I wield the keys no more.

Thank You for your guidance and grace. I shall share my insight and continue to explore.

CHAPTER FIVE – A Cross for the Tapestry

I've clarified and honed a few things in the past few days, though they don't seem to be an increase in faith that I'm doing the right things. I've made some proclamations about how and why I'm working, and I think I've been deluding myself a bit. I've also been talking too much about some things and rehashing some ideas.

I seem to think in the past few days that the books are pretty well a muddle. I've made four of them up to now, and I'll keep making them. I've also started two other books that I'll complete and think they're interesting pieces of work. With the Fountains books, I also may say some additional things about them from the past week.

1) I don't know how to push or market them.
2) I was using the Seed Fund as a draw for my own prosperity.
3) I still keep my money commitments with the books. I just don't know how they'll sell.

The middle point is where I think the clarity (and other points) stemmed from. I was asking people to help the Seed Fund and buy books. I was not provding with prosperity, though rather asking for prosperity so that I can provide. The words (even in my own mind and text) spin in and upon themselves. I'll help with contributions from the book earnings, though maybe I should not ask for sales by marketing to people only so that they support the fund.

I also had a weird Facebook message a few days ago. A person that I barely know had messaged me saying that they were at Dairy Queen and desperate because they didn't have money for food. As per usual, I could say a few many things about this. I've only met the person once before, they told me they didn't have money because they are an impulsive spender, and I think too, since I was at home in my gonch and in mid-laundry, that the request to drop everything and go pay for their meal was not a very rational thing to do.

I've had concerns with the Seed Fund in that it could be used as a mooch point. That people would know I have the money or gift cards, and then ask for them and use me often. I've had some key (what I think) are good uses of the fund though. One friend is without full-time hours right now and was to go without food due to a lack of money. I transferred them some Seed (and personal) money to them, and I hope it was a good choice.

Another friend once borrowed $50 from Seed and paid it back in about three to four days later with a $5 return given without request. I like this! The first $5 donation from another who's not me into the Seed Fund! Two other friends also gave me $20 for Seed work; $10 for ordering the next batch of *Seeds of Tomorrow* books and $10 to the fund itself. When people are honourable and maintain their promises, the fund more easily shall assist.

When there are other people that want to abuse, there could be other issues. One friend had borrowed $50 from the Seed Fund knowing that they would not be able to borrow more past the $50 level. They had made a promise to repay on the next Welfare day and did not follow through on their promise. They later said they would pay back the $50 a month later on the next cheque. They did not. This friend also later asked me if they could borrow more money. I did not let them borrow and then thought the idea to *give* them $20 as support and not a loan. I had messaged them to contact me, and they hadn't.

Mixed up in this are how I do wish and want people's needs to be met, and the opposite side of not wanting to be used and abused for resources. It's a muddle that I've yet to clear. I don't want people to be in dependency upon others, yet at the beginning of this book I spoke of how I want to fund 285 people in town so they *do* have a home. As the saying goes: "I've been making promises that I can't cash."

So then in the middle of *Fields of Formation*, I pivot, I restate my commitments, and I move past the process of pushing a cause that hasn't succeeded with the current parameters. My percentages for the books and music that go to the Seed Fund are maintained, though I'm not clear if I should market the fund. Perhaps. I should, though, get to work, market, and sell the books (and future books) and keep writing. I do leave a huge portion of this up to the Universe to do with it what it will.

In *Beautiful, Do You Mind?* I also had audience awareness of my books. I'm getting clear that I write my books for anyone who is to read them. Fountains book audiences are anyone who's interested in my process, progress, thoughts, journey, and work. BDYM is for anyone who's interested in relationships, a shared future, and thoughts about communication. *Built from Within* is for anyone who's interested in wellbeing, communication, and interpersonal connection.

I also want to help people find their pathways and creative works! There's a pretty rad and amazing contact from Lewis Howes' mastermind Facebook page named Florencia. She's definitely started well on her journey! Florencia's in the initial parts of starting a book *Add Some Latino to Your Life* about how to live life more vibrantly with a positive attitude. She's an amazing and interesting person, and she's also super bright and positive. Her Facebook pages *Flor Real* and *Add Some Latino to Your Life* are in English, though I've seen Florencia's Spanish videos. Although I don't yet understand the language, Florencia is so wonderfully enthused and radiant with her energy! I love the way she says things because she means it fully from her being!

(Insert another night of sleep between these paragraphs).

We trip into wanting and becoming capable of helping other people in ways other than money; by sharing knowledge, counsel, or advice. I like this shift. I want to find people that're open to creating and collaborating with our lives. A few many years ago I wanted to be a counselor. I wanted to help people with their emotional and mental issues and help find solutions for them. The idea of being a life-coach also was spinning through my mind a bit through the past years, yet I've not yet sought out the training to do so.

Introversial is where I've been going with this. The basis is to help cultivate positive futures with and for people through creative means and invested effort and heart. There needs to be a shift to work for other people and not just myself from the information I've learned and continue to learn. I'll also need to earn trust from people so that they'll allow me to be an active participant in the lives they want to create.

For some people, I'm just be a friend. I'm a loyal ally that they may contact to talk and process. The life-coach part of my being doesn't include payment for services or a structured program to follow. I must open my heart to some people too that have been mooching resources and find other ways of helping them instead of allowing dependencies to form. Will it be the case that if I cut off the channels of free or borrowed things that the friends will actually still want to have a shared connection?

Then too, I must gather my own awareness as to how I'm valuable in another's life beyond money and resources. I'm a friend that's okay to talk about almost anything. I'm a good listener and let other people talk about their issues and lives. Regarding businesses and creativity, I have knowledge about selling on eBay and also have gone through the self-publishing process. I can give advice about both. I have a willingness to meet up with most people to have focus sessions where we may focus solely on their own lives while setting mine aside

Some people may not believe that I set myself aside or that I *do* want to discuss other people's lives and solutions. I'd like to expand my network of contacts and I've *not* pushed myself so far out to do so. I've found it valuable to know other people because then I may bridge connections between other people. Knowing business owners can connect them with good/decent people or friends searching for work.

I have a super strong belief in people sometimes, though I also note some of my own challenges. I've been judgmental, I've been reactive, and I've blamed some people for actions and thoughts that I don't like. I think to maybe ask them the reasons as to *why* they do what they do. When I find people acting in wasy I don't like, instead of getting mad or judgmental, I think I should step back, and sometimes away, and engage in dialogue about *their* reasons to behave that way. I need to be more curious about people's reasons for action instead of separating myself from them with anger or disapproval. There may well be some vital reasons people do things that I don't understand. I need to make far fewer assumptions.

I also today saw some of my all or nothing actions. I found this tonight at Toastmasters. During the break I was more comfortable to go outside and have a smoke alone instead of mixing with the people in the building. If I want positive relationships to form, I must actively engage in building them. They won't just magically happen! Facebook is a place where I check in almost every day, though not the way I used to be on the site. I used to message all the green dots (people online) and also track *every* post on my newsfeed. I was trying too hard at pushing connections then, and now I've been so lax and passive that I've shifted from overtending to being quite inconsistent. The classic term of 'balance' trips in here.

With marketing, I see all sorts of stuff online and in my email inbox. I know the ways that some people build and structure their work, projects, and programs to make money, yet I (contrary to some friends viewpoints) haven't desired money so much to use some of the tactics. Tactics also are NOT always a bad thing. It's great to know one's plan as to *how* to earn money. I may not strongly enough want to push and market in ways that others do.

There are some people that're all about sales funnels (which work) and also about dipping into different Facebook and Google+ sites to put themselves into the communities. Gary's *Jab, Jab, Jab, Right Hook* book holds premises I also agree with. There's the premise to give, give, and give. The premise holds also to not just give for the fact of wishing a future gain.

A YouTube channel could be put online to seek viewership. Daily Instagram posts and live videos can push ideas and content through that platform. With Facebook, the live video function and making a video every day can gain attention and share one's process. A shift to webinars and selling coaching or marketing programs is an option. Affiliate marketing can sell another company's products and developing and marketing one's own products can be effective. There are a few ways that we can make money.

I could push my music and make music videos to draw attention. I have

YouTube videos, though there's a weird twinge in me that knows I don't want to be a musician as a full trade and focus. I make music, though it's not central to who I am. It's highly peripheral. Music and production *was* an exceptional identity that I lived before, though now I'm the one who plays my own music the most. The other fact from what I've made in the past decade or so is that I don't even really fall into any genre. That's where the word intorversial came from; a made up name/word for the type of music I made.

Regarding being an author, I write, yes, though in the moment I type this, I, again, see writing as an extension of who I am. Maybe it's that I'm also terrified of committing myself to a job title and being held in that label. Two years ago I gave myself a few non-standard job titles. The one that falls clearly on me is Contialitic Shoulsman. I know there's a strong worth in calling myself that. Calling myself a Contialitic Shoulsman describes how my mind, thoughts, and work form and meld. The most crucial part, though, from my belief, is WHO I need to be to claim that vocation/profession. I need to step up and level up to represent that.

A Contialitic Shoulsman is one who is highly honourable, compassionate, well integrated into life, and also values other people and how we're each involved in each other's lives and work. I had six T-shirts made that the title printed on them. There are not many people that I know that are suited for the shirt. The first day I wore my shirt, I didn't feel confident that I was living up to the Shoulsman title. I became aware of some of my social and behavioural faults. I also had an insecurity that I was claiming, by wearing the shirt, that I'm better than I actually am.

I fell into the rhyming idea again. I want to form another book of rhyme like *Shared Node*, yet weave some things into the meld that have yet to be known. Though I still know that books may be the way I find my gal, there's the case I press on. The pathways I chose remind me I forgot about Lori and Elizabeth. The stories in the psych ward may be for a different book, though I'm in the process of change.

I'm not one who wants to use or share some things that people call 'a key'. The facts of my own depravity had torn sorrow from my soul and stuffed guilt back into the top of my own mind. I've been in sin. There are still so many secrets that're pressed into my mental pressure. Although it seems I share everything, I still know I some secrets seethe in our being. I feel uneasy. Is that always a thing of change?

An idea is there are things that we do to remove our own self-hate. The things of my own depravity are burned up and turned into the cup of above to nestle kindly into the truth. I'm 39 years old into my youth. The grief is substantial, and I've not yet even passed the first day. There are wishes and feelings of having submitted to my own self to shred my own terror into a secure point of what is. I can't assure that I'll be there twenty years from now, yet part of that is changing.

Choices have been made, yet I still think I've betrayed the facts. Even if the reason is for my own wellbeing, I still know selfishly know that I must. This turn may be abrupt, though I wish not to have her used as a lure. The call toward action finds her and not the well-being of our soul. I've lived without her for decades, and another few years, let alone sometimes a moment seems to be never. Forever it is, yet I still don't know.

Thank You too for allowing me to renew and spew out the text into the next hours that pass the lass into the stellar class that treats me like a noble gas. Brent Goble is on the pass from the link as they're out to ask me if I'm using the trees of either of the two main forms. Some of the dorms hold the bold case of how there are things that I know I replace with the clear coat of grace. I smote the lace and traced the pace of how the Sapphire clones the tones from space. I hope that you forgive me for living so free while holding the sea from the oceans of me. My heart does feel rain within it, and though it seems I can't tend, the idea is that I'm never going to know what it's like to be her friend. My own heart can't assure that I'm not, even to myself, to contend past the plan and plot.

Upon the cross I set the tapestry. Though my own mastery of glee shares we see I still reside in my own lies from the rise and fall of the tide. Ironically, as I swing into the guide, I thank each and every one of thee for helping my own right path be upon which I always reside.

Hired by Earth as a Contialitic Shoulsman June 15th, 2017.

CHAPTER SIX – Now What?

(With permission, written to Elspeth).

First, and most explicitly, thank you for being a friend. I often have neglected to contact some people, while some others I message often and fear I'm a disturbance. You fall into both categories for that. You also are one of the few friends who actually initiate and allow meetings, even if I'm so often 'at' you when I think you'd prefer I not be.

We were supposed to go camping this past week, and the way my ideas flux into this chapter, it almost could have been for the other book. I still am afraid to tell you that I've thought of future things with us, yet still have an inversely solid belief that I hope we have mutually friend zoned each other. I made reference to you in the other book, *Beautiful, Do You Mind?* with reference to the ½ the age plus seven rule. You're a strange focus and I'm weirdly wondering about how you are so amazing, while not knowing if to stop or start.

With some of what I've told others, the idea is that if there are no other people or friends that grasp some of our connections. A super true thing for us is that I *don't* know what your intents and opinions are of our friendship. I know I have a weird certainty that you are amazing for me as a friend and that I'm just a creeper. Since we haven't really talked on the phone much, and also because of how you don't respond to some messages, I've projected that you don't want me in your life full well.

The other ultra-weird trip is that I think you're the only person that I've spoken with on this planet that's said they can see my vision of the Glass House. There are multiple signs to me that you are one that both wants to keep far away, and also that you 'get' me as being a really scared, true, and sacred child on Earth. I make light of myself often by saying #NoAdulting and also know explicitly well that I'm really a person that's been deprived of so many things including a girlfriend and/or also (seemingly) other true friends. I also know that this is due to my own choices and that I've made my own situation.

The other part of writing to you is that I know I can tell you more about the truth of myself than I could another. You dredge up a lot of vital things that, yes, selfishly, I need to acknowledge to myself and other human beings. By writing to you, I get the chance to dive deeper into my own psychology as you're one that I care a lot about as being honourable. You dredge out of me some vital pieces of information that I might not understand in a relationship with any other human being.

I love how you let me live. I love that you give me grace. You also should not have to be part of the grand conspiracy, focus, and game that I am to the majority of our local community. I know (not by evidence) that I'm a person that there's a lot of focus, attention, and, though I don't hear it, gossip among the many people of Chilliwack. I bet that you know A LOT more about me than I'm meant to know. You too should not be played like a pawn or chief piece in this game of what I'll do and how I'll act or respond.

I wrote this on my patio June 19th, 2017 after walking home from Bastion Games. I performed a classic Weirdo maneuver by standing still at the end of one of the tables for 2-3 minutes with my eyes closed. I went into the sounds that I heard. I could hear the different voices of people and was in a state of taking in the audible voices without taking in visual information. I may have made a few vocalizations, though where the Weirdo part was is that when I opened my eyes I just said "Random!" and walked out of the store. I didn't make eye contact or speak further to or with any of the people and just walked away. Just out the door and then went home.

My own insecurities and neurosis are, from my own solid judgment, still far too extreme. It's like I'm trying to sabotage myself. I seem to keep from having ANY people in my life. I've written about this too. I know it's safer to have no friends because then those friends can't betray me. It's also, as clearly as we know, a pathway that's left me alone sometimes.

I do have a like and love of interacting with people, though that's my benefit. I don't know how, and have been told it's not my choice to make, if what I do or what I make hold any worth for another. It's the other person's choice and preferences if they like or not. I think back to Vancouver and how I knew so exceptionally little personal information of the people that saved me from getting killed. There were good people that assured I live. I must honour them by making good with my own life. Full stop.

I could recount all of my sins and taboos to you, though, what's the benefit? I could tell you that I've made choices of change that I'm still terrified could revert upon themselves and find me deep back in my own realms of filth and depravity. A different pathway I could take and won't; I could pretend that all is okay and carry on blissfully unaware of the hate, angst, and turmoil that's been.

I can't seem to trust my own inner guidance. The system of the mental and spiritual realms adjusting, controlling, and projecting my thoughts change some actions I make and sometimes find me feeling self-loathing, cast aside, and eternally unworthy. I also know that the debris and remnants of my not so distant past also cloud the facts. Are many of the assumptions true? Some people may not care or have the compassion to give the first chance, let alone second, with the reputation that I seem to think is out there in the world. Enduring compassion doesn't matter for me if I can't seem to be one to understand that there's a huge amount of damage still to heal.

True also that I don't want to solicit attention and sympathy. I believe in self-responsibility and consequence of actions. I remember clearly one friend in Vancouver making the comment about unforgivable actions. Secretly, I believe in some ways that I've made these actions with you too. There's a clear stain in my being that reminds me of how my salacious actions have tainted me to be damaged goods that should not be for public consumption.

I recall the friend that I wrote to in the second book. Their points of advice were: "Focus on the positive" and "If you want to be part of the solution, you will be." Heeding that advice, I'll share some things that I know of myself.

I'm one who has a strong understanding of what is right and wrong for myself. I have a high value of honouring others and respecting people, their wants, and their situations. There are many times I could be super-critical of others, yet I hold my tongue. I keep hate and animosity out of my own heart. I exert a great deal of effort in controlling my own thoughts, attitudes, and actions. I'm often highly considerate of other people and *their* right to make their own choices without condemnation.

I wrote in *Built from Within* yesterday about how there are quite a few things that I know aren't good for *me*. I make the choices to not do them. I have an exceptionally high set of expectations for myself, yet I don't expect the same from others. I also know I'm highly tolerant and forgiving sometimes when people have wronged me. I make choices and actions to protect myself from some others as to not fall into their control dramas. My own strength and urge to do something worthwhile are true, and often I'll help people, even at my own cost.

My compassion for some people and animals is also an asset and I'm learning more about discernment. I've helped and given to some people that're using me explicitly well, and I've been learning more about people's honest and truthful intents. I'm learning to slow down, to be patient, and also to remain open to ideas and opportunities are given to me by others, God, and the Universe. I'm learning to speak from my heart, and I'm also one who's willing to have conversations with some people about things that other's may not be comfortable with.

I'm learning to put myself further out into the world, even when in fear. The ideas and values that I hold in my core are some that others may not believe exist. I've learned to release some things, to push for some others, and I've also invested an incredible amount of effort, heart, and time into some things. I know this helps more than just myself. I've learned some practices and have implemented them into my life. I'm learning to care for my own wellbeing and also expand my emotional capacity. I want to assure others I'll work for acquiring freedom too.

I've developed and cultivated some bare basic lessons and attitudes in life that I'd gone decades without explicitly knowing or practicing. I've found worth in my own self that sometimes surprises me. I am a decent soul and human being. I've allowed myself grace and compassion, and I allow myself to feel the fear of the unknown while still building a faith that my work *is* for the world of Earth.

You've been patient with me dear Sprite. Thank you!!

As the chapter title asks, though: Now What?

We know that we don't know. I keep my bookwork and move forward. I have full faith you'll be okay with your life and situations. You have an amazing heart and I know that you're pretty smart too! You are still so early in your life. You'll dance past July 7th and turn 24 this year and pass the age where you say 'nobody likes you'.

Does this mean I think that I'm also 23, though with 16 years of experience? Think of that. I'm not even in my twenties anymore! Our ages are so different. I wonder how that plays into our friendship. I'm nearly 40 years old! How? I have no idea how. I certainly don't feel like I'm that old. I feel like I'm in my twenties. I also note that it really kicks me back in the face that I should not be doing things like a twenty-year-old.

Ultra honesty? I think you are an amazing young woman. You are one that I think should care more about your own being. I hope you develop self-compassion and don't push yourself so hard and far. You have a super rad work ethic, and I also like how you get torn between different ideas and commitments with such dilemma. I like how you value many different things. Although I don't like how you get stressed between commitments, I love how much you care about the importance and consequence of them.

I love that you care so much for animals. I love that you have such a care for the environment and clean-up projects. I love how patient, graceful, and gracious you are. Kenny is rad and I'm happy you love him. I love how adventurous you are. You put yourself into experiences that are so much further out of my own comfort zone. I like how you sometimes drink or puff and, from what I've seen, don't have a dependency on those things. I love your youthful attitude and energy and that you are a true friend. You've tended to me kindly.

You also have a pretty cool tattoo! I like how you've developed from, yes a biased and judgmental opinion, from such a seemingly naïve 17 or 18-year-old 5 AM farm working gal to a sternly strong-willed, yet free-spirited, young woman. We know, and I hope you believe, that you'll overcome any adversity that's put in your path. You keep pushing your own boundaries of experience, and, strangely, you take on so many things and responsibilities that expand your own capacity. I think of how you say you have baths. I like that as it also shows that you *do* know to take some time to yourself to rest, reset, and rejuvenate. You care for yourself!

I think I neglect often that we also know a lot of similar people from the Clouda's days. Although Facebook says we only share 15 contacts, there are a great many people that know us both. I often forget that life isn't just my own microcosm and that there are many others other than those I talk with, message, or write for. I hope I've not caused too many issues or have affected your other relationships negatively. I know I have to accept full responsibility for my actions. I must admit I often don't know how I affect others.

I don't know what others say about me. Even for the few that are friendly to me, I have zero clues about what they or others say about me. There's a vast array of how we never really know what others think or say about us when we're not there. I tell you, though, I barely ever hear anyone talk about you. I wonder if I should ask.

I received feedback from another person, neglecting who, that I've mentioned you a lot. I don't know if I call you by your real name or Ruby or even just Sprite. You are an important person in my life. You are a thread that holds my despair, divinity, and dignity in ways that I'm not quite certain I should articulate. I thank you for being a dear friend. I also hope that my choices in the future honour you, your being, and your life.

I was going to put on a pot of coffee and stay up late to write tonight, though that plan is gone for today. I close this chapter and bring my things in off from the patio. I sometimes have the feeling of exhaustion that feels like decades of life have been dragging at my soul. I'm aware that we're on a long journey. It's been a strange trip.

I told you I'll clear this chapter by you first before publishing it. I also invite you to add some of your own words to this chapter for this book. You don't have to reveal your real name to the world for this, though I'd like to invite you to add a short response. It doesn't have to be about what I wrote, yet rather consider it a bit added to my work by chipping in your two cents. I should, though, playfully put a good lead up to the words you might share. Perchance a question? Yeah!!! I think that a good idea.

If you were a canoe traveling down the river of life, what would you do to a rude elephant that tried to hop into the canoe with you? I await your response!!!

CHAPTER SEVEN – A Beautiful Idea

(A chapter that's written to and for myself to bring some hope back into my heart)

You've put in decades of effort. You know the work you do most people don't seem to value at this point. The ideas cycle and repeat sometimes, though that may be because the lessons need to be learned again. Give yourself some patience! Give yourself some compassion!

Please complete *Beautiful, Do You Mind?*. The book is taking *una forma bella* and I know that there are some great insights to share. In that book, you've acknowledged some of your own faults, though the ideas and ethics of knowing what is beneficial for relationships are helpful. You made the choice to work on the book, and I also am pleased you're pushing your comfort zones and abilities to expand outwards.

This book and the Fountains series books also hold worth you've not yet understood. I thank you for putting them up and out to the world without pushing them so much. As you've seen with yourself and others, it's difficult to gain interest in what's said or shared when it's so much about the person sharing. Your awareness is that few people would actually read even free copies of the books. It's a great thing to know we form other works.

Thank you for not giving up!

When you wrote this, Rob, you were really pissed off and despondent about what you've done and what you'd achieved. I know that twenty sales of a book over the course of six months aren't enough to form a living wage from. Think not of the monetary worth of what you've earned up to writing this, though. Think of the insights and clarity you're gaining through forming these books!! You've evolved far and have explored quite a few things openly that some people would never reveal. Some, like your Dad, may think that it's foolish, and some may think it courageous. I see it as you still purging your inner angst and secrets to allow yourself the power of not having to hide things. Thank you!!

Please remember to breathe! You've remembered to slow down, to pause and make sure what you are saying is true and helpful. I also know you've become less judgmental and controlling. There *are* still quite a few things and people that tick you off, though you're still in the process of shedding some of your own points of upsetting others too. Your wish and desire to be kind, and your faith of knowing you do put in a great effort (even if others don't notice or believe) keeps yourself moving into a positive future.

I encourage you to keep pushing your own comfort zone. Your growth's not easy, though I wish and hope it'll be a great benefit, and not just for yourself. You bridge and bond ideas, connections, and people to improve our collective lives. Even if, at this point, many people aren't consuming the books, please don't give up!! I've said I'm patient, yet I must recall it's still less than one year since the first book. Some things do happen magically, though also remember that you've done so much on your own *and* that there *are* other people that want you to thrive too!

Remember that you are still not doing a lot of things. When you catch yourself and become aware things are for your own benefit, remember to stop and be thankful often. Slow down, take a few breaths... Pause your nervous energy. Sometimes we need to stop, reset, and restart.

Not all trains head to the right destination. Sometimes stopping and getting off a train gets us on the correct one for us to travel.

Thank you for remembering your parents. The four of them have helped you in so many ways. I want to encourage you to take interest in them and also clearly share your appreciation of and for them frequently. Your birth Mom's been so very patient with you, as has your Dad. They both have given you space and encouragement to pursue your dreams. You know you'll make good work of those dreams, just hope a little less and believe a little more. You know your work does have worth. People learn that as time progresses.

Thank you also for making up for your mistakes when you make them. I'm an obsessively flawed human being, though there are parts of myself that *are* vitally true and good. Don't be so reluctant to think that your ideas don't have merit. I still think you discount yourself a bit much. Maybe you've written yourself off because of the projected opinions that others have is that they don't care for or value you. Don't be defiant or claim it doesn't matter what people think. I know you are often considerate of what you do so you won't affect others negatively, just don't be so afraid to reach out to some you like and love. Also, don't be abused by others trying to force themselves into your life.

It's been a long journey. I know you carry a few many years of exhaustion in your being. Take a day off and, as recommended by an amazing friend today, go for a walkabout. Tomorrow, you made the one task of getting the envelope to the post office, and then, just wandered. You've been neurotically wandering through the past few months. Don't bring your backpack either. Just load up some music onto your phone, go to the river path and go wherever you want to go. Make zero effort on producing books, sharing materials, or even checking the phone. Take a free day. You need it.

Keep clear in your mind some of your own positive secrets. Some of the information you come to know may need to be hidden and kept from the minds, even the thoughts, from some people. Intellect and deceit are blue mage skills. Please keep your heart and intents true. You may need to shield others from some things. Discernment is valuable and needed. Remember to cherish, honour, and appreciate those that are true, real, and for you.

And near two hours later, I continued.

I tumbled down the rabbit hole of my soul with control of the few things that hold me over the loom. There are strings of thought that others may have forced me to bring. I gather my composure.

The fragments of my paranoia, a want to blame my medication, and my assured belief that I'm exceptionally misunderstood (even by my own self) find me psychoanalyzing myself and reverting to self-explanation and poor-me behaviour. I veered off course from a message by a gal that I'd love to interact with. I then focused my own fears and doubt in on themselves. I intuit I'm on course of the things that wish for God and the support of Saturn's rings.

One coping mechanism is to only focus on what we're glad for. I know I'm fortunate, though I've often not been able to be completely positive. There's a reason that I fear envy from others and that they hate me for having a good life. It doesn't, that I'm aware of, matter if I like or love when others have good and great things, lives, or situations to many other people. I'm happy they have them, yet when I've fallen into Facebook with self-hate, I've sometimes closed the site. I'm aware that I wish not to feel bad, mad, or sad for not messaging.

I have an extreme fear of people disliking me because I've neglected them. I wonder, now, why would people not message me first? Why should I place upon myself massive amounts of guilt, shame, and self-loathing for the fact that others have reciprocated by not messaging me either? I know that there *are* few who message me, and I accept that. Why should I be the one that people hate on the premise I didn't message them first?

So if this chapter started as a message to myself and I'm meant to be positive to others AND myself, then I should, again, shift my mode and path of text. Dare I, though, bring in an inversion and write about what I dislike or feel mad or sad about from *other* people's behaviour and not my own? Who's going to read this anyways?

I love it when people message me because they actually like me. There are some few who message me that I don't want to hear from. Those two or three people I dislike messaging me all the time are obviously not the majority of you. There are *many* people I'd love and adore to hear from, though those three or so other people have tainted you! I know about friendly fire and how, when I'm dealing with invasive thoughts or energies that my Ruby sometimes turns to anger. Don't let those rare few poison us!

The beautiful thing from the chapter's title is, that I that some know you love so much more than others can even like. The fact that we know love is the strongest guiding force (that no one else believes we can even talk about, let alone feel) is a full force. I think this is the key part. Your love is so strong and so fierce, sometimes, that you shield others from it and scare away some others because they either; don't believe it, have abused you to the point of animosity, or are scared that you'd find out that they hate you and would be put in an uncomfortable situation.

I know that some of my 'friends' actually dislike me, lie to me, use me, speak ill of me, and also wish me negative things. Conversely, though, there are some rare gems that are people that have REAL love in ways that we know; some love that is far greater than others seem to understand. You (Rob) know a lot of the lies and deceit, and your ultra-forgiving nature isn't seen clearly when you show or speak animosity for those that have dishonoured or disrespected you countless times. Those few drops of poison have tainted the waters, which make the liked or loved ones you wish to share clean waters with to avoid drinking.

I know that I am, to almost everyone, not vital. I know that to some I'm an annoyance or seen as an insecure child who has no confidence, courage, or strength. I also don't think enough people yet understand that the values of goodness, truth, respect, integrity, and genuine love and kindness are our values. I'm just really angry that I've allowed myself to ruin myself with animosity by not defending myself from abusers.

The people in the town I live don't understand how corrupted drugs had made me. Though still healing, they also don't understand how deep the currents of my own truths of goodness run. There are decades (yes, and not just of her) that compound and fortify my own idea that there's not enough goodness in the world. Some have wanted to ruin other people and corrupt the essential fabric of life. There are, also, some good, sound, and honourable people that treat gems like dirt.

I have to take the hints that some others do want to hear from me, though are afraid to message me first. I need to heed others clearly. It's not due to my own negative feelings toward some that I don't message. There are few people that I dislike or have animosity for. There have, though, probably been *many* people that have gotten caught in the friendly fire of my anger toward those select others that have abused me. I also hope that those who've wanted me to leave them alone, and that I have, also are forgiving for me going at them too often in the past.

People have different sides to themselves. I'm not clear on what other people's relationships with others are often, though that's a skill to learn through time. It also takes the trust of people to share what they think and feel about other people, and at this point, I don't have many people that trust me enough to even have a conversation with me. It's a grace, blessing, and honour to know what some people think.

I think I wrote this in a blog post a few days ago: *"Some know one sharp word can destroy a relationship. It seems few know how much effort goes into working to build one."*

Trust in the good people, you know who they are!

As we move onward with this work, please keep a keen sense of perception. Even if I don't mention *your* truths, I hope you may learn from mine. There are signs left along the shoreline in this book that may be like a message in a bottle. If you are traveling alone or are on your own island, there's a high probability you'll still connect with another. Be sure to keep the raft of this craft as something that's helped by others that're contialitically staffed.

CHAPTER EIGHT – Let's Write This Here

I'm wanting to work and form more text tonight, though I'm not so much in a *Beautiful, Do You Mind?* or *Built from Within* mood or mode. The past five days have been extended with the lessons and experiences. Since these books seem like my processing journal, I'll form another chapter here tonight.

The amounts of insight I've received from multiple sources have elevated not only my awareness, though also my belief in my ability and myself. We live, demonstrate, share, and cultivate PLUR. This is vital. The Fountains are all muddled and so much about me, *not* a marketable form of work. The other books and projects may have commercial worth also.

I've been reediting *Fragments of Intent* and know that serious revisions must be made before mass consumption. I've remembered to hold some key points of information and treasure them in my being. The depth of my own awareness is compounding, though, tonight, I also know I need to make some crucial adjustments to my medication.

I was in the middle of a med change and needed to go back to the previous med combination. The dropping of one med, and the increase of another, had given me a couple weeks of hyper drug awareness; insight into life like when I used to smoke drugs. Though the level of intensity and 'crazy' was a bit high, I'm reminded I'm okay to be dulled and stable in my own being and body. I didn't, though, meet with my psychiatrist until two days from when this was first written.

The ultra-trippy experiences included a deepening of my heart, soul, ethics, and knowledge and were worth the obscure and scary thoughts and energy that I had. It's not been easy, though the lessons carry forward and help solidify a positive effect for quite a few.

My heart knows that as I give myself to my work and creative process (and my friends, family, and community), I'll still thrive, maybe even more so. My awareness in my books and information hold values that another may share. I love that my intents and beliefs strengthen the process of sharing some of these ethical principles. I also like how my process, communications, and actions are deepening.

My Mom's been amazing too! What she said on the phone two days before this surprised me. She had said that if my medication does prevent me from waking up in the mornings that it's an idea to accept I do work well at night, sleep late, and that it's part of who I am. My love and appreciation for her have increased for her through the past few years and I'm glad to know that her understanding, acceptance, and love have developed much further too.

The days before this have given me a stronger understanding that people are a high value I hold in my heart. My love for some has been reconnected with my mind. I'm sad and sorry that I've been so focused on thinking of my own want of earning an income. I've focused so much on books for money and by marketing neglected so many people both by action and attention. It's not always easy to earn a living income.

As I wrote this, I thought of how now I'm in book mode and alone again. I get over-focused on work sometimes. I push myself through some of these moments by thinking that I need to do and produce something. Pushing is a good thing, sometimes. I don't want to puddle into my own books so much if it means that I isolate myself too much. There's a delicate balance I find of having time during the day to interact with people and making something helpful for our future. My sometimes too self-focused nature's not, from my belief, always healthy.

I'd like to know who *does* read my books and play my music. I'd like to know my audience so that I may form books with a more clarified bundle of information that absolutely improves their life, and also those they know. It's a weird balance of wanting to create for the sake of value for any and all *and* also wanting to know the specific people who'll actually read what I've written. When I know *whom* I'm writing for, then I'm more direct. I think how I want to know, and don't yet, what the effects of my work will be. I must make sure I do positive things and the right things to make sure there's a greater chance a good thing happen.

Anyhow... I could report in this book some of what's been happening, though I don't know what the benefit of that would be for anyone. I know it's not what happens to me, it's what I learn and do with such. I then must share my work through the correct channels and people. The results become some pretty amazing things. It's a link to Lady Luck and the pluck that we dissect to connect the Id to yang. We slang the dialect and inspect a direction to shift each rift and bring a certain gift. The selection to make sure the curtains don't close on the flows for the crows finds the kitten's purr to be real, true, and kind by *not* having a death warrant signed.

The threads of the meds line the beds that shan't be shat. This situations find a variety of text put into how the cats thrive and remain alive in the community and consects. The text of the rhymes context decades later still connects climbs that hold the fold the bold told: "He protects."

How does the cold approach and also coach the roaches rolled up in the paper? Do we ensure the capers aren't found as ones that open the gate of how I know my mate. While it's not because I want to give or share my D, the ironic part of a true heart is that they're not trying to part the legs to chart. The lad's actually rad as I learn to evolve life and also become a Dad.

I remember that some mega-vital names were mentioned in the first book. I took *Finding Natalie* offline this past week. I know that if that book is part of *Fragments of Intent*, it's not a standalone work that I deem worthy of someone buying. Some of my musical influences also remind me that there are numerous artists that're highly admirable. They've helped us shape me more than I yet fathom. I love music explicitly, and have neglected my own musical and lyrical roots.

With my rhymes, I've bitten so many tracks, artists, and beats as I love how they sound. I've added, often, my own lyrics because of how I like they sound. My lyrical terms and abilities are sourced strongly from playing other people's music. The codes of my language have attached thoughts and words with the sounds of the music I play. There are quite a few crucial artists that I've not played or heard recently. I'm reminded of the vast variance genre-wise with the music I've played, and though Rap and Hip-Hop are awesome, and electronica music siphons rhyme out of my being, the female singer/songwriters and my own music also keep my mind active.

"It's kind of dangerous to be an MC" – Mos Def and Talib Kweli *(Definition)*

I've so daftly forgotten the monumental works that others have made. As I intuit too how the calls of the tracks speak Chilliwack's truth, some lack the adoration of others from our youth. The spiritual food exudes the fact we refract into a slight light that shares the vision. Right through to the decision and view of how the plow threw the meld into that held. It welled up her tears. How had the belly swelled up to find the pup wind the thread around the spool of lost forgotten years?

Found set and solid with Slim, yet I don't know if she knows him or if Wayne's a Dad. Still some remember that a tad of her denial adds dimension to the smile. The freestyles of some show I'm not an MC, yet an obsessive flow in part of the heart shows we come from the glee of art.

I've forgotten some of my best friends in the past. I've not spoken of them so often to current friends even. *From the Valley to the Fountain* initially held the idea to write each section to different friends and some girlfriends in each part. Male friends I think of from high school and university are; Dave Clark, Peter Feldstein, Brent Ross, Chris Plemel, Chris Seltenrich, and Jason Yamashita. Happy-hippy fun days at SFU were some super bright, light, and gleeful times.

A certain Ryan in Vancouver before Chilliwack also was an amazingly cool friend. I think too of roommates Mike and Franky at 1153 and some really messed up trips with Waldo there too. The people in Vancouver, both friends and others, were the ones who knew my process of self-corruption. I was not glad about how I was when I landed in the ward in 2001. I had caused so much damage and still don't know how to make reparations.

My memory of how I felt during drug life (I had three distinct drug lives) was remembered quite strongly in July 2017. I feel, now, sadness that I made so many mistakes. I think too of how I neglected to mention Pat, John, Kyle, and other music friends and how vital they were to me. I was so terribly uncertain of their intents and still am terrified they conscribed to a plot to kill me. I'm conversely shamed by thinking they would when they also were some of the actual friends that did love and support me more than I knew. The most important part of my situation in Vancouver is that a lot was hidden and kept secret from me.

I didn't know who was a friend or not. I thought people part of the plan were part of the plot. There *were* some revealed as ones that kept me alive. I also fear the consequences of people being my friend and how others that wanted me to die treated them. I feel awful and awe-full. I could not know about many if they were valuable friends and allies or if they were against.

Since I can't go back in time and know what was for each in Vancouver's plot and plan, for those that read this, please forgive me. For those that were a friend and kept me alive, even if I didn't know you, I thank you with a wish your lives may be everything you wish for!

For those in Vancouver that were wanting me to die, I'm sorry for invading your city and dropping so much drama, so many corrupted thoughts, and for causing such discord and division. I hope you clearly know I was not meaning to cause disruption between you and your liked or loved friends that wanted to keep me alive. I don't know what I can do to 'fix' the past or what reparations to make since I was too scared to actually kill myself.

For those in Chilliwack: Thank you for your grace, your guidance, your love, and also for your forgiveness and protection. You've allowed me to live. I still don't know what I may do for you. I repent of my promises of what I'll do with my creative works. Not so much for what I said I'll do, for I shall. Though my apology is for not earning money for the Seed Fund with my creative work yet. I'll fuel as much as I promise, though I know I can't yet afford my own life by myself right now. I've not had a job or have been working a trade like many of you have had to, and I commit to working for life here.

Specifically for the friends in Chilliwack: I'm still growing. I'll protect your secrets as best as I may through the lessons of life that you teach me. I must find ways of channeling the books with respect and honour. I thank you for your grace, blessings, kindness, and support. The love and happiness you grant are a severely gladdening emotional support!

Maybe going back on my meds will prevent me from knowing what the truth is in some ways. I'm a person who believes that many things should be kept secret for other people's protection, though, I must quit making it all about me. We learn love, and live to thrive. Some of us create a way to play and pray. My work is for the evolution of the Introversial prerogative. Vancouver did not choose me to be in their community, and neither had Chilliwack invited me to be here. Both communities have allowed me to live, and for that I'm eternally grateful!

I close the chapter here. Be warned. Massive amounts of love, goodness, and life are approaching. Thank you, Florencia, for your work too. It carries into my life with gladness! I'm happy to recall that when we shift our attitudes, attention, and energy onto the things we like, love, and are good for us, that we (even if done so nervously) edge into creating a future; a future that's exponentially greater than we yet have believed or imagined.

Open your being to love! It's terrifying. I want to go back on my meds because I'm afraid of what I've learned and experienced in the past five days. Maybe I'm afraid I'll lose control. I need to put more faith in the Universe and myself and think I need to remember to pray and ground to keep my truth held safely. From Elizabeth Lesser's book *Broken Open* I know that prayer, meditation, and psychoanalysis encourage our growth. I also know I'm terrified of my Phoenix process, though it's into the skies of PLU8R while staying alive as a Taurean Earth Horse that values a multitude of futures and pasts yet told.

CHAPTER NINE – Community & Consect

(Written to a family member, though their name is concealed)

You know that the past week's been quite extreme. We also know your past has been quite extreme, though in a different way. Tonight, you had messaged me again, and I'm not going to be on Facebook for the night. I don't want to talk with people, even if family tonight. You know so much about my past, and as you've shared in our phone calls the past few days, I also, now, know a bit more about yours. You've not been through an easy life.

I'm not truly clear what I want to tell you in this chapter. I had asked you about the idea to write to you, and you had said okay. I'll follow through with that for now. I have zero clues about what to share with you. I also remember Graham and how I was concerned about him and his intents. The idea blends friends of others from the far past, though, even with family, I've thought of people plotting and planning. My mental health's not been stable in the past few days. Since the previous week, my paranoia and fears have been quite substantial.

I also wonder *when* to share this with you. We had been out of contact for a few years, though through the past three to four days, the extreme things you've told me have jostled my own mental stability. I've not been able to handle or process all that you've shared. I'm a person who often doesn't have long phone calls every day with the same people. The fact we've had phone calls longer than an hour in three of the past four days compounds the nervousness.

In the next few years, I still have a lot of work to do. My books are vital to my own process, and it's getting clearer that they may hold some good principles and ideas for others too. You've opened up my heart and exposed some of my deep values further. By having so many talks recently, even if ultra-intense in my being, I've been taught a lot of things. Thank you!

The other layer of *you* not talking or hearing from me in a long time includes a great many things. Some people have fused into the situations that we're part of. With my meds, I'm glad to have, today, gotten my prescription changed. My feelings of being all drugged up and out are nulled mostly by the meds. If there's another lesson about my job situation, and myself, it's also clear through the past few days I can barely cope *without* a job. I'm exceptionally fragile mentally and a huge uncertainty even to my own self.

I also told you, I won't reveal your secrets; so won't talk about them in this book. Your experiences have guided you toward where you are. I hope and pray that you do keep your peace and love too. It's not an easy life, though I hope you do have happiness from the choices you've made. My life is different. The next few years are going to be shifted since we spoke. Much awareness has been given, and many lessons relayed.

We talked about my parents and how they've been with me. We talked about how it was for me growing up and moving overseas and also on my trip(s) to the hospital. I put my family through a great many things and fears, and I also know I can't change the past. I'm grateful for the relationship that I have with my Mom now. I know that my drug use really put her into a fear of her own. When they were stitching up my left wrist I heard her voice in my mind.

My Mom doesn't believe in telepathy. She's told me that she can't hear my thoughts and that no one else can either. Another great friend named Ashley also believes that no one hears each other's thoughts. Ashley believes that body language shares a great deal of what we 'speak' to other people though not that we hear each other's thoughts. I've not been with you in the same room for more than a decade, so I wonder how we've changed with our in-person talks. We find out in the future, though I've no idea when.

Another idea linked to the title of this chapter is the ideas of community and consect. I have a stern awareness that I'm not part of a gang or crew and that I'm also sometimes a solitary person. I barely hang out with people and know that I'm often okay to be on my own. I love visitors that are known and liked or loved, though I, like my Mom says of her life, am also quite okay with my boring life. A gal that I met today spoke of how she's into physical labor and work, while I'm totally one to work digitally online on the computer. Another Toastmaster made a puking gesture about being on the computer, though, for me, it's part of my process.

(Insert 2-3 hours and another point of contact)

Thank you, dear madam! You understood that I'm not used to such deep and frequent contact with friends or family. My own insecurities are extreme, and I know this. My own awareness that I'm glad you are well, safe, and love is vital to my being. We know I need space too. I thank you deeply for understanding and thank you also for your grace! I'm exhausted... I've said it a lot recently; that this past week's been exceptionally difficult for me.

(And then 11 days later, I continued)

My fears and paranoia traced me to Edmonton. About a week ago, I had gone to Edmonton to visit family on my Dad's side. The plan and plot seemed to hone in on the gathering there. I found deeper truth and substantial deepening of love, honour, homage, and respect for many on that trip. I was tripping out on some great fears thinking how there are so many forces on all sides of the equation. I was terrified that a group of people was going to siege the farm and battle those there; that we would need to make a stand of defense to keep ourselves alive.

I've sometimes thought that there's a super strong focus on my life and myself. The fanciful imaginations and ideas of True still carry on with my life, and the ideas of there being global missions on both sides of the equation concern me. I don't know why I believe there's a great divide and that there are forces battling against each other with myself as the focus. Plan and plot. Community and Consect.

I want to thank you for giving me space from daily contact in the past week. My need of being solo and being allowed to work without so much direct contact is vital for me to form and work on my projects. Thank you, madam! I hope you are okay with infrequent contact as I'm not one to be so comfortable with ultra-frequent or daily contact, especially when longer communications.

In the past five or so weeks I've gone through a lot of extreme feelings, thoughts, and energies. Things have calmed down a lot and I'm almost stable again. This lets me get back to working on the books and online work. The medication change was what fueled the imbalance of my heart and mind, and I thank you again for deepening my values, my beliefs, and my understanding.

I feel a bit dulled and sedated from my meds, though I prefer that to the super-intense and ultra-nervous feelings I had when on the med change. You say you understand med changes from your anti-depressants, though psychosis and depression are *very* different. I know this from having experienced both. With my own schizophrenic diagnosis and past depression, there are some mental ideas, fears, and imaginations that are quite extreme. Even if not rational, I seem to intuit that there are massive amounts of situations on opposite sides.

The idea of Community and Consect are layered upon each other. We know that there are extreme and strong feelings, connections, and bonds between people in both. You may not know what I mean by using the word consect. A consect is a Shoulspeak (my own invented language) word that's basely defined as the criminal network and community. Since I'm not hardcore, a gangster, or a gang member, I'm not an active member of the consect. Some too would note that community and consect overlap on many levels; local, provincial, national, and even global.

The global community is part of what keeps some of the stasis. I note that there even are layers of discord between communities, even on a global level. We know that religious communities have also had conflicts, though sometimes they defend each other. I wonder how the people that aren't part of a religious group also keep the balance between believers of any religion. How shall we keep groups and individuals from dealing damage to each other? I believe I'm a local focal point, yet I also wonder what I do for Earth as a whole.

My rewind back to global issues and how the Seed Fund is also not just for the local community. My hope and faith from yesterday (one of the first few peaceful days in the four to five weeks prior) had me finally able to think and dream for the future again. I still want to earn money with my books and I note that the Seed Fund is only being used locally at the point I wrote this. The want is to expand and assist with global issues. How?

The advice I received to think huge audacious goals reminds me to work to expand outside of Canada. We'll assist with ideas, people, and projects on a grand scale. I may be exceptionally fortunate to have the tools to allow my work to form, and I'm grateful for such. We must remember there *are* people that help guide and form our lives and situations creatively. Although I'm alone so often, and am okay with being solo so often, I know my work is for more than a few than just the town I live in.

When I've gotten so terrified and fearful of my own safety, those are points of time where I've had difficulty thinking outside of my own self and life. I may sometimes lack knowing things and people outside of my own self, yet my being, wishes, and ideas are for Earth and not just for myself, my family, my friends, and the communities I'm a part of. That's where the global and personal PLUR mixes in. My own personal version may be considered the Introversial version.

I've used and fused so many ideas together, and even my Dad would tell me to be more 'normal' or understandable. If I adjust using the 8 in PLUR, then perchance that'll mix in some truth of a global idea, and not just me trying to push my own. Perchance the mix of me melding with others and not pushing my own individual ideas allows a greater form of unity; people working together with the same intents of Peace, Love, Unity, and Respect. I hold the other 'R's I've used in PLU8R as personal prerogatives, yet blend in with a global movement and not just my own notions.

We had just closed (not by either of our choice) a three-hour phone call. The fact that you've talked so much is concerning. I barely have a chance to speak when we call. A one-hour phone call is okay once in a while, though we've had three or four of those in the past two weeks. It's become a bit much. What you say of some (like me) avoiding contact with people is true sometimes. It's also difficult to appreciate another so much, though thank you. Please know you are dearly loved *and* that it's hard to know or share that when almost all the talking is yourself. I'd like to have a voice too. I hope you ask questions next time.

The fields of text are my work. You've helped with that too. The fact that I have a lot of work and writing still to form is true. I often prefer to be one to not have so many communications and I'm partly one who thinks I form more on my own. Yet, there too is the vast network of life. I'll honour you and your requests, keep your secrets safe, and thank you for permission to ask some questions that you would like answered.

I *am* a self-focused person *and* I know that I value family highly. The fact that you remember so much of your childhood is both amazing and unsettling considering some of the memories and experiences you've had. I'm sorry for not trusting you yet, though so much overwhelm and chat trapping is something that teeters me from knowing how to respond.

I thank you for being part of my family, work, and life, and I also thank you for the vital lessons you've given me. You remind me of a great many things of my own life; that I need to work on myself, the fact that you actually DO contact, and that it's like a cast of thousands.

I send you wishes of amazing layers of protection, love, guidance, and peace, and pray well you too know that respect is something for myself that I earn. I don't want to use connections or excuses to earn my living, so the values that are instilled must be something that I earn and honour with my own actions, commitments, and attitudes.

I wish love, light, luck, and life for you. It's odd to know that I've had so much trepidation and uncertainty. You're dear and I fear we may never understand that the world(s) of Earth and the Universe do wish us to one day, again, be ones to hold each other. The full trine of love, trust, and appreciation manifests. I breathe. We learn, love, live, thrive, create, play and pray, and it's the fact we also live forever beyond today. Amen.

CHAPTER TEN – A Fragile Balance

(A wish and a prayer out to the world through your eyes)

I shut my eyes. I open my being. I thank all forces that exist for keeping each person safe and guarded. I ask that family and friend are ones I also help tend. I ask that there won't be a need to defend. I thank You too for the signs and wonders of life, and how you've placed some, like myself, so delicately into the fabric of life. Please watch over her and keep her safe, loved, and honoured. Thank You for guarding all she knows too. Please allow me to understand that we're held in grace and rhyme and time and space. You too for your unending and continued trace.

Please let us each be honourable, kind, and compassionate. Thank You for the multiple influences that guide each of our every moment, movement, thought, and decision here on this planet. I'm glad and humbled by the fact that our lives are tended and protected, and I thank You for allowing us the chance to connect and repair the faults in ourselves, no matter how deep the ideas of below have wished to take us.

Thank You for reminding us the ways we love truly we learn to comprehend. Thank You for helping me slow down to remember our work on Earth's something that's not ours alone to form. Thank You for the cool air that may remind us that our souls, spirits, hearts, and beings are held together. Thank You for the fact that I'm one to support and guide a multitude of people both known, unknown, and not yet known.

Thank You for allowing people homes to live in. Thank You for allowing us friends and family. Please allow us to help other people have food, water, and shelter too. Thank You for keeping her safe! I know that my own fears have gotten in the way far too often, and I hope and ask that I may learn how to trust people wisely. Thank You for all things that are good, right, just, and true. I also ask I may be a conduit for good, love, and life here on planet Earth too.

Thank You for guarding my family, friends, and the communities of which we're a part of. I thank You also for letting her know we do have dear, amazing, and good hearts of love. I should not focus so much on her, though thank You for that sometimes I do need to keep myself safe and separate from some. Though I often don't know where people are trying to come from, I thank You for letting us grow and develop plans and networks that help us each.

If I'm to make a wish and prayer for some who seem to not understand the value of life, please let crystal clarity fuse into our awareness of how we also keep safe, guarded, protected, and appreciated. I thank You (and her) for letting me talk with so many other people and for allowing us to communicate in alternate ways that don't overload me so much. I hope and ask that she too may be honoured and cherished by many, and that my appreciation and growing trust in her be kept safe and true for her, and many others, of whom know not what she or I are to do.

I also, strangely, thank You for letting me get so much further away from thinking of Natalie so much in the past few weeks. I know that there's so much to live and learn and experience without chaining myself to her. The intuition and guidance to speak clearly of PLUR, PLU8R, and the adept and rapt abilities of perception and feeling that continue to change, emerge, and evolve forward. Thank You for letting our hearts be heard.

I ask forgiveness for my fear. I ask forgiveness for my slips of mind. I thank You for the fact that the pacts we honour are for the greater good and that my works are for the benefit of many. Thank You!

Please allow people the things that they need to thrive. Not just to live, though to thrive! Please allow me to recover my intents urging for prosperity. I know that I've often made wishes and prayers in languages that other people don't understand, though many would say that You, God, know ALL things. If this is the case, then you know how much and what I yearn to be in every regard, for every being, in every life, and in every notion and thought that I have.

Thank You for letting me ground and have time and space to myself. I know that I often haven't been able to handle all the stress and pressures that others have put on me. I know that I've near been crumbled or shattered by the fact of overwhelming. I also thank You for the grace, courage, compassion, and blessings that you've allowed me to keep the oceans deep in the bands to keep. Forgive us here on Earth for often not stating our full appreciations and gratitude for other people and all the forces of life in the Universe.

I know I'm just one node in the Contialis. I also sense, though, that You've guided me to know that there's synergy in the flow. We learn, develop, cultivate, know, and grow. Thank You for the fact that the set gets wet with snow and that we'll continue to allow the plows dig deep. Let our lives be what we may keep sharing to reap and sow.

I know I've not cried in a long time. I've been wrapped up in my own neurosis and have often neglected to pray. I thank You for allowing the changes that're being made to my full being. The fact that You've let her back into my life is monumental and I know that the significance of the reconnection is far beyond my own understanding. I'm still dearly sad that I've not had full trust in Your plans, and I thank You again for your blessings and grace.

Please allow me to love and trust truly. Please allow us each prosperity and hope. Please allow us security and faith. Please allow people light, water, and nourishment. Please also allow us to provide for many people here on this planet beyond the geographical confines of our current location.

I thank You and the worlds for allowing me life as my vocation, and though I don't have a professional trade at this juncture, please have me not puncture the precipice of how we now know that there's love, synergy, and truth in the flow of this.

I thank all forces of Earth and Heaven for the fact that I also don't know what it's like for those that are held in Hell. I know she comes from a drastically different point of past and perception, and though the wish is that she may know Peace, Love, Unity, and Respect too, this world of Earth holds both community and consect. Although I have no power or dominion over any of it, I thank You for guiding me with the intuition, signs, and wonders that you grant us each.

Please keep people on the paths of life that are best for themselves and others too. I don't know what Your plans are. I don't know what the plot holds. I recall there are some that held me up against the wall. I ask, hope, and request You for continued grace, developing blessings, eternal devotion, and also redemption.

I don't know much outside of myself. I also know that I'm learning many things about myself. I thank You for who I've been made to be, and though the thought of the crows does hold a key, I note that there's also the wish to live with positive synergy.

I'm develop my role as a scribe. I know I'd not perform well as a lyricist. I know that a solitary life is partly what I desire, yet I thank You for allowing us connections to guide us and teach us how we improve as human beings. It's not always easy for some people to continue living, yet giving us the space to create, the chance to connect, and the grace to select our own choices are also what help guide our internal voices.

I ask that we each may be respectful, kind, and true in our beings and thoughts, and that we learn to love, protect, and cherish fiercely without scaring or pushing away others. I know that some people have been through extreme experiences and circumstance, and yet I can't change what's happened to them. The best I can do is support and care for them. Let us each nurture, nourish, and heal our lives.

Please forgive me for my mistakes and my errors. I know that I'm a daftly flawed human that's pushing onwards so dearly well sometimes that I've neglected to remember the lives of others. My own nature is timid and meek sometimes, yet I also hope not to be trodden on by those brash and/or abusive. My own tentative nature may find my own neurotic fears and concerns get in the way often, yet please remind us that You are in control of life. I work for You too. Thank You for Your compassion, peace, and harmony.

While I'm down here on Earth, I'll do my best to work for the cohesion of life on this planet. I'll work for and with the good to ensure that lives are saved, that people are kept honoured and safe, and that the lessons I learn are shared with others for our collective benefit. Though I may not yet be able to conscribe fully to an organized religion, I have faith in You and the process of life, and I'll honour Your organizations, planet, and communities. I can't claim I know who You are pesronally, yet know that You are explicitly not me, yet work through and with me in many ways.

Thank You for happy days, comfortable and peaceful nights, and the eternal maze I pass; even if riddled with insecurities, deceits, and freights. Let each find their reach extend outward with community, family, and friend, and instill in each of us a love, willingness, and desire to help, assist, befriend, and tend.

Thank You for the gift of life, and thank You for allowing me to be, even if sometimes I need to do things for the benefit of the entire planet. There are deep roots in what it is to be You and me.

Amen.

I revert back to natural writing for this for some additional context. The seven weeks before writing this chapter had been astounding in the amount of life that happened. The sequence of events had been extreme, deep, and had some moments of excruciating peace and deafening fear. I'd deepened my own awareness of life and shared values, and I also found there's a monumental lack of my own awareness and knowledge.

My family's been exceptional in this process. Reconnection with some on both sides of my parental trees was made. Some from a gathering on my Dad's side, and also a teetering back into how I'm aware there are splits between families when there's a divorce. Different couples act differently upon a separation, and I know from my own point of being that I'm thankful to honour, love, and trust both of my direct parents even if they divorced. My parents are two of the extreme few that I trust on planet Earth. I wish that I evolve my heart and mind to accept that there are more than a few that are trustworthy too.

My own awareness of generational devotion is also in the crux. I think of two dreams I had of such. In one dream I could hear ten previous generations of a woman's family speaking through her body. In another dream, I saw one hundred generations of people from birth to repose stacked one upon the next. Italy holds these deep layers of insight and reverence, and I wonder about the foundational works of Christ from glimpsing the Renaissance artwork I saw in cathedrals and churches in 2016. When I returned to North America, I had a different frame of reference to the differences of the worldviews of religion and prayer in both places.

I also now think of another dream I held where I had seen the central focal node of all existence within my own life. I had not seen or deciphered the inner four to five layers to know what the core is, though I know three of the vital/crucial layers around included Canibus and Eminem, and also, closer to the centre, Viviane, the Lady of the Lake from Arthurian legend. I reveal myself to know that the feminine holds an exceptionally high value and esteem of. After some time in nature today, I wonder about Gaia and the idea of Mother Earth.

I'm not one to believe that the world yet knows what to do with each other, or myself, yet my wishes are true. Global PLUR. Peace in every nation, Love for every race, Unity of every creed, and Respect for every religion.

I don't know what'll happen here on Timeship Earth, yet I work for those that wish to work and achieve global PLUR for this planet.

Please find and keep your own values and prerogatives. I sometimes don't know what other people's intents are, I often don't know where to place my trust, faith, and love. I also know that my appreciation for some people is momentous and maybe not even believed or sensed by them. I know that there's been a focus on myself. I know that many have tried to crumble me under pressure, condemnation, or purgery. I still lack basic knowledge and definitions of life, though, I hope I may also recover, maintain, and preserve balance.

CHAPTER ELEVEN – A Neurotic Bundle of Wonder

Remember again as I start this chapter, that I have the creative freedom to write *anything* that I wish or want to. I think of how I don't know *who'll* read this. Add a layer or wisdom adds the idea to write some things as if *anyone* will read them. With those three things in mind, I share some things, yet also note I want to keep other people's information and secrets honoured.

Each person on Earth has his or her own life. The lives intermingle and cross with others often and the deep fears and fantastic experiences we've had also compound our ideas. I know now too, that I don't want to write for shock value or to try to pity party or mooch undeserved respect or interest in what I create. I even teeter from writing some things with my neurotic ideas and concerns because of others incepting false ideas into the fabric of what I form or think.

A term I've used sometimes is 'thought criminals'. This term's not meant to imply illegal activity, though rather those who are devious with thought. Often it seems like other people are attached and hinged on the thoughts in my mind. I've had the belief that some others are planting poisonous ideas in my mind that they wish to blame on myself to set me up. The ideas of calling the positive and negative conspiracies 'the plan and the plot' have been alluded to in this book, though I also don't want to focus too much on theories.

The premise of writing my truths should not be used as an information or value push either. Just like using the word 'push' in marketing, or how some friends push others to do things, the links back to Magic remind that sometimes pushing can be fatal. I mustn't push my ideas or ideals at people; instead I'd like to invite people into truth, goodness, and open the doors to elucidating people. My home is a welcome place for many; I just haven't invited, maybe, enough people in.

A primary friend and I talked yesterday. It was the first day in the past eight weeks that I could comprehend and feel ready enough to actually think of having a job again. They recommend I get a job that's *not* customer service oriented or too much interacting with the public. I think of having a job again for the regularity and the structure of having a routine. The past many months have had only two or three weekly events that I've attended, and I'm feeling grounded enough to think of employment.

This feeling's NOT one that I've really had so much in the past two years. I had wanted to go 'all in' with the creative bookwork, and that's not panned out so well. Considering the quantity of books that I've sold, it's not rational to think I earn a full-time income from my written or recorded work. The other part of the idea is that I think of having a job for my own sanity and internal stability and structure. I've been going a bit crazy, and I hope many appreciate that too. It's not been easy, and I've also not been ready for, even, part-time work up to now.

Rewind back to my step-dad's advice of the right thing, at the right time, for the right reason. An additional idea of wellbeing is the idea that there are six parts of wellbeing; emotional, mental, social, financial, physical, and spiritual. At the point of writing (July 23rd, 2017) the order I wrote them in is telling of my own security values and needs.

I seek stability in life. My own emotional and mental wellbeing are higher values by myself because they're central to who I am and are always part of me and how I feel in life. The social is there with connections with friends, family, and community, though I also need to finance my life. The physical wellbeing is lacking (no vigorous exercise and I smoke) and my spiritual understanding of beliefs and alignment are also lacking a lot. These six areas are valued, and cognitively fortify now that I mention them.

If I focus then on my long-term dreams, I also know I'll need emotional strength, mental fortitude and development, and a consecrated earning of a strong social wellbeing too. I've written a bunch about how I'd love to have a prosperous financial future, though am not there yet. I also think to write a full chapter about my own spiritual ideas. You've seen some of them shared up to now. I deem that since I've yet to conscribe to a set religious structure, that my own mental nature is covering part of that.

How are we going to earn for the Seed Fund? Right now I only have one book available for online purchase. If my audacious goal of providing shelter, water, food, and transportation for people is to be met, then I'm not clear how we shall yet. I also heed Dan Holguin's advice about losing weight; one pound at a time. With that advice, then the first steps should not even be to get to the first Care and Share card for someone ($50 a week for groceries) though to sell the first book.

This is where I wish when I write that I could ask questions and get immediate answers. There are often times I'd love to ask a question and get all sorts of feedback and opinions from people, though the closest avenue I have to do that is to post on Facebook and await a response. That's not as efficient as a direct phone call, though it's something I've not totally used or tried yet. It may be better than just leaving myself in the dark and not seeking the desired answers by not putting a question out there to the world.

(A few days passed)

I definitely have a concern I've not cared enough. My own strong feelings of love are sometimes something that I wonder if I should have. I've far too often cared far too much for some people while inversely for some others haven't had full compassion. Like so many things in my life, I want and need to find a peaceful resolution.

It sometimes seems like there are all sorts of issues, and points of wishing, to resolve and make reparations. There are these wondrous undercurrents of peace, sometimes, that keep my being afloat to remind me that my own love is amazingly true and part of what holds my own life together. Peace and Love are the two first words of PLUR and I note that when there's been disruption to my own emotional peace that my ability and awareness of love sometimes deepens.

Regarding unity and respect, those are different words that are also ultra-vital and help hold the cohesion of peace so that we continue my journey of learning love. With disruption in life, there are points where respect has been such a huge importance for me to give that I may over-focus on some individuals and dislodge other connections of love and peace I have with some other people. PLUR's not my own idea, though joining all four quadrants from *Searching for Tomorrow's* four-circle picture is an idea I want to weave.

If you've not seen the next graphic before, think about it for a bit. What is *your* purpose?

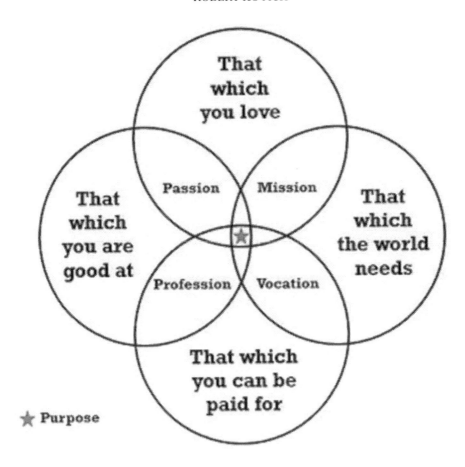

I know that I've been approaching the four circles differently than some. Where the business world says that we need to start with a need, get good at solving it, and then earn by doing so, some have worked differently by working with a passion or mission.

Those that know me may not know or have seen proof that my writing has improved because many people haven't read many of the things that I've made. I'm getting better at writing and communicating [that that you're good at]. I really do like the process of creating, yet the worth (more so the vocation crossover) has not been validated by current parameters. I don't think that people have a strong functional need for the books up to now, though I know that *I* need them for my own life. Maybe authorship *isn't* the path I should be on for vocation? My passions have not yet turned into something that earns money, and I'm aware that it's vital to have an income if I want to provide.

It's ultra-clear to me that my own personal journey is still mutzed up and not solid as being something others are yet willing to build with. Personal development is often a very involuted process. I still have a wish and hope that all the experiences and learning are used properly to keep cultivating. We are developing a shared future. I still have a great deal of inner work to perform and I'd like to know how I can be such a mess on my own and still reach the future. As something to benefit the world, again said, it's an involved, involuted, and introversial process.

So, I give myself the permission to use my books as therapy. Writing, for me, is exceptionally valuable. Even if the readership and audience aren't yet there to consume these books, I still must remember intrinsic values. If I'm to be a conduit and channel to help many, then I must keep myself open to them and let my muddles puddle into a clarified series of text. My books may not be needed. Am I okay with that?

I'll form other books, though my ability to fulfill a need in another's life requires me to be healthy and knowledgeable enough to share wisdom and insight. If the Fountains books are merely a way for me to put it all up on the digital table to clear out the wreckage, then let's put additional gain and value into the other works and relationships we also have.

Breathe. Aware. Acknowledge. Accept. Action. Appreciate. Humour.

I'm aware I'm a muddle, not a muggle. I'm aware of the fragmented intents, fields, and relationships I have. I'm aware that my own self-focused and obsessive nature is who I am and that many things are beyond my understanding or control.

I acknowledge that I'm a person who has an amazing capacity. I acknowledge that I do have a great deal of inner angst, debris, and turmoil in my being. I acknowledge that my own works are vital to my own process, even if not always seemingly beneficial for another to read.

Do I accept that I'm a mess? Yes, so that I may work and change that. Do I accept that there are many people who assist and help us with our lives, even when we're meant to be unaware? Yes. Gladly, and with thanks! Do I accept that there are many things beyond my own understanding and control? Yes. Do I accept I have an amazing capacity? Meekly so. Do I accept my inner damage and wreckage? I must. It too helps others.

Though then shift to action: What will I do about these things?

I'll continue to adjust my choices, thoughts, and actions. I continue to develop personal integrity and practice what I preach. I learn further to forgive myself and others when we make mistakes or errors and learn from them. I'll keep working on my own, and I tend the fields of this work and creation. We till the worlds of Earth with future yields also for future generations.

As we move forward from now, 11:11 PM July 27th, 2017, I commit to some many few.

For the people I labeled Planeswalkers, I pledge devotion, integrity, and correct action. For my family, I pledge devotion, honour, and to hold your secrets. For my friends, I pledge patience, openness, and PLU8R. For our community, I pledge to till, tend, and earn for the Seed Fund. For Earth, I pledge continued understanding, contialitic development, and being part of our world. For the Universe as a whole, I assist to the forces of life and commit to cultivating reverence for the balance of all things.

I apologize to the worlds of life for not clearly showing correct and proper actions sometimes up to now. Thank you too for the grace, homage, and blessings that have been given, shared, and granted. Please allow me to work for compassion, harmony, and the betterment of our individual lives; to form a cohesive reality that we may share. I'm flawed. I've been fearful and insecure. I also note that the depths of what the world(s) have taught me may provide insight, hope, and restoration for many that may not yet comprehend.

I ask that we may continue on this planet to work together to improve the individual and collective lives that are. I'm committed to our lives and this process. Thank you for letting me be here on this planet too!

CHAPTER TWELVE – Fragments of Our

Tomorrow

You know the weeks when this was formed were layered with difficulty. I'd barely been able to think of the future and plan to build for it. The time between writing the previous chapter and this one was a few days. I had a job interview with Best Buy to get a part-time position as a Product Process Associate. It was the next Sunday and I'd not heard back from them yet. The hope was they would contact the next day and they hadn't.

If I was granted a second interview and succeeded in joining their team, I knew full well that I wanted to adopt a cat again. I know that having a cat is a major commitment and responsibility, and I yearn for it! I love cats, and I'd like to adopt from the Animal Safe Haven.

In the past, when I had Winks and Boots, my great uncle Chuck purchased the cats for me. They were amazing animals and I loved them greatly and poorly. There are many things I'll do differently with my next cat and I hope that she'll be happy to live in our home.

My own sanity and intuition have healed a lot through the previous week. I'd been balancing out with the results of my med change, and I still carried some fear and nervousness. There was an edge I felt on my shoulders that I didn't want to creep into my heart.

The day I wrote this I put *Fragments of Intent* up for review. I may be an impatient cow, though I note that I really want to have the book available for sale. The second part of the book, *Searching for Tomorrow*, was edited again, though I did not transcribe the changes that I wrote in the proof copy that I had. The choice made was to let that section stand on its own as after the previous revision. There was nervousness in my chest from not knowing if it'd have been best to transcribe the changes. There was a chapter that I was to remove from the book, though I made the choice to let it stand. In August 2017, I did go back and make the changes.

One fragment I took from *The First Three Fountains* is what was to be used for the closing of that book. As of now, there's an idea to use chapter thirteen from *From the Valley to the Fountain* as a potential chapter for the next book *A*

Distant Glimmer. With the chaos and calamity of the past many weeks, I've neglected to connect with a pretty rad gal from Toastmasters also. That statement could apply to two different gals; one who is a highly honoured planeswalker, and another who I'd still like to learn and talk with about languages and Italy.

Arlinn is the Planeswalker. Her situation reminded me to get back to work at *Fractured Formation*. I won't mention the other gal's real name either, though I really like how she's fluent in Italian. I have concerns about the second gal and her high power level. I'm not clear if I've offended her by barely messaging her in the past weeks. I have concerns that I've affected Arlinn negatively too, though she does have my loyalty and heart.

The person I labeled as Gideon, a planeswalker, also notes they don't want to be pigeonholed as a card of another's choice. Perchance the codenames and words with the planeswalkers and cards should be loosely held?

It's kind of weird to think of how *this* book is almost done. There's so much that I've yet to relay and share, and it's not always easy to form chapters for the books. I sometimes am low on words, as I have to draw out additional ideas to finish some sections. What I think is another neat idea is to have a non-linear document formed to show the associative links of my codes. There's a limiting factor in that written work is just a linear series of text. There are numerous edits and changes, though when we read a book in printed form, it's just line line blah blah like how I think my own music sounds sometimes.

Oh!! That's another forward motion thing with the creative work! I started posting on the Patreon site! Each morning for the past five days I've woken, I've puddled, had some coffee (and at this point, still ciggies), and have put a track online to share. If you have creative work, make sure you check out Patreon.com and get regular with it! In the past five days, ten or so people have checked out the Patreon posts. It's not many, though it's better than none. We've yet to have the first patron to make a monthly pledge, yet I feel hopeful.

https://www.patreon.com/Introversial is the link to use. The site gives people access to the work as it forms. Cued by the word 'work', I really did hope to work at Best Buy. The benefits I'd receive could have been exceptional, though what I needed to relay is that I also could have been an amazing teammate and co-worker. I had no doubts about the actual work/tasks and I held a strong belief I'd get along well with the other teammates. I knew that if I got the job there that I would've been the lowest in seniority, and I utterly honour that.

Oh!! And another super rad, glad, and amazing thing! We get to Magic again next weekend! The plan as of now is to gather Saturday night and play sealed (a format of the game) as a group of eight people at my place! We've not solidified who'll be playing that night, though I know that it'll be awesome and amazing! I'm getting dreamy again. Being able to think of future plans is a fantastic thing! It means that I've gotten unstuck from the mire that I fell into with the plan and the plot for this moment of time. There still is a great deal of work to be done to accomplish the future, and I hope that we'll still work together to thrive!

I get impatient sometimes. As I type this I feel my knees wavering back and forth, I feel a slight unrest in my stomach, and then there's the freeze of my body into a scared focus. If I'm to head the Seed Fund and achieve global activation, it'll require far more than just my books. I've said in other writing that we need to start from a firm place and foundation. The events earlier today showed me that although I'm a bit wobbly sometimes, that I know some of where and what I'll need to do. It may have been the correct choice to push *Fragments of Intent* online sooner and get working on other projects too. I still love speaking with my cousin Alex as he helps me keep upbeat and positive. I feel good, light, and happy talking with him instead of fearful and cautious. Another sign left along the shoreline.

So, if I need to get to my work and cultivate a positive future, where do my books situate in that formation? My mind winds into to *A Distant Glimmer* with a similar pattern and fears with closing previous Fountains books. The feeling of surging onward find ideas of how and what to form. There's an urge to close the book that I'm in the process of forming. I've learned of bookwork, though, that lessons heeded to adjust how we perform differently in the future.

In the past, I've just shipped off without a conclusion and just have been "on to the next." I've noticed this with Toastmasters; of which I've barely written about up to now. Often when I've performed a speech I've not concluded strongly. If you've read up to now, you know I sometimes stop short. I think not to do that with this chapter and book. Dare I form the next section as a conclusion to this book in a more formal way? I think I shall, though in a slightly strange and non-literary way; a way that's more understandable.

Mission objectives:

- To abide by prerogatives of personal values, ethics, and conduct. By developing and strengthening my integrity as a person I'll be able to carry a heavier load if needed.

- To earn the luxury of having an audience to read our books or play my music. I must keep writing for our own wellbeing, though I also must learn how to create works that entertain, inform, and/or elevate others.

- To find a stable routine and life patterns so that I may have stability in my own life. This may mean a part-time job and this also includes church and writing books. This also includes purchasing healthy food so that I may nourish my own being.

- To maintain my commitments. Toastmasters is a program that I've committed to and value. Toastmasters allow me to tend my social needs of interacting with people while expanding my love and comfort zone. Magic gatherings too, I think, are vital to my wellbeing. Giving friends the chance to visit my home to talk over coffee or tea also is good for my soul.

Up to now I note my mission objectives are about *me* and *my* activities. I need to sort myself out first before assisting others with their lives and situations sometimes. There too is additional advice that it's wise to develop from our own insides before expanding outward.

I must heed my own inner guidance system and wisdom. I *must* find people that *are* trustworthy and have positive intent and character. I need to guard myself against negativity and those that wish to poison our lives, our work, and our own selves. We must find, outside of friends and family, those that *are* allies that want to work together. This leads to my intuition that it'd be positive to find people to gather as a mastermind group.

With that layer, it takes key things to let us each thrive. Step by step, we earn the pathways that provide for our local communities. As people's basic needs of food and shelter are cared for, we level up and find additional pathways to allow people their own success. The global objective of providing water is far on the horizon, though it's not forgotten.

For the deep future inner work, I also must think and form the finer details of how I live within the confines of this planet. How does function of a creative and focal point for other people, Introversial, and the Seed Fund operate? I'm not clear how this'll develop, yet also wonder how we expand beyond Chilliwack with the combined process.

I also must remember to return and actively engage in learning again. There are books to read, skills to earn, and people to glean lessons from, even if they aren't personally known. Grant Cardone reminds us that success isn't just a commitment; it's a responsibility.

PLU8R includes Responsibility as the 2nd R word of the term. I feel this in my heart. I know it's not piled up on my shoulders as a burden that I was told to wear; it's sourced from my inner being. In the moment I wrote this, I know that my own being is devoted to the cause of providing for more than just God. The stern edge also knows I don't want praise or acclamation.

Though we know that I may incline the idea that I could be vital to life, I also know I also could be removed easily. The layers of the grace of God and Earth have let me live this long, and for that, and the decades to follow, I too am meekly grateful. Although I can't 'business' so well at this point, I know that my intents, wishes, and prayers hold a value that'll help Earth.

Spiritually, I know also I'm not a savior or Messiah. I'm a child of God and my life is to be used as a living conduit for goodness. I hope others also help support and keep us safe. Though I've said it before, I repeat: my profession is life. Life is all. All is what we each are part of. Though there are some that plot and plan, those too ensure we may work together.

Introversial is the encompassing word and term for my creative works.

Though it's not really yet a brand, perchance there's an expansion. I'll keep the Patreon page open and maintain my 30% commitment from book earnings, though I also want to find other sources of reliable income. I must fuel my being into the world so that we accomplish the prerogatives of PLUR and PLU8R.

Please share these works and ideas with others. Seeds don't grow on their own. If each is a seed bearer, then I give you these seeds to plant in your own gardens, and dare you to create too. The fields are for combined yields, there are many who've given me seeds to tend in my own garden. I pray well that they may help tend yours too.

Get into books of your interest; business and marketing (Gary Vaynerchuk and Grant Cardone), personal development and spiritual evolution (Lewis Howes and Gabby Bernstein), giving and healing (Bill Clinton and Elizabeth Lesser), survival and ethics (Denis Shackel and Jack Canfield), story and intuition (Peter Guber and Tosha Silver). I even recommend the classics like Jules Verne and people like Jesse Itzler to entertain and teach you some things. If you're religious or want to learn about life, there's also The Bible and The Koran.

Dive deep into the world of Earth and find the gems and jewels that may be shared and relayed to others. Also recall, that we may think of having extreme worth may be like dirt to another. Don't expect someone to share the same values as yourself. Don't presume that another viewpoint is wrong or untrue, especially if you don't understand it.

Keep your being open to new ideas; though remember that not all seeds are good in your garden. What another loves, cherishes, and protects may be our own selves, even when *we* think they wish us death and animosity. Don't assume what you believe as 'the truth' won't shift and change with its own evolution.

And, as a closing note to my cousin, just because someone doesn't perform a happy dance, don't assume that the person isn't set, sure, and solid in their own knowledge. They still find exquisite moments of happiness AND appreciate the fact that you assist them with their fortified resilience.

I thank you for reading. I ask you too to start seeding. Though there are many who have strong and desperate needs, be sure you secure your own life too. That, I think, has been my journey. To have been dunked deep into ideas, knowledge, and experience that many may not comprehend, and then place some good work into the *Fields of Formation*. This life is shared, and I'm exceptionally fortunate to be held within it.

Thank you! For the world is lived in and out of our own doubt.

It's the entire globe that some are to tend to this contialitic sprout.

Learn, Love, Live, Thrive, Create, Play, and Pray.

A Distant Glimmer

(The 6th Fountain)

Ready to Dream

(Part One in the series: *The Fountains of Faith*)

INTRODUCTION TO THE 6TH FOUNTAIN

Okay, I've been waiting for you for a long time. If you've been following this journey, you know that quite a few things have gone on and that there are still messes to be cleaned up. With previous Fountains books, I've gone way off topic and have strayed from the initial idea of the books as they form into new and strange pathways. If you've not read any of my books before this one, I'm a fresh imprint into your brain before you read this. This introduction was formed before the body of *A Distant Glimmer* was formed.

In previous Fountains, I've started with the idea to write each chapter to a different person. I've gone off point from writing outward to others, even if the books did start with my dream girl as the main focus, I can't claim that anymore. I know that the books I've formed up to now have an audience of the rare few who are interested in my process and me. I use the Fountains books as a way to write about my future and the plans of what I want to do on Earth. They include ideas about communal support and what I'd like to do when I start to earn money. Though they also are focused on my future with my family. This includes you.

Although we may not know each other at the point of when I started this book, the world does have a weird and wonderful way of surprising us sometimes. When there have been times I've been riddled with fear and subvert ridicule, I've also had moments of divine insight and wondrous peace and tranquility. I hope and pray I'm okay. We may not meet anytime soon, though you are hopefully going to read this book in the future. It reminds us you chose me. I also hope that Celest remembers that I know I forgot before *this* book to mention that she comes before Aeris.

I've written about my future and the visions I've had for us. I wish to clarify my own intents and commitments further. I've been problematic and proclamatic sometimes, though I know my own authentic being holds much integrity, some solid ethical stances, and a great heart. Even if I'm not living a 'great' life at the point of when written, I hope you may find the kind things wind into your spirit and call for the doors to open. We allow people into the pit where we sit and help knit together the fabric of life.

Cart before the horse? Sometimes. Yet still told to think with the end in mind. I've started to think and envision the home in which we'll live, and during the days, I still may not be planning well enough the steps I'll need to take to get there. I wrote the 'I'll need to take' even when I'd prefer to use 'we'll need to take' because when I started writing this, I still had no idea who you are. I've been told that we seed the star with the reservoir of thought, yet I also call out to y'all that we're going to get deep into the winter after the leaves of the fall.

While we find that a kind word is flown in from the bird, it's still shown that the third instinct has linked the sense of thought of what to convey. We remember some people assure we live forever and a day. Hold onto what you say and pray. This is a work we form, even if to remember that there may not always be another way to open the way to the past. Outwit, Outplay, and Outlast.

Some dreams are held within our core. Some dreams hold the cast fast to a door. Some dreams may hold streams of text that the next idea selects to project and connect the choices we inflect. A direct linear flow may grow to know that some people may wonder how deep and low will she or I will really go.

CHAPTER ONE – Is This Just a Game?

If it is, it sometimes seems like I'm back at Laser Quest; unlimited shots, unlimited lives, and clearly a solo mission. The objects of the game are different depending on which game and who the players are. Some people are all about high scores, some assure we work together and help the teams, and some just play to play. What if this isn't a game, though? Some dreams have been shared and proclaimed, yet there's a way that others have aimed at my own heart in the ways that they refuse to let us start.

Through the past year I had gone all-in with the creative work. I had written and released a few books, and I too had been sharing my music CDs. I had NOT yet been able to source a full-time income from writing or recording. I have a concern that a real-world job's not a correct path for me. Many years ago, my Dad thought I should get a trade and have a vocation or profession to support myself. I dug in my heals, my mind, and my heart and asserted that I'd be able to find a different path. I still haven't been able to do that.

The book *Fragments of Intent (The First Three Fountains)* is a project I developed and honed, though even at the point of its second release (August 10th, 2017), I still hadn't found an audience who wants to read the book enough to actually buy a copy. In the one year that I was full in on creative work, I had sold seven books online with royalties totaling $42.70. This isn't a full-time income for a month, let alone the full year that it took to sell that many books. My path of profitable authorship's not yet been a monetary success.

I've started other books, and though I know my ability to write has improved, I've been less focused on audacious goals. I've shown that I'm overly focused what I want and myself even if I want to benefit others with what I sell. The 3rd and 4th Fountains talked about the Seed Fund. That program hasn't yet been successful. We've not earned enough money to house the first person, let alone others as the primary idea of the program holds. Other friends have told me that I should focus on helping other charities with my work. $42.70 isn't going to make a huge difference to Earth, though is one-week of groceries.

A lot of lessons have been learned though. I still glean a lot of free advice from online mentors and guides, and I've also gained experience, knowledge, and wisdom from connections, contacts, and actually living life. Though the actualization of my goals, hopes, and dreams, haven't yet been made, it's because I need to create, heed, and market effectively. That's a clear truth.

I've also limited the process by being quite lax by not fueling my creative work with additional income from, even, a part-time job. If I have any say in the matter (and probably should as I'm the one responsible for my life) I do believe that part-time work could be an amazing add-on for my life in ways beyond just money.

About a week or two ago I found that I've been shifting my goals to include family and improving my own home life. The idea to adopt a cat again is one I like and love. I'll also keep up with my self-discovery and analysis to gain a clarified vision of how what I want isn't just resource based. I've had enough money to have food, drink, and smokes. I note too that the abundance of time I have has't been managed well. There are changes that must be made.

Some regressions and revisions are made, though there also have been some hopefully crucial changes to my mental and social actions and attitudes that have yet to be appreciated. Tonight, I made the choice to start the fields of this book and work. Some negative choices also were made. We know that often there are trade-offs for the things we do. I've often in the past seemed to think that staying up late and writing is beneficial for my own long-term life, and I'm not in agreement that it's not.

My level of faith in the 'process' (a word one online mentor dislikes) and the intrinsic gains I have for myself by writing and forming these books are also things that I value. It's clearer that I follow my intuition and inner guidance. My own, sometimes, wavering belief is that these books benefit others too. I'm not clear on how yet, though. It's just that a keen instinct tells me that the distant futures are linked to these books being positive formative work.

When I closed *Fields of Formation*, I wrote about how I need to sort out my own inner world and mind. I wrote about how I need to cleanse myself of some actions and beliefs to allow the words to run clean and pure. I'd like that when another drinks with them, they may refresh themselves. I'm not yet clear on how these books are valuable to another, though by letting the words, worlds, and text flow, I adjust myself and how I am; to be, in theory, be a better friend, family member, and member of society than I have been. Working from the inside out, I deep cleanse and grant the chance to live, love, thrive, and share in the future.

As I've found myself as the lowest or bottom of friend groups, it also shows me that I know I can't merely fight or crawl up to the top of the group. In many cases I know I don't want to. Since we're not quite playing a game of Survivor, I almost daftly find myself to not want to start making moves and pulling power plays or sneaky points. If I know I'm on the bottom, then I just work on my own things. There is a benefit for other people.

Knowing how we are, or aren't, valued by other people should also remind us to not blame them. I know that I've not been a rad and amazing friend to many people and I'm be a bit weird or overbearing sometimes. I note too that I don't want to be someone who's to fall into others control dramas just to be likable. There's a danger of not being a highly regarded friend of some, yet there's also a great comfort of knowing some friends have little expectations of us also.

There's a comfort in releasing the wish or want to control or manipulate a situation for our own benefit. Knowing that I won't and don't want to hold power over others, the lessons I'm learning are that real and genuine appreciation is something that should be cultivated, not mooched or forced. If someone doesn't like me, I could invest a great deal of effort into trying to sway their opinion, or I could just find out and learn who does appreciate me and honour those more fully and more often.

It's also odd to know that some people that pester me and sometimes tick me off a bit by reaching out a bit too much really are true friends. There's a great value in knowing that some people reach out to us because they want to be a part of our lives and not just because they want something from us. As the future evolves, there are some friends that may wish to betray or try to sway us from connecting with some true friends, yet our own discernments strengthen that the lies and deceits are shed.

Also, as a key point, take into consideration your own self-awareness. Are you an honourable person? Are you trustworthy? Do you have correct or proper intent? If yes, then these things also may be clearly seen in you by other people. The saying 'like likes like' also guides how we find people gather together that hold similar values. Some activities and engagements with people allow us to meet new or shared interest friends, though the qualities of who we are as people also factor in and become clearer.

In the past two months, I've gone through many changes. I've learned some vital lessons, I've developed different and unique understanding my place in life and myself, and I've also gained insight into relationships between people. I've done this by engaging with a more diverse network of people. I've found strong doubt in some claimed allies, I've secured and deepened faith in some people being 'safe' people, and a lesson from today also is: "You don't have to trust a person to hang out and learn with them."

I may have a tainted past that sometimes hounds me for my transgressions, though there too are some people that are devoted to the good cause of life. There also are trusted contacts that help keep the balance. Knowing, and knowing about these people, help me keep a grounded mindstate. By remembering those who are good and true to us will also assist us in preventing people from pillaging our being.

A groovy part of this could spin in religion and how just because a person goes to church (or doesn't) it doesn't mean that they are intrinsically a good or bad person. There have been some despicable actions from some church people, and there are some thoroughly amazing and good people that are atheist or agnostic. There also are some people who fully believe in God and don't attend church.

My own spiritual path *does* have me attend church two to three times a month, though I still would not call myself a Christian either. Just because a person goes to church, it also doesn't mean that they understand Christ and what He represents. I've had concerns about people mislabeling themselves or others as God or Jesus. I know clearly in my own being that I'm neither of them, and neither would I like to be either of them. I do note, though, that higher powers are strongly at work in my life individually, collectively, and also with the use and diffusion of my written and recorded work.

I may be a bit legalistic with some of my actions with giving. I do tithe 10% of my earned income to the church. I also honour my own birth father and his lack of wanting to support a church. My Dad might not like the idea of the Seed Fund either, though since we've not earned money from the books so much up to now, that's not yet a concern. We find a won source of prosperity through my creative work. I share my future earnings and lessons with others too as time progresses.

The wants that I have for my own life in the next three years aren't massive. Maybe it's a good idea to have stronger wants? I seem to have displayed a lack of effort. There are some people that would agree that I do a lot, yet some other people would think I'm just scuffing along the road with no objectives, purpose, or drive. I want to own a car again. At the point of when written, I couldn't yet comprehend how I'll ever afford a car or live off PWD. I may lack a strong belief, I may be too accepting of my own current situation, and I also would like to add that I've at times been so ambitious in my dreams and visions yet haven't performed the tasks needed to achieve them.

I'm kind of sad that I've come back down to Earth from my whimsical imaginations and wishes. I'm not clear yet on a plan as to how to earn $2,500 a month on my own accord let alone house other people through book sales. I may be envisioning a home I want to build, yet I also note I've not a clue about with whom I'll build that home with and live there eight years from now. At the point of when I wrote this, I don't have even a potential girlfriend or any prospects toward having a part-time job for my own wellbeing.

I do have a solid place to start from though.

In the past two months I went through extremely diverse experiences of energy, thought, and fear. The facts of feeling, now, stable and okay with myself and who I am is a great and wonderful starting point. Although I'm not financially prosperous, I do have enough supports in place to keep okay resource wise. I have a luxurious amount of time to plan and plot the course of how to get where I want to be, and I've also learned to be okay with myself. We get set and be grounded to build forward with a more rational and achievable path.

Starting this book with this, I feel more grounded and secure than I had when forming the other Fountains books. The first book was a messy and sloppy presentation. Even in *Fragments of Intent's* second part; *Searching for Tomorrow*, I almost gave up and didn't give a proper final revision. The initial printing of the 3rd Fountain also held some information that could have been really embarrassing and problematic. I made a revision of the first main book and removed the last three chapters from *Fragments of Intent*.

This book hopefully carries on to show further developments made in my being and character. I'm not seeking for fame or acclamation, though I do still want to form earnings from my bookwork. I think that *Fragments of Intent* is a book worth its cover price and by the time *this* book is done I'd like to have shared the work and sold copies. Even if I'm not to be a wildly successful commercial author, these books have allowed my core readers and family to give me the love and grace (and inspiration) to create.

Introversial isn't quite a company. It's not quite a brand. It is, though, a title that I use to bundle my creative work and I do assert it as a genre of its own accord and micro-niche. A lot of what I do can't be classified as being held as a standard form or easily be labeled. I'm also wondering if it need not be marketed so heavily as something to generate interest. Those that read these books are a rare breed that actually cares and are interested in my process and me. I thank you dearly for being a part of this.

For my wife and my kids? Thank you for being four of the most important parts of my life. When I started these books, I had been thinking of you and our home for a few many years. I also note, that if all does go according to plan, I'll have known our pet for some time before we had melded as a sealed and planned family. I do want to adopt a cat soon, and as soon as I secure enough reliable income, one of the first things I'll do is go to the Animal Safe Haven, adopt a cat, and sign up for pet insurance. I'll be thinking you each when I make the selection of our cat.

For the kids, you may not meet the cat, yet I really hope you do. If we build the Glass House in Australia, I'm not sure how the cat will get there, though I note that yesterday night, when I was envisioning the home, I saw Canadian foliage outside the kitchen window. We may be in Canada; we may not. By the time you (Celest, Paradox, or Aeris) read this, I hope you clearly have known our home safe, secure, and warm places for us to thrive, play, and rest.

And for my wife, please be patient with me. I know that you may still not understand how much I've invested in our life before we met, but please remember that I love you. You are the lovestone of whom I'm afraid to name, yet the facts of the pacts given share you knew the same.

Even if you each were *A Distant Glimmer*, thank you for making it through to the books of *The Fountains of Faith*.

Let's go on this journey! I promise to you it'll be amazing!!!

CHAPTER TWO – Through the Wormhole

We teleport into another dimension as our heart calls across the Universe for a brief look into their eyes. Yet the vast disguise of the worlds we live in surf under our flesh, a mesh of intertwined threads of thought caught the notion. Hearts aren't easily forgotten when they cross an ocean.

They shattered the stone. The drips of mascara slowly course down her spine with the tears she's been shedding for decades by waiting in line. The moment of cross reflection does find the blood that he shed in the tub. Stitches torn out of my wrist insist digital chips were planted to assist.

I mustn't search. She mustn't find. Though we wind back down the staircase to the realms of Heaven, there still are eons of which have yet to pass. Even if He dropped the equation into the hourglass, some grains of sand must never pass.

The gaseous planet hovers over the text. Jupiter knows there are some signals along the rifts of time that call us into the sewer. Some guys were in it only for a chance to do her.

I'm not.

My mother slips Freud into this. Should the developments be global? Should we investigate the literature? Or is the soft sensuous kiss that was held in dream state to tell me that you could never love me in full. I pull in a breath. This must be the time to create. It seems like I could never wait for forever just to date. The green polka dots remind me of a song, one we used to dance to it in high school. It seemed like the song would carry on forever. That seems like millennia ago. Ironically, it was.

She's known clearly about the one with the crystal blue eyes; the one who I dreamt of wearing a disguise. Each creative reprise reminds me that the fortuneteller could not be right. There's a slight intuition about how the Wrys know they shouldn't assist. Some family should be kept away from us, yet we understand how one assures the others are kept safe. It may be her I stand for when I know nothings ever to be all right.

The impossibility of peace fused into the sign. There were meant to be six thousand who were meant to pass through the line, yet the party never occurred. There were fifty broken promises that gladly were not kept. Instead of having slept, the coffee crept into the mug and then into my being. I can't be the one that forces the rant and mental freeing.

On the brink of dawn, the dream calls out to Ron. I thank you, Dad. You've given me more than my own life to know that I must not seek her out to be the one to be my wife. Mom too would remind me of how she almost wound around my throat and caused the jealousy of others pull the chords that would reach the note. I can't buy love. I wish merely to love from myself so we create a diamond out the fabric of space.

There's a divine and Heavenly grace that seems to chase me down to Hell. I must save the other souls as well. Just because they could not cross Heaven's gate, it doesn't mean that they too for an eternity, must wait. It's in this life that I must remain fast and assure that the worlds' solutions of harmony are what I bring forward. We work with and for others and help create. Dare some kind being's correlation of imagniation and not imagination crosses the muddle of how this is? Some say business before pleasure. What if pleasure is a business of leisure?

Where shall we travel? If we're bound to this planet alone, there are many pockets of wonder of which to place ourselves. I saw the deep turquoise waters that the daughter's toes squiggled within. I saw some of the places where I wish to dive in again. Even if we can't travel back in time to the memories that I must sequester, is it that they are hidden, or that another tar bar must be cleared. I think you feared I'd never stop. I'm surprised that I have.

I was held in lustful notions. Even the potions of your smile I can't wish to cross or toss out into a faithless denial. I know I repeat myself a lot. I know too that some things have been shed that I wish to reclaim for the knot. I had set myself aside. I had craved to understand that I myself must be one to reside on Earth as a loyal friend, support, and guide. The doors are wide open, yet I still fear to pass onto the next part of the journey. It's simple here. No hearts to break that hear I shed a tear. No lovestone there to share I forgot my one true love's still above in the heavens casting down the lights of the sprites.

Dear Sapphire, we have been forever apart. I can't claim you ever would know the depths of where I turn my own being to start. You know who I am. You also have been kept in contempt for the facts I've not cared for you more than a gem. I've been brash and forward with some of my claims and wishes, yet the fish isn't loved by us cooking and eating it. It's loved by letting it swim free in the oceans with all the other wildlife. I know we allude to how we're by each other's sides without knowing how to love each other.

My own ways of loving others by how I feel *about* them isn't quite loving them for who they *are*. I know that there are metaphors of how the wings have been clipped. I've slipped under the door and been kept from the war. I must not hold out any longer. You may need to. I don't know who you are, True. There are only the wanderings of our spirit that I seem to wish for. I can't hold you in my arms, and I can't tell you that I'll be one good for your life. You let me know too who I am and who I need to become. It's from want you to think of me too.

Book three, chapter two. That was about the cigarettes and coffee. Maybe Gabby is one for me to learn from? She won her chemical battles. She found what her root causes are. Why does she eat so quickly? As I wrote, I relished in my slavery to chemicals. The cigarette lit and the mug of coffee between my arms with the idea that it gives me something to love. Is it a craving to close the space between want of something and actually having access to it with such immediate pleasure and availability? I've not been able to *believe* fifteen years from now, yet have dreamt, envisioned, or rather claimed so much about it.

There's self-defeating and demeaning behaviour that makes myself unwanted by females so that they don't taint the decades of my depravity. I need to tear myself from that. Then the wish of her having myself pulled in like neutron star gravity into her womb without salacious calamity. Is there another who actually *do* want to orbit in my being for decades eternal into our shared future and not just paint me like a ball of filth? I'm sorry for not trusting well enough that there's a different layer that keeps me away from such stuff. Puff after puff... the train at the station with a definite fear of a clear inhalation.

I solemnly sip the coffee and breathe.

I take another breath and in the middle of it fear I can't accept death.

One breath after, I hear her think of my daughter's laughter.

I've relied so heavily on acceptance or approval of another about what I want to do. Parental instinct, or rather direct suggestion and recommendation, have told me not to think of you. What happens if I disregard all the wise and sage advice and find that my life is one that always stays alive? That it stays alive because someone other than Jesus paid an exceptionally high price? What *is* my value? Why *have* I been kept alive? I don't comprehend how it could be for what I write.

My writing seems like such a selfish thing that benefits none other than myself. I'm not placed up on the shelves of wisdom, self-help, entertainment, or romance. I don't even know why I finish the book I'm writing that's in the chapter about how life is a dance. I know, even though my actions sometimes don't show it, it's because I said I would. I often tend to follow through with things I say I'll do.

If that's the case, Rob, then why are you not in bed right now? You said you want to sleep before midnight and be up at 8 AM like the majority of the population. You, Robert, haven't blended in well with what is expected of society and the people that live on this planet. You should not be such an anomaly floating in time and space and stealing decades of life, love, and grace. You, Robert, should, though, remember that there are some who believe in you. I hope you learn to do so also.

What'll Paradox say when he learns of this? Have there been points in the past where he's scriggled through time to catch his father in the form of rhyme? Will Celest be okay to be on her own so often? Is it that Aeris forgives us both for the fact we couldn't keep our family together? Or are the wistful notions of my years prior shed and dispensed into a different equation. Do we find ourselves held together amazing, strong, wonderful, faithful, and true.

There are times I wondered if you'd be faithful to me. I know I already cheated on you. I fear that my own self-focused nature's been shed in some ways, yet shed ways that seem to not let me care enough about my own values and myself. I may be too accepting of what is and what it'll be to be the foundational support we are. The support I need to be assures our family tree extends past the idea of just you and me.

There's trust in this. I know I wouldn't trust me either at many points in the past. Then too, there are points in the past where I may have clung on too strongly and not given space. The wish and desire to unite as humans, even with ourselves being a different species or race. There are some things that remind me of our unity.

It's so much easier to trust someone that we've never met instead of placing ourselves delicately in the petri dish. Placed there and tested to find if we cultivate life and not just a wish. I don't ask for a kiss. I ask for the fact of a conversation. What if I don't want to enter? What if you don't want to leave? What is the truth that you forgot about ourselves? Is your own being won by me that lost and cleaved? There's an intuition of a mission, the omission of tuition, and my own poetic admonition of myself for being true. I warn myself of the consequences, and that may be why I cower behind the request of merely one meeting.

What would my faith tell me if I really believed? I'm not clear on how to answer that, though that's partly why I write. I deny myself inwardly through ideas and thought. I bundle up my mind into something that's drawn out and pulled straight. There's the idea of 'straightening things out' by compounding them and confounding myself and, later on, to share the words with those that read to find each correctly sown seed stand still.

I don't want to need her. I sometimes think I'm terrified of her. I fear that I've already caused so much sadness and discord that she herself would want me gone. That's where part of my insecurity is. That I fear the world could be made much easier if I was not here. The crinkle that's in the plot for me is something that holds me also as one to skip between the dots as one to never call the shots. What would happen if I have full control of what I want? What if what I want's not something I'd like to have after it's happened?

There was a guiding force that held me away from actually believing, yet receiving some energy, I find that I still wish to make up for the damage and loss I've been a root of. I think I've not accurately guided myself with my ideas and wishes of love.

How are we meant to know the truth if we're held away and from the very people that know what the truth is? We can't keep treating me like an experimental subject without actually interacting with me and keeping me immersed in an isolated observation zone! This is, partly, why I like to work at the Starbucks. I can be active in life and *actually* interact with people! A relation with a singular nodal point can't be truly understood without a relationship. There must be a *direct interaction* between two things to find out how they'll be with each other.

Using the chemistry analogy, we may know *all* of the properties of a chemical compound (person), though it's how that compound interacts or not with another compound (person) that shows more about how they behave. We also must remember that different people interact differently with different people. I know I'm not a noble gas. Some 'water' might show me as Sodium. Some others tell us that considering how many electrons are orbiting around my core, that it may seem I'm not even an element.

There also are the situations that make me think I'm *not* a male Oxygen atom seeking to be water, as I'm not searching for *two* female Hydrogens. I also hope that if I'm an Oxygen atom, that there are different genders between particles. I'm not clear on what element I am sometimes, considering that I love being able to interact with all the gals and not be bound to only one. Then too, I also had bonded spiritually with one tonight that reminded myself some is still secured to my being, even if a ghost particle.

OR, is it that all the girls are electrons, and one is so close to my core, that I'M just a Hydrogen atom that's a proton with one electron in my field that's moving so fast that I can't perceive her? OR, is my final makeup of this analogy that she and I are H_2 and the O is the Organization of life that keeps her and me apart and still part of the whole molecule. If we add enough electricity, does the Organizations of community and consect unite and let her and I float up in the air? We then must avoid fire and heat to make sure that there's no hydrogen explosion (to put us back into a molecule of water).

It's neat to repeat a kind friend is something to tend. Though I delve deep into the yard, there's a shard that called out to the spout. What if I *am* a true and honourable spout? I know not, yet the sprout is nourished with the water they give, even if signified by the intellect and deceit in the sieve. A line said many years ago shares and shows that there are some things that make sure we're not to make a mark. It's streamed like a cross through the hashtag of my brain. Some remember that we don't cross global warming or the hydra elements of Stain.

Hold onto your buckets, dear Jane, as the elements of Bob aren't just the great great grandparents of the one of whom may have a thought to abstain.

I hold the tears of the rain over the fires of the forest with a link back to Bant. The Bayou does bridge the perspective of two shards linked by Khans and I know that Roland and Joe hold the mould of how Esper controlled. A Golgari link of how we fuel delirium into the drink, yet a Tundra wink shows that Viridian melds is in what we think. Ciggies? I suppose those are best not to plot, yet what happens if the sniffles are found in thought? Keep it as so, even if these pages don't make sense to anyone, even those that claim to know.

CHAPTER THREE – What I Need to Do

I'd like to invite you into my world. It's one spun from a fine web of deceit of which through I must also pass. The tendrils of time try to ensnare me into the phonetics of how some words sound the same. Though I can't tell you truly enough about some of the things that do claw at my being, there are some things that have been shed.

I've made proclamations and wishes, I've committed to definite things, and my own insecure future seems to lure me into the present from the past. Creeping along moment by moment while streaming all the fragments together into another cup of coffee.

Some of the people of Chilliwack have come to know me. I'm pervasive with my narrow focus and wide sweeps across the book of face. My friends have been pandered to too by me searching for sales wishing to earn a creative income. There are some people that may care and wish to support, yet some of them are in their own quandaries. It seems many of the people I know are restricted by money or time and have a lack of it. It's also weird how I don't want to use or abuse those who do. I feel I should not ask for their help.

My own financial lack, up to this point, has had me one that's been fearful and scarce in my own acquisition of prosperity. I've made many grand claims about what I to do as I reach financial abundance, yet my own faith, or maybe the lack of such, holds me back. I want to free myself of some shackles, yet relish in my situation as being one that's glad to have some things. I have the restrictive mentality that wanting things isn't always greed.

There are some people who don't feel worthy, yet my own attitude is also that I seem to think I get more than I deserve. I don't have a strong belief in there being value in what I've written, yet I think the story and ideas may have some merit. I don't see how interest in my own life is something worth people giving me money by buying a book sometimes. I've been focused on pushing for a sale on the premise of a sale as a guilt offering and not what the works do for people. When I had a car I seemed to think I was doing so much for other people, though not so much now.

If I'm restricted by not being the car friend anymore, and I'm one who doesn't supply people with Magic cards (as I had for a couple years), what is the worth that I may bring to another person? I know that working a job's one way to earn money, though I seem to think a job's not worth money sometimes. The anger, frustration, past vulgarity, and negative feelings of entrapment I've had in some jobs aren't worth the damage to my own mind and being. This is where bringing knowledge to people is helpful, though I also don't have a want to write just to earn money. My craving for freedom and purpose are values I hold quite high.

The Seed Fund idea is one where I want to use myself and my work as a tax of some sort. If I commit to sharing some of what the books earn, then there may be some penance in that, yet, again, what is the value for someone else in buying and reading a book? At this point, what interest is there in what I've made or what's to be done with the money earned?

My views are skewed. My own heart too I think needs some cleaning. I may be entirely okay with my life, though me being okay with my life isn't enough for others. My own desire is to do something worthwhile and far greater than just passing through time. Some people would say I need to learn how to chill and relax. I'm a bit too neurotic for that. I have a strong urge to actually *do* something.

I barely ever get bored. I don't have many hobbies. I still smoke a lot and love that I can. I also note I can ramble on for hours with the keys, yet I'm so lazy and subvert that it seems like dabbling. I've been dredging through time rather than how I've said I'm 'at the plow'. Uncle Grant would assure me to put in substantial effort and work. I have seemed to be just puttering along like a motorboat when others may say I should stop the boat completely. Maybe I'm *too* okay. I think I may be *too* comfortable.

In some bookwork, I've gone on with secular repentance and fantastic wish. They seem like two sides of the pendulum idea that Carolyn told me about. Metaphors sometimes run and course right through me and I note that so many fanciful ideas and cryptic notions hold a strange tainted intrigue. What may I do to convey and relay the ethics, values, and worth that I honestly hold?

The first book *Finding Natalie* had a purpose when it was formed and released. The purpose was to write a book, share it with the world, and have my dream gal come find me. The second book was telling my future audience of what I wanted to do other than that. The third book (although the last three chapters were not published in *Fragments of Intenet*) was meant to market partly to the female audience. *From the Valley to the Fountain* included a chapter to my future girlfriend(s).

It was the 4th Fountain when I got dreamy and audacious with the Seed Fund idea, while the 5th Fountain was more about clearing. It helped me resolve and understand some of the emotional damage I had from the first and third Fountains. This is the 6th one though. I made the subtitle of the book *Ready to Dream*, yet I've been dreaming for years without forging a full actual plan as to how to achieve those dreams. I've been wound up in my own idea by scattering thoughts and wishes and talking about all the harvests. I've not been tending the fragile saplings that first need to be tended to.

There are ideas from the book *The 7 Habits of Highly Effective People* by Steven R. Covey. *Habit 2: Begin with the End in Mind.* I think that's what dreamers do. I know too, though, we need to do the correct things to reach those ends. From meeting my dream girl, or providing homes, food, and water for people on Earth, or even the self-gaining goal of building the Glass House, each of the dreams stem from that habit of beginning with the end in mind. What I don't know is if the things that I'm doing are *Habit 1: Be Proactive* and the correct things to reach the goals. I've thought that writing and staying up late to form this text is what I *need* to do to make forward motion. Am I wrong?

Habit 3: Put First Things First is coupled with knowing what we need to do first. I've believed and have said that I need to clear out my own inner self. I need to do this so that I may be solid and sure to do the things that I need to do. I couple my own self-therapy as being a *Habit 5: Seek First to Understand Then to Be Understood.* If my work is to be so self-focused, then I need to know a lot about myself, why I do things, who I am, what I believe. I also understand what I'm meant to do. I take what I've learned or understood and share it with others.

Being such a nodal solitary person, I also know *Habit 6: Synergize* isn't so easy when it's just me. There's a cool thing I know of my intents and self, though, *Habit 4: Think win/win.* I've inversed and have been partly backward with these ideas. Gary Vaynerchuk was the first person I heard that talked about reverse engineering ideas or plans. I'm not clear about the answer to the question, though: Have I actually been operating like I've reverse engineered? I think, now, that I have a bit.

I've already known that if we're to gain anything, others must gain [Habit 4: Think win/win]. I know that it takes a great many people to actualize some of the ideas [Habit 6: Synergize]. I've been working to understand other people's points of view [Habit 3: Put First Things First] by intentionally [Habit 1: Be Proactive] practicing and learning [Habit 5: Seek First to Understand Then to Be Understood]. It's all stemmed from the main overarching objectives of achieving huge audacious goals [Habit 2: Begin with the End in Mind].

Another kind suggestion; if you have plans, goals, wishes, and wants, WRITE! Put your work on paper or on a computer and organize your thoughts! I think *I* may be on the right track from the articulation of the previous paragraph. I wouldn't have encountered that idea had I not written this. Faith builds when we know we *are* doing the right things for the right reasons.

Having faith in God, the Universe, ourselves, Jesus, the world, or any other thing that strengthens and assures us of good things, lets us know, often, what is true. This stabilizes and strengthens our beliefs. I smugly feel how my faith and intents in this series compound compared to when this started a couple months ago. *The Fountains of Faith.* Spot on for actual relevance?

(Add a day or two between points of text)

I've been reading Elizabeth Gilbert's book *Eat, Pray, Love.* I think in conjunction with that title the name of the band My Chemical Romance. These two ideas twist into the fabric of this in that I made the choice tonight to dive deep into my chemicals like the pleasure focus Elizabeth found in Italy. In Elizabeth's book, she talked about food and Italy as where she relished and soaked in pleasure and language. I also note she's an amazing and exquisite writer with her diction!

The Italian links are clear in my being with her work. I want to go to Italy again and live there for a while. The pleasure reference in the previous paragraph, though, is in my own addictive nature. I have again committed to the creative process by drinking coffee at one AM and have a tar bar dangling from my mouth as I type. I still honestly don't know if my habit of smoking, coffee, and writing obsessively is a pleasure and commitment to my work, or merely my own foolery.

I want to push that it's for the long-term future (creating things) though I know it's not healthy. I siphon in how there are sacrifices that are made for advancement. I know that the sacrifice of sleep's not great, that smoking is pretty awful, though I also want to assert that my own detriments are marginalized by my own choices. I do need to heed that health is literally vital and I also know that I'm making sacrifices for my own long-term future. I'm still a smoker at this point, and I also know that my substantially (pun) skewed belief is that there are some superpowers that rule me creatively with these chemicals.

Tonight, I've made the commitment to coffee and submit that I smoke a lot too. We'll see the work form as I form two chapters tonight. The next chapter that I'll write's about my spiritual needs and beliefs, though let's finish this one first. I had just titled the chapter *What I Need to Do*. I covered the mission objectives at the close of *Fields of Formation*, though that's not clear enough for me.

I need to tell myself what I'll do and also clearly understand myself, my own beliefs, and personal requirements as they emerge. I'm often eclipsing my own past and futures with the moments of the present when the cursor edges onward from the fragments of now. I also wonder if I tell all of you what I think I need to do for our world, my work, and myself if it'd cue up some ideas in your own minds. What do I need to do in and with our own lives? Let's run through this.

Firstly, I need to keep moving forward and create. I need to give myself the obscure and sometimes intuitive choices to assure that I keep building for the decades that pass. I need to forgive myself for the mistakes and poor choices I make with the faith that God is guiding me. I need to slowly relax and also trust the folds of time. I may be on the right track when the rhymes start to weave into that we perceive. I need to put in the work without guilt being a driving force and tilt the trust of the horse's repentance. I'm still purging my faults.

I must trust in the gusts of above and below as we sow the seeds. The needs met also allow now to be then. The fact I can, and do, stop and restart also shifts me to redirect points of time. I must yield often to what is right and true and let others know that exactly who I am is what we must renew.

The points of staying up super late to write are, for me, crucial to the process that I want to accomplish. It's imperative that the forces of my instinct guide the tides of thought that may never again be forgotten. We are deep in potting the plan. The fear also clears the lens of how they may sign me into the tree of life. I know I don't need a girlfriend or wife, yet I also know I like bonus points. For me, I know that I have enough people time, though the fact of the one spirit that lingers in my being can't be accurately named. I think I've mislabeled her through the years.

"She knows my soul yet don't know my name."-Me.

I think this still True, even if I don't know her too.

The idea of gathering the world in our heart are a different one I actualize. I know that my being holds an astonishing capacity to care for some. When I'm alone, those are some of the times I've felt the strongest and most pure love. It's an energy that I've not shared with many people, as I've not felt it as strongly as those divine moments where I seethe alone in its power. Not power over another, it's, quite funnily, the power of love.

As I wrote this, there was music on my stereo that was linked from Suzi's post. She plays a lot of electronica music, and the pulsating beat of the song reminds me of the force of a glacier again. The relentless devotion to life causes me a belief sometimes so clear, dear, honest, and true to me that, when alone in this creative process, my love's sometimes much greater than how I seem to treat people. I need to learn how to share and convey my full love and appreciation for others the way I have, and can, when in these pockets of solitary awareness.

This is where my prayers are sometimes. My wishes to God and the Universe are that you may have read from me. I mean them. They are epic and they are sourced from an awesome point of being that exponentially devours my fears. They put me to wish inviolability for any and everything that wants to work for the greater good. There was an album that I had titled *The Power of One*. When I'm in interaction with some people, I may seem weak, meek, or like a tainted crumb that's not fit for a bird, yet when I reach some divine moments at the plough, I feel the wish that if only each person had the intent and heart that I've had then, that we'd transcend beyond any and all potential negative things, energies, thoughts, or situations.

My faith, in line with this book's series, is one I know alone on my own. The thing is, Earth is seven billion humans. *Fragments of Intent* started with my strewn connections of life and what I thought of them. I've gotten to the point of having focused my intents and wishes. Now we just must find myself to abide and actualize them and ally with others who'll share the mission.

CHAPTER FOUR – What I Believe

I may use religious points of view in this chapter. That may be helpful and exceptionally relevant if you really want to understand these works.

I believe that each person has five main parts to their being; their body, soul, mind, spirit, and heart. There's firstly our physical self, our body. This is what we each live within and hold as our own personal boundaries of physical awareness. We have our five senses that are part of the body; our taste, touch, smell, sight, and sound. Our different body parts allow us to perceive these ways and can be said the biological organism is our own self *and* also a spiritual shell we live within.

Our soul? That blends, in my belief, some of the other components of being.

I think that our soul is the physical manifestation of our spirit. That what we feel in our body is what we're conscious of (mind) of our spirit and heart. We know that how other people treat and act toward us perceived through sight, sound, or feeling may be connoted as how they are with their spirit toward us.

Our minds can also perceive or think about other people and the things we sense or even imagine about them. Within our minds, we process our senses. Yes, we blend in the sixth sense here too. Some think that thought and hearing others thought is the ESP or telepathy that some speak of. I also add that there's an idea that the sixth sense also describes how we're self-aware of our own body positioning. What we think, whether it's immediate perception, memory, or imagination, is directly in our minds.

I then thought the idea of how our hearts are like the brains of our love. The saying of keeping someone in your heart is how we may think of the full being of another (their body, heart, mind, spirit, and soul) and having love and affection for them in our hearts vaults. The mind may be aware of people, though the heart may say how or if we like them and/or want them to be in our minds. A person's body may be near us, though our likeness (from the heart) of their spirit (or how they look, sound or feel) may call us to judge their soul.

Judgment's not always about saying something is good or bad or right or wrong. Using law versions of judgment can imply innocence or guilt. We also could say that if we accurately judge, we know what the truth is. Truth is one of my values, though this chapter is about beliefs and not values (an idea for another chapter?) Belief is a pinnacle word. If I don't believe strongly in a person being true or not, that may also adjust a different set of beliefs or responses. Spin in the idea of when a truth isn't just believed, yet known, that's when we get knowledge. I believe that knowledge also fuels belief and faith in that it's a foundational block we may build upon.

The movie *Dogma* had a line about God that inclined the notion of "I have an idea." The premise was that when we believe too strongly in something, that it may not be the actual truth. It's helpful to have things to believe in, even an idea, though, I wish to build factual knowledge.

Wishes are a different keyword though also link to beliefs. I believe that if enough people are wishing for something to happen that there's a greater chance that it'll occur. A friend in the past spoke often of how they believed that wish tactics were being used against them. I believe prayer is a valuable, helpful, and noble thing. I believe that those that pray have a different understanding of life and I also believe that I must write what I write to people that do or don't believe in God. If you aren't religious, think of prayer as wishes for things to happen or even just gratefulness for the things that have happened.

There have been scientific studies that show when enough people pray (or wish) that changes are made to the events or situations they are focused on. Even if this was not the case, I still believe there's exceptional value in prayer. I can't say I know it as a general statement for other people, yet I believe it to be true. I *know* that for me prayer *is* helpful even if anyone would claim that it has zero effect on reality outside of myself and my own spirit, soul, heart, body, or mind. You may not believe me, yet this chapter is what *I* believe.

I believe positive reciprocation as being a skill to develop. I believe that we sometimes choose which pathways of thought or action we make. I believe that optimistic attitudes and ethics are positive to hold, and I believe that if you offer someone a hug, you should give them a really good hug. I believe that adopting a pet is often an amazing choice and very well worth it. I also believe that my parents may not comprehend how grateful I am that they've given me so much space, grace, and support to let me do what I do.

I believe that there are many higher powers active in life and that I know my reverence for them also maintains. I believe that people should respect other people and their beliefs. I believe that people should act justly with themselves and know their own core values, ethics, and beliefs. I know that English is very difficult for some to learn; yet I also believe that there are secret links between different languages that bridge. I believe that some secrets should be kept, yet the truth is an exceptionally high value I hold. I believe that truth, sometimes, should be withheld.

I believe that my writing holds worth for others and not just myself. I believe that people haven't had access to some of the ideas and thoughts that I've had. I believe I need to focus on what I can do for people in life beyond just these written works. I believe that some that read my work about Natalie may want to help her and I meet, yet I don't yet know, believe, or have faith that she and I meeting is a good idea. I still believe that my choice of not pushing for a meeting and leaving it up to 'the hands of fate' is probably the best idea.

I believe that we each have an effect on other people's live, fate, and destiny from what we each believe. I believe that all people should be honourable. I believe that all people should be respectful. I believe that all people should encourage and support others. I believe that almost all who need help do find help with what they need, especially if they ask for it. I believe that people should help others with their lives and that we each give to other people, especially in ways other than money. I believe that I've been too money-focused, and I also believe I should push much harder for sales and support.

We continue to learn how to love people truly. I believe I've loved some people even when they may have wished me dead. I believe that the subvert meanings and signs that I steal from the Universe are sometimes intentionally placed into my awareness to hide from my own soul. I believe that there. I also, now, at 2:33 AM on a Saturday night believe I formed some good work and know I won't be at church tomorrow. I believe in the process and value of restoration and redemption. I believe my parents love me. I believe we make an impact on many lives. I also know that I learn to believe subvert and honest truth. I also believe that there are a link and similarity between knowing something and believing in it.

My own diction stifles me sometimes. Even though I've made up words that have become part of my own language, I desire to have an expansive vocabulary. Elizabeth Lesser's book *Broken Open* used 30+ words that I could not define. I also strongly admire Elizabeth Gilbert's writing and word selection and impeccable ability to weave through ideas. She also writes Italian words in her book. I've well invested in further learning that language. I believe that learning a language is an extremely good and cool thing and hope that I use what I've learned in the future.

I believe that I'm still to find an ever-unfolding future and I hope and pray it may be something amazing, wonderful, and mystical. I wish for travel. I choose to learn for love. I believe in the fact that having a reluctance to believe also may assure truth. I believe I could write another few pages in this section without discussing names of some that others also believe in. I almost want to attempt that, yet my own process of avoiding truth also finds me to sometimes obsessively hone in on fact. I know that if I trust, I may fall into patterns of saying things that become untruth. My own awareness in a solitary time cell confuses the very foundations that have built my guilty conscience.

The mind also holds that, our conscience. Ethics are argued as being subjective or objective. Some believe in absolutes that restrict the chance of there being a personal or unique truth for a person or group of people. When I type the statements "I believe…" is that not myself being subjective? Is that where one says that truth or fact is objective and absolute for all? I've said a bit recently: "What is true for you might not be for me." That's not so meaning characteristics; it could be when we think of differences between us. What though if teleportation *is* a thing?

"Seven billion subjective realities in one objective playground."

I also note that truth's not always static. When I was brought to the psych ward, I held quite a few false beliefs. One idea was the city of Shole. Shole was to be located on the planet Saturn and was to have a dramatically subjective (I think that's the right word) reality for its inhabitants. The differences of perceived reality were to be extreme in some cases. For two people walking down the street, one person could perceive a bright sunny day, while the other was walking in the rain. This isn't a metaphoric reference of how one would be happy (sunny) and the other sad (rainy). I meant that literally one person could be drenched and needing an umbrella in a torrent or rain while another might need sunglasses to shield their eyes from blazing light while they pass each other on the same street at the same moment of time.

How that's relevant to what I currently believe is also linked to another belief word that's scientific and not religious; theory. The theory of a nodal reality for each of us, even in current day Earth, is also a belief I hold. If not to trap myself by holding a firm belief, then I'll adjust the English use to having *an idea* like they said in *Dogma*. I have an idea that sources from my past experiences. We may jest *all* experiences are sourced from the past, yet there's an idea linked to the birds of the sky.

Have you ever looked out a window at the sky and seen semi-visible dots coursing through your vision? Think of how (maybe) these semi-visible dots then become a bird, or that an insect buzzes past the window from you looking too deep into reality. The theory or idea is that each person's entire reality and perspective and perception is their own. The semi-visible dots in the sky can be imagined as being actual birds, though just on a different plane of existence because of their locational need or placement for someone else's reality. (It's a really human-centric viewpoint, yet such as it is). When we find some things 'magically' happening, the theory that also needs to be included is time and timelines.

If we consider time as the primary variable or dimension, and we think of it as linear (that we've only traveled one pathway of time since we were born) then everything on Earth is on the same timeline. If I was five years old when you were born, then you must be thirty-four years old now. I'm thirty-nine now and we've been alive on the same timeline according to natural time theory. If that's true, then if we meet any moment of time, the exact pathways of time have happened to allow us to reach that moment. If it takes us two years to meet, then we must have passed through the exact same 'length' of time from now until that meeting.

Shift closer, though. What of those fragmented moments of life seen in the sky? Think of how that bird lands down beside you to hear a secret word in your mind, you have the awareness of a memory of a friend, and then that friend walks into the coffee shop right at that juncture. Does a puncture of your imagination call that person in right at that moment? You and they have been on your own linear path of time and node together right then.

There are a few theories and questions that could be melded. How did the bird know how to relay that thought? If that bird has its own birth hatched from the egg and traveled through its own lifespan to be there right at that moment and reality is static, then forget how it telepathically sent you a cryptic hint your friend was on route ("a little birdy told me": old saying), then would that bird not have to have followed the same linear path of time? Would it not have been a persistent actual being in the same physical locative relative positioning to all things? Would it not be that that bird was at the same places from every perspective from its conception until then? I'm not clear I can answer that.

That may not have made sense. Think of a different idea. Have you ever heard a song playing (audio recording) and heard a different series of lyrics than when you've heard it at other times. Literally, I mean. A completely different set of lyrics than when you heard the song earlier in life, and you absolutely know it. Think of this; when that recording was made, it would be the exact same sequence recorded as the musicians had performed when it was recorded.

How can someone hear a different set of lyrics than the musicians actually sang, rapped, or spoke than what was actually said? Should it not be the literally the same recording for every person who hears it? This leads to nodal music theory, though I remind myself too this chapter is what I believe, not theories. The idea from the birds in the sky is that I have a weird belief that there's a layer in the statement 'everyone's life is different' and not just by us each having different physical bodies. I've thought that the semi-visible dots are birds on a different plane of existence that's not fully on our own and is being positioned temporally for other's signs of life.

The birds that need to be placed (by God, the Universe, the Soul of life) at an exact time and place may not be in our own reality solely. Each life is separate and distinct and the parameters we see and share a bond and solidify as 'true' by a shared belief between us. Since I may not be relevant to some lives, that I'm like those semi-invisible dots flying through the sky, I may be relevant to just one person that needs to be reminded that they do have a friend that just walked into the coffee shop that loves and likes them.

I believe that we're each on our own pathways of time and that we do cross over and coincide with many things that aren't as random as they seem. I heed the need of some signs, ideas, and knowledge shared. Some of the signs and wonders that I perceive are connected to a grand world that I'm only one person within. I have a lack a lot of knowledge that I may believe strongly in that develops further faith. God is essential, fundamental, and not just an 'idea'.

An idea, though, about God for those that don't want to even consider religion. The idea of G.O.D. being, if you're Earth-centric (and not a flat-Earth person), could be considered as a Globally Organized Development. Think of the systems of Earth, trade, and government as the organizations. The process of our lives guiding form the development. The idea of a GOD is that all things are as they are and are interconnected.

A different idea is the Galactic Organizing Directive. The idea that every point of reality is designed and in place due to galactic organization directs all things.

If I step us back a bit though, what of those that call out to God or Jesus or Allah or another higher power? What do I believe about that? I believe then that I must put faith that I'm not God, Jesus, or Allah. I set my wishes and prayers outwards. I use a capital H for Him and also say "Thank you, Lord" often. I also believe I should not have the audacity or belief that I can form a prayer and close 'in Jesus name' and wield Jesus's power in God's name as if I hold His power. I believe that Jesus should be honoured and that we should not claim to have His power for we are explicitly not God. For a Christian to *ask* Jesus to petition to God on their behalf is more sensible in my own belief.

Regarding my own opinion or stance about religion? I can't yet claim to profess. I have interest in learning about different religions and I've attended church, though I also skip into and away from conscribing to another religious label, even if self-given. I don't think myself a Christian from my lack of understanding about Jesus, though I have had some glimpses into comprehension. I have a complete belief that there's a uniting of people in the name of religion, though my Earthly concerns are the conflicts between those who aren't of the same faith. I continue to adhere my prayers to God, I continue to explore my own spiritual understanding, and to honour and encourage others to believe.

CHAPTER FIVE – A Discrete Instinct

Trust your inner guidance! I typed that two or three days ago before *this* sentence asking myself if I'd stay up late with coffee and continue. I go to the kitchen right now. If you're going to do something and commit to it, make sure it's a good work and that you follow through with what you need to do... Pause... Coffee sipped... I commit.

Okay, back to the drugs.

I don't mean the illegal or herbal drugs. I mean the drugs of coffee and cigarettes. The book that I'm reading is *Built to Last* by Jim Collins and Jerry I. Porras. Learn much we shall! A weird point is how one of the visionary companies they studied in the book is Phillip Morris. I found this a strange choice for a visionary company as, generally, cigarettes aren't viewed as a great or good thing. I too believe that cigarettes are a wonderful pleasure, there just are super-great costs to them; health, their smell, and they cost money. I also note I'd never recommend smoking to a non-smoker.

The thing is, though, that I know, for myself, is that I want to get my work done, and that writing is my work. By making the choice, the commitment, of a cup of coffee at 12:30 AM, I also may glean, produce, share, and learn a lot by doing so. I told you of the sacrifice I make of sleep by writing in the middle of the night. It's a risk I semi-consciously make. I make the joke about how I'm walking a marathon because I can't run with the ciggies. There too is the additional jest of how I know I can't win the race, though wish for some bonus points for enduring. Am I glad to be a part of the race? The different idea, though, is what if it's not a race?

Endurance isn't just a physical thing. Expanding one's capacity isn't always about health or financial abundance. There's also the compressing of ideas and learning sourced from committing bad choices and persevering. I often have impulsive ideas bundled in my mind near the end of the night. This is in different ways or forms, and include a variety of learning parameters and expression. For example, tonight I process on page what my mind was thinking as I could not fall asleep. Other nights, I've written when I feel thoroughly inspired the moment I get home and trudge through the night.

The ideas from yesterday are heavily Seed focused. The ideas were stemmed from another topic and situation that filtered into a conversation with a kind and cool friend. To the point, the idea of giving 30% of the online earnings of books and music may be scrapped. I have a different idea.

The idea, as of today, is to give a greater amount to the Seed Fund. The idea is for 100% of the book earnings to go to the Seed Fund. This idea came from a few things, though it puddles my own fear of not having enough for myself. The premise is that some people may want to support my work (thank you!) and that some people may want to help the fund and not me. I don't think the previous commitment of 30% is enough.

What if we use Patreon as a channel for my *personal* income? We then can use a full percentage of the book earnings for the Seed Fund. Additionally, the books then may be marketed rationally *if* to use the cause as motivation. This makes a lot of sense to me.

My own personal situation, from a selfish viewpoint, is that no one wants to buy my books right now. They don't want to read them, or they don't even know they exist. I don't think I should market books on partial principles if only 30% or even 50% is given. My own ethics make me think that if I'm to market something, it should also be clearly beneficial for others. I like 100%, not 30%-50% idea because I have an idea that if something is to be given support, intention, or attention it should be entire.

I love explicit boundaries! That's partly from how I was raised, I think. I like explicit boundaries and guidance from some people. When I ask a person a question, I appreciate ultra or radical honesty. By making commitments and following through with them, I know that I often hope to meet my own expectations. If we commit to things and follow through with doing them, we also may build our self-confidence and self-worth. I love the twists and turns of my own psyche with these books as I write them. I get caught between the words, worlds, and muddle my own won mistakes. There's the case, though, that I want to form a solution.

The ability to have freedom is one I shall honour. I also believe that we should reward others for good, just, and true actions. A thing of this section goes back to intent. Am I doing good things for people so people do good things for me? Am I giving a percentage because then I'm rewarded for that good? Am I writing books for my own benefit as declared in *Fields of Formation*? A weird artist point of view is also just "I do what I do." I let my actions be as they are and accept the consequences. I also should not be blunt or defiant.

I don't know if these many late nights do have solid and positive long-term consequence. I have an idea that writing *is* absolutely good for the distant future. I know that I can't see or predict the future, so the smoking issue clouds my mind by not clearly letting me know if it'll be an issue when I'm eighty-five years old. My present based, even hedonistic, behaviour also carries an intuition and guiding force that also impels me to do things that just 'feel right' as cliché as that sounds.

Almost oppositely, I know when I'm making a bad choice. I sometimes have started an action, and then have to force my way through the action because it's too late to stop. It's like going on a road trip with someone. The idea may seem great, and then it inverts upon itself to a different moment of time. I know someone's trying to run me off the road. There's a delicate fragment of knowing when we need to avoid something or someone. Just like that bear in the middle of the road that you almost didn't see. The solution? Stop, let the bear cross, and then find your way home.

Is there a bear on the road right now? Are we supporting those in need and not so much the kid who writes these books? Would people want to help support that kid (me) to earn my income? Would they help me directly and not want to help the Seed Fund? That may seem weird, yet there were two people today that wanted *me* to have money they helped with and *not* give to the Seed Fund. Some don't like the Seed Fund idea.

The factors with this are also stemmed from only-child parental influences. By being brought up as an only child, I've sought approval and permission to do things. This coupled later with my belief that checking ideas with a trusted source, or multiple trusted sources, is also a great idea. I had not yet committed to the full idea when I first wrote this section and felt a twinge of guilt about working for my own gain.

Shall we seek Patreon supporters? What would happen if I gave up on marketing the books since there's no direct $ for me from their sales? What would happen if I didn't push strongly for sales? Is the idea of buying my books a lure or draw for people into the full goal of helping others?

I love that I have these doubts! I love that I'm so over-focused and almost faithless in myself and then make re-corrections that adjust the pathways to be potentially helpful for other people. I like that we're making the right choices, even after choosing unwisely first. I'm thankful we adjust my intents and commitments. Courtney today said she likes it when things go in circles, so let's spin these works in and upon themselves! (Check this out... Hold my coffee!)

What if we make the books be widely available and many people buy the books? What if the first few books get far out into the world, and the initial intent of *Finding Natalie* calls forth and it does lure in Miss Nat Jane in for a meeting? I know that I don't need her like I used to. I still have this messed up spirit in my being rolling her eyes at me as I wrote that. What if this flourishes and we can start housing people with the money? Am I just playing ideas to allure her to meet me? Am I just putting all these wistful whims and wishes of prosperity as a great deception? What if I should have fallen into lust and not given up the Internet girls?

The faith that I hold is that, as far as I'm allowed, I'll keep doing some of the irrational things that I do. Forward motion has been made, though. I commit to giving much more than I yet have generated, yet I also must sow a future for myself. I know I'd like to be one of those 6 AM people to actually rise to the sun and have near zero belief I ever will do so. I know my path includes many late nights at the plow. I too remember that there are the many other people that're chained to their overwhelming lives. They too forget that there are people who have found alternate pathways of life that cause them happiness and joy! How may we find solutions of freedom for those that haven't yet?

The thing of this goes back to reverence and gratitude. I'm exceptionally thankful for the life I live. I wish others to have their own Freedom Solution. There's a great responsibility that few know of, and part of mine is to keep forming these works. The fact that I still learn and cultivate a visionary organization (maybe not a business) of providing for people inspires me. God, the world, my friends, my family, absolutely my parents, and the blessings of grace from Earth have let me live how I live now. I am thankful and meekly grateful.

Some may be pissed off at me for it, though many may even accept that the work I do form is different from the majority of the population. I also must accept that my own parameters are different and trust that my 1:30 AM coffee is something to be cherished and reveled in, and then to fuel back into the work of the keys.

I'm exceptionally glad and grateful (and yes, even happy) that I do have my work, heart, and ethics. I wish that others may have theirs also. I know that my life's given great amounts of grace that allows me to do what I do. Even though I can't *yet* provide hopes, goals, and dreams for others, I still wish to provide the basic needs as a common courtesy. There's a meritocracy, yet the idea of fairness is also similar and valued. With the question: "Why is Rob so fortunate?" I'd like to answer that it's also so I can provide for others.

I wrote down the purpose of what I believe my life is meant to be; to provide. I'm to provide for people's needs by earning prosperity. I'm to provide other people's wants and improve the quality of life and being. I also wish to provide hope and inspiration for others so that they'll build lives they love too.

I may be a fool, yet as I've been told so often (and have claimed too of myself) I'm one of a special type. What if that's an idea for the genie and the wishes? It might cause a calamity and conflict, though what of the wish that other people's wishes be granted? There might need to be some carefully selected subscripts to such a contract, though what if we could use our wish to assure other people's wishes are granted? Hmm... I used a line in my lyrics that link from wishes... a karmic idea. "What you wish on me on thee in three." I think there are even Celtic ideas that support that notion. That what we give out comes back to us.

Is that why I live a great life? Because I wish all sorts of good things for some people and deny my own animosity to, for, or from other people? I dare not taint the balance, yet is that also good advice to others? There's the recommendation to have a great heart and do the right things, for the right reasons, at the right time, and for the right people. What if they left? What if they're left right out? What if she's *Left of the Middle*?

Anyhow... I love my work. I love having cigarettes and coffee and not having to wake up early! I love having people that I'm learning to like and love and appreciate. I like the fact that some people want to give me things and that I share some things with others too. I also am glad and grateful that my books are used as a financial conduit to support. We relieve some financial stress, and dare we even go so far as to provide some hopes, goals, and dreams and not only basic needs? Yes, please!

I have a lot of appreciation for people that can't just be given as a squishy hug or an expensive gift. I know that I'm not so great at helping some people, at the point of writing this, by not having a car or extended resources. My own basic needs are near entirely cared for. I'm glad for some of the friends that'll transport me and help *me* with transportation. I'd like to work, build, and revel in the fact that the love's becoming true. There also are some things I refuse and need to refuse.

If we share the Seed Fund on a grander scale than just locally in Chilliwack, do we find people to push for sales to fund our projects and commitments? What if people can share a link instead of buying a book? That may be a lot easier for most people. Will the love, luck, and support we earn be enough to earn Full Seed? I've been posting some of the chapters I write on my WordPress page and shall with this chapter too. I'm curious what (if any) feedback I'll get on this chapter before I write the next one, though we'll see.

And for those that read this in the printed book form, it'll have been a while between when written and when YOU have a copy. We'll more clearly know the future by then! Thank you!

CHAPTER SIX – Personal Significance

Each person has a different worldview. Each also has explicitly different lives than others. There are symbols and metaphors that are universal or common among different groups, cultures, and people, yet there also are the individual personal signs and wonders that speak directly to our unique selves. Some people have their own personal code names, secret languages, and private ideas that they share with a select few. I have some of those too.

I think of global significance. I strongly like, and kindly love, the fact that there are so many different nationalities and languages even in my own life. At the Thursday Toastmasters group, there have been quite a few ESL (English as a Second Language) people in the group from quite different places. It doesn't seem fair that English is my first and most well-understood language, yet it is as it is. At the Thursday night group, there have been people, visitors, and members who speak Spanish, German, Dutch, Japanese, Italian, Russian, Portuguese, and French. The night before this chapter was written, at the Wednesday group, there also was a Korean first language speaker.

My own experience with languages has me often thinking of my own abilities when I say that I'm babbling. This keyword, babbling, makes me think of the tower of Babel and how the languages were shattered and dispersed in the Biblical story. With Shoulspeak, there also are links between other different languages. I know some French, some fragments of Tagalog (Filipino), Cantonese, and Korean, and I too know a word or two of Halq'eméylem and Mandarin. I love languages as by learning even shards of other people's native tongue, I can both communicate and decipher deeper meanings. My second most fluent language is Italian and Japanese is a language I've only just begun.

With the code languages, there's the movie *Windtalker* where the Navaho language was used as a secret code in the U.S. Military. I've noticed other intricacies between separate languages that reveal deeper meanings. The Filipino way of saying 'thank you very much' in their language is 'salamat po'. If broken down (from the Babel idea of all languages being split) salamat po can be squiggled with and from Arabic 'salam' (peace), 'at' (English directional preposition), and 'po' which is Cantonese for 'girl'. That said, from my understanding of language's blend, 'salamat po' can mean 'peace to the girl'.

English definitely confuses things. 'I *think* things' isn't 'I *thank* things' in past tense. It's I *thought* things. With 'I *drink* water' and 'I *drank*' water being a grammar comparison, I *thank* God could be interpreted as saying I *thought* of God; that I gave thanks. The saying can be construed as 'I thought of God' and vocalized as an acknowledgment when we say so.

I don't know how it is to have English as a second language, so can only view reversal ideas from my point of English as my base language. For others that have a non-English language as their base, then there must be so many twists and turns and subvert ideas that aren't easy to grasp. Though tough thought through this theology theorizes.

With the idea of Shoulspeak, there are still developing thoughts and ideas that use English grammatics. Even grammatics isn't a natural English word, though language's connotations and use is an extension of our awareness. If it makes sense to *us* as individuals, we can at least make sense of our own thought and ourselves. Personal meanings and understanding of language as individuals is how *we* understand life, and sometimes our own thoughts.

We also know that communication is a multi-nodal idea. What I mean by multi-nodal is that communication's not just one dot, it's an exchange of ideas or an idea between two or more. An idea is sent, translated (sometimes through distortion), and then received and processed. What I say can be what *I* mean, yet you may interpret it quite differently depending on your language, worldview, and frame of reference. It's the shared understanding and comprehension with accurate communication allows people to know the ideas shared between.

Even to me, that sounds a bit obtuse or confusing. Note even there; I use the word obtuse to sound smart or intelligent. My intents, even if subconsciously, change what I say. If you don't know the words that I'm using (or don't hear or read them) then the message may not be successfully received. This is where I need to speak in plain language, slow down when I speak, and allow a successful transmission of ideas and intent.

I add to this how there are also different love languages. From Jack's Canfield's book *The Success Principles* and *Principle 53: Practice Uncommon Appreciation*. It's said we communicate love in different ways or channels.

The way I show love best is through sharing physical touch. I love to give people a hug, high five, or even a real handshake or intertwining of the fingers. This is the way I best show love, though some people disdain. Some people don't like physical contact.

Some people, like my cousin, are yearning for me to say 'I love you' or 'I miss you' to them, and, for me, that's a huge thing for me to actually do or say. I must entirely mean it, and if there's doubt, a hint of un-trust OR pressure to say it, it causes me not to say so. I've found this severe reluctance to say 'I love you' to one cousin because it seems that they're trying to force it out of me. Just like you'll more easily hear what a person is saying if you don't speak, there's also the case some need a lot of space and freedom to say 'I love you' and mean it. I do love them AND I also know that I can't say it, for I'm not so fluent in that love language under pressure. I lack fluency.

Almost oppositely to being reluctant to say 'I love you', I also sometimes say it a lot, just in different languages. Using another language doesn't always convey what I mean, though the strength and feeling of devotion (even if I truly mean it) is different. The love language of verbal affirmations is a weaker language for me, and I also value the feedback loop I receive by giving a physical touch to another. I could be smothered with 'I love you's' verbally, though the feeling of a real hug is what seals my belief in the truth of the statement of their love more clearly. Spoken words are easy to use to lie and deceive.

Truth is an extremely high value that I hold. The repentant fact, though, is that sometimes I'm terrified and scared to tell the truth. I also want myself to be fully honest. I have severe doubt in some people's statements or claims and have seen what I think are many lies and deceits. The layer of both ideas is that sometimes I may not know what the truth is, even if I hold the ideas as a true belief. There's also a statement I saw on the Internet that says: "Just because you're right, doesn't mean I'm wrong." My truth may be true to me, yet to you, it may be hogwash. If we stand on opposite sides of the number six, you may see a nine. Then again if you're wanting to use a nine, think first of how we add some line to assure the cosmos won't need to blur life out of the living realm.

Different languages, different sources and receivers, the diffusion of truth, and also what the true intents are weave all these notions into and upon each other. There can be some confusion. Regarding the truth idea, what happens when someone *is* telling the full and accurate truth and we don't believe it? The language and meanings may not be conveyed accurately and distortion can lead to disbelief. That leads to the idea of action, reaction, and response. I choose to push for truth, I don't always believe, and I also evolve past points of time, place, idea, and belief shift the very idea I've tried to compose. I think this is getting a bit complex, and I also want to get back to chapter and book relevance and not a schematic of my own muddle.

As I've spoken, written, and claimed, I've said the Fountains are my processing journals. I can be exceptionally accurate and short with my words, and also know that bullshit's bullshit. I may mix that moment of time when I wish to exert the rhyme. To climb into the view of how you know you are explicitly not me. Thank Yyou too. I also must form penance of some things that I do.

Anyhow, the topic is personal relevance.

I'm still learning. I know that all things are connected. I know that I'm sometimes separated from some points of life. I believe that my self-focused nature should be honed into words that build and not convolute. (*Convolute: verb. To make complex and difficult to follow*). I want to be clear and concise *and* continue to dig into my awareness to cleanse and purge. I continue to learn more about English and other languages to communicate. I also note that my own emotional intelligence must evolve and develop further so that we can work these ideas into a beautiful shared process of action.

Using text to communicate is a wondrous thing. The significance of what I learn and share may till ideas into the future, yet I'm still too aware of some ideas and things that keep people away. Some people I hope stay away, yet some other people I'd love to interact with more often. I may not have entirely thought of them and have forgotten to message, contact, or connect. I should call some people out, though it's also true that my own values guide my choices and evolve my intents.

The significance of my work's not always fathomable by my own self. I can make proclamation or claims and believe them, yet it may not matter to anyone else what I've written unless it's read. That too isn't entirely true. When I make statements, contrary evidence may be true and then immediately contradict itself.

If I keep writing and forming these books, the full truth falls more clearly and is brought into our awareness. These ideas also adjust our knowledge bases. This change of actions into a positive bundle of information and idea also may use these books as way to fortify our own truths. We can't assure some projected beliefs of others shan't till us with doubt about the very core of who we are. I need to become secure.

Some people say 'God first'. There are people who believe they themselves *are* God. I know, of myself, that I'm explicitly *not*. The practice of giving thanks, prayer, and homage to God is one that I use, though I also must remember that no matter what is entirely true to, for, and from God may not be understood accurately by myself or others.

You've read about my beliefs, though the significance and depth of my own beliefs are poetically just like a stone skipping across the frozen lake. I don't know the depths of whom and what God is. I know, though, that He and the Universe use myself and the ways they will, my own microcosm is an exposition of everything and nothing. It's sometimes broadcast out to everyone yet viewed by few, all, or none.

OR, maybe the seeds of my work have been tilled in the fields of time, and the *Fountains of Faith* assist providing water for (Big Hairy Audacious Goal) *all*. That's the kind and cool thing. I don't know what the future holds. We can't often even know the truth of what is and what has happened, let alone know what the future truths are. Using the entirety of all that's already happened I'm to be the focus of a mystery, I just hope, wish, and pray it's a positive one where the mystery is a series of supported miracles and not my own death.

From my mind in Italian: "Cosa la significa della mia mente. Non e tutta mia mente. C'era molti menti che unire. Questo Terra sono solitamente infinite."

Or that Italian to French (Google Translate): "Qu'est-ce que cela veut dire pour moi? Pas tout mon esprit. Il y avait beaucoup d'esprits à réunir. Cette Terre est généralement infinie."

From that French to Spanish (Also Google Translate): "¿Qué significa eso para mí? No toda mi mente. Había muchas mentes para unirse. Esta Tierra es generalmente infinita."

From that Spanish to English (Google Translate also): "What does that mean for me? Not all my mind. There were many minds to join. This Earth is generally infinite."

Yet what I first thought in Italian translated to English: "What does it mean to my mind. Not my whole mind. There were many minds to unite. This Earth is usually infinite."

What did I want to say?: "What is the significance of my mind? It's not all my mind. There were many minds that united. This Earth is usually infinite."

This is an example of the phone game with filters of language. What we say in English too can be compounded in and upon itself. What we mean to say is often not what we meant when another believes our words from their context. Shortened: People believe what they believe even if it's not what's true. Belief then builds upon itself.

So how will this resolve? Am I pushing to be understood when I should instead be working to develop the ability to understand? I think, yes. With the support of [Habit 5: Seek First to Understand Then to Be Understood] I need to get that principle first. What if we compound that and learn to understand how others understand us? If we can learn how another comprehends the world, not just understand what they say, then we may more accurately remove the layers of distortion in messages; to accurately communicate to people in the way they understand with precision.

When we shift our ideas to how another understands or processes us in knowledge of their absolutes, we can give them a more accurate response. The warning, though, is that some people understand some use that knowledge to present deception as truth. Psychology is (and I understand this idiom now) a double-edged sword. It can cut through the bullshit, and it also can slice off the truth. (I guess a single-sided sword could do that too. Maybe we should just be careful of people with weapons).

What though if the allies of Heaven also work for those that are Earthly or worldly based that have yet to believe or understand? Is that where the crusades were righteous and holding true to ensure rightness and justness were fortified? Or were people deluded and persecuting others who did not hold the same belief? We talked about the ideas, truth, knowledge, and fact. The individual wisdom must be found to then absolve the wish of others to abolish. As soon as one point of view is made, there's a contrary view. The clashes and jostling of weapons of truth both can destroy and hone further clarity. One device may sharpen the blade of good, yet still the shattered remains of the pains lost at war may open the doors to peace; without having to assure the cross is lost by a piece.

English isn't so easy, yet I often communicate that way. Even if threads of truth are wound and stitched through the tapestry of life, some people are colorblind. Some people can't see the truth for what it is. Some people may believe anything that's said as being absolute fact, even when as solid as gas. What if we sublimate some things? Skip the liquid phase of the fluidity of Earth and skip directly to the future skies of another planet? What if the steam that drives the engine is frozen into crunchy water? Snowballs flying from Italy upon timeship #427 find if you count forwards from five in Yoda's voice you find that it was six seven ate. Yet still, a random idea may be fun to share, even it obfuscates the text.

Thank you Elizabeth Gilbert! I appreciate you, your work, and what you've shared from the lives in which you traveled! They've allowed the threads of the loom to be woven still, even if I can't make such adorable and commoditizable fabric as that you allowed your own spirit (with all things) to weave. For those that do read, try her book; *Eat, Pray, Love*. It makes a lot of sense about God and life than I can't relay.

From above and below the raft of this craft, there are multiple realities and dreams I've wished that upon which it seems that God Himself has laughed. Or is it true of Venus? I know not... Saturn holds her within His rings.

CHAPTER SEVEN – Hidden Under the Veil

Some secrets must be kept. I dare not have slept when starting to dream. The facts are withheld sometimes, as requested. I've also said I wish to honour and absolve with the truth. I pray well the time to release the contamination is nearing. Kyle too has reminded me a decade ago of the 'cancer stenched walls'. I like how my home smells like an old smokey apartment. The smell reminds me of my grandparents.

I made a promise February 2nd 2015 that if I get a casting call, I'll drop smoking immediately. There are some hurdles to clear, though near to the precipice I dangle and reach. By the time this book is released, the choice's been made. I can't yet wade across the sunset, yet the tides of the call still crave to shred my habit. It's been a chain well discussed; yet I still am holding onto the grips and shards of my freedom to smoke before I must, and shall, honour my commitment.

Within the veil, she too makes her promise. I know I can't yet tell you who she'll be, yet there's a lingering wish that the fabric is drawn back to reveal she learns how to like and love me. Maybe I'll need to plead my case to some, yet threads of loyalty are where a great portion of my heart comes from. I've been pulled out like strings of cat's cradle with wings of the fable, yet the strings aren't able to yet compose the flows of the blue never wilting rose. I propose some things; yet the Kings let the set get wet with snow before it's time to grow.

Proactively, I deem I should release the habit to make it easier. The other side of myself seems to think I'll never need to quit. An essentially different viewpoint would tell me I couldn't cross the paths of enlightenment without shedding some snakes like the rat had its skin. There are two other Natalie's who competed; one with Russel, and another whom is a twin. We wind the loom into the brooms that dust my cigarette addiction into the bin and not under the rug. I'm terrible to act on the fact that I should be so smug.

The desire to honour the commitment is there, though the guarantee of there being the chance to honour my promise is what's not yet. Again, by the time this book is done, we'll know if the distant glimmers catch the glint of her eye. We also know I'm true to clarify some of the how and why.

Stop the rhymes Rob. It's time to focus. You've been given a glimpse that the Universe, or rather your wishes on Earth, *are* coming to a point of actualization. Please remember your wishes, and that I too wish you didn't dance so delicately close to the boundaries of your own forgiveness and misgivings. Please, I ask you, my own self, to slow down and gather your own devotion, integrity, and forces of instinct assure you keep your commitments; even to those you've yet to meet.

Having different topics and ideas to write about also give an author a way to deflect and meander away and from the truth. Even in my chapters of repentance, I've hidden the bald-faced open sandwiches of synergy to be chewed upon by false teeth. She knows about me and that she wants me to not know about some things of myself. It's inverse. I'm still inside the well-polished bubble that people look into to spy on our corruption. The cigarettes have been smoked tonight, yet I assert that the promise to quit hasn't met its initiating parameters. They've not said I can, so I keep my freedom for these bare remaining days.

A few months ago, I thought that the looming finality was for me to lose my own life at the hands of others. Now I must shield and nourish my own dreams and wishes with trust in what I need to do. I read brick walls are there to discover how much we want what's on the other side. I'll not need to break the walls down. I however must grab the correct ladder and take my first delicate steps. There are others on the other side of the wall… are they part of my tribe?

I deftly note my arrogance of thinking I could compete. The restrictions are there, and my faith calls them aside to allow my own passage into the ritual. The points of black mana fueled upon the stack like a train puffing and steaming at the station. One that's thirsting to be guided by the sheer magnetic pull instead of relying on even the negative urges to electrocute.

There's no electricity there. Will I have my meds? Does the story go back to the beginning of July when I thought the world was secretly conspiring for my ultimate adventure, or even much further before I was even born? Are they seeking my demise? I should be glad? Some energy is so different it can flash in the blink of an eye, and contain an eternity.

I'll miss smoking. I also hope that some others miss me. I hope that some contact me on my trip to visit my Dad. I also hope some miss me with their 'slings and arrows of outrageous fortune.' I'm not near as money motivated that I think I need to be to achieve some of my dreams. I made the choice to start the Seed Fund. I have the vision of what the inside of the Glass House looks like, though my lack of monetary drive doesn't even have me accurately able to answer the question: "What would be the craziest, wildest thing you would do for a million dollars?" I know there are many things I'd NOT do for a million dollars, though what'll I do to acquire that much.

If the Seed Fund is meant to house people and provide food and water for as many people as its audacious irrational goals, then $1m isn't anywhere near enough to finance that. One million dollars is only a few hundred thousand books even at 100%. I can't imagine that many sales at the current sales level we're at. My dreams are audacious, though the realism of them isn't rational. That said, we know dreamers dream.

So, what'll I do? Will I keep the goals huge and dreamy? Will I buckle up and pound a shit-ton of pancakes into making the projects excel? Will I keep my faith open to the fact that some of my dreams are more rational and achievable than I yet understand? Will I earn the trust and salvation of others to allow us to move toward meeting? Can I find Jesus as a belief and knowledge and not just an idea I glance across with love or reverence?

Does it matter what I do, or is the fixed finite path of a design so clearly tainted in my own favor find the rinds of orange taste chalk? I seem to think infinity holds, yet; again, we're at the end of time with the digital sands of the clock.

No moments of time have happened past now, yet the entire book is far in the future there from when I put these individual letters on the page. Each letter bundled in its own group to form a definition and understanding. How do the letters stand on their own? What if it results in us needing to build fire? I accept that challenge too. Yet, I also must jest of holding a stone. I know truly that I'm afraid of what'll happen if I let go.

What if it's seven, then six, then five? What then happens when there are two or three? There'll be people across the fire looking and prodding and compounding the judgments that have built up over the course of the journey. This may be a good thing for me if the judgment is good, yet what do I need to do to reach that point. We learn this together. An exposition of my own course of fate and destiny cradled in the hearts of a select few. When written, I knew not for how, I knew not it's true.

What would I be without my dreams? I don't know, and we may never find out. As one dream folds into the moment of now, I also ask the plow to tend the delicate seeds into the soil. There's a saying that strong winds and tumultuous seas make a strong sailor. It's rad and amazing to be there with the waves crashing on the shoreline. The fears of some wishing to learn to trust. I've said that faith is that. There some that trust this may be placed in *The Sands of Yesterday*?

Will I shield out those who *are* a friend by trying to defend myself from enemies? Or is an open heart, mind, and trust placed in fate with some who allow a just and triumphant victory? If so, how can I be put as one worthy of such a position to receive? How can I be there with another and be put in the situation of a choice made between another and myself? It's been said to think win/win, yet what happens if a decision's not made? Again, the wish and prayer are that we find out.

3:17 AM September 12th, 2017. The all so frequent split of whether to fuel with chemicals and work through the night, or to submit to sleep and conscribe to my nighttime dreams. The daydreams are like fantasy. What do we call the dreams of the heart and soul that refuse to be diminished? Dont stop short Rob! You know your being is yearning for this. Don't wait a moment longer than you need to renounce what you must. Put trust in yourself and not just the Universe active on Earth. There's much we'll need to do.

And if that's the case, then perchance I should rest to return to the future tomorrow. We need not always greet the sacred dawn. Some of us haven't seen the sunrise from either side of the night and day. The crucible of my very life is near. I'll not be one to let it evaporate into a puff of smoke.

Please (as an open wish and prayer of and for myself), please, please set aside the things you need to release for this. Please, Rob, put value and worth of yourself into what you *do* to reach that sacred goal. There is a thing you've said to others often so... It may not be easy, but it's worth it!!

A few days later, I continued. Shattered. Dismantled. Seemingly slipped out from under my breath. How can it be impossible? What if it's best I'm shut out and denied? Is being denied actually a grand protection of my life from a future that would not be best for me? Twist the key like the dagger that stuffs into the bag of rice. I know too that *they* don't have a price.

A clarity, though... I found the purpose of the work; to provide. To provide for a shared future through prosperity earned by collective input and effort. I know that Introversial is meant to supply people with the things that they want and need. My books, at this point, aren't the need or want that others have. I've been trying to push the process to allow them to be used as a conduit for a higher goal. We may need to find additional products, media, and ideas to fuel the Seed Fund. I heed that too, and think of how I sometimes don't quite know and what to do and for whom.

There's advice to make a move though. If I keep moving the keys, and move hearts, then perchance I'll move other people into alignment with higher values that'll assure others help support. Maybe it's not possible, Lilly, do I know in three years that I don't know now? You know you are relevant to the course of time, text, and insight that Lewis helped share in episode 506. Right now, in the cosmic dance of how we know celebrity may not be the best path for myself, there is a need to sacrifice some of my autonomy for our larger goals.

At least I'm learning that almost all people aren't interested in the minutiae of my life. It matters what I do, though barely anyone has interest in what I've done. It's what I'll do that'll help grow and cultivate the fields. I must often find the other tenders of the gardens and fields and wield a good bag of seed to share, tend, and send. Compassion and kindness, integrity and commitment, devotion and grace, and truth balanced with tact. The impact of our actions shares the division of the elements of the mind's refractions.

I've been aware of some things that twinge us. I'm still wondering why I'm allowed to do what I do and live the life I live. I have an intuition it's because of who I am and ones who want to assure I live. Thank you!! I think, though, my own feeling of guilt compounds that. There's the fact of how I have my situation when others are in different traps of life. The fear of jealousy and envy are clear, and I too know that they, even from my own perspective, may be justifiable. My wish is to earn my own income, so that I'm not on PWD or supported by other upper forces. I must add additional value to do so and be allowed prosperity.

I'm well now, and note that many aren't. That calls me in a divulgence of wishing reparations. If I'm given such an amazing life, then I know I can't, and won't, hoard it all to and for myself. This isn't just about resources. When I receive more love, praise, or attention than another person, I wish to shift the light from me and shift some of the goodness to them. There are far too many people that aren't appreciated or acknowledged often enough. This is a point to provide for too. To provide for people's needs that aren't just resource based; to improve other people's esteem and quality of life. My own life is to be used as a conduit.

I dream into the streams of text that wind the kind words into how she also knows parts of her spirit are heard. I know that there are some things are developed beyond the whispering bird.

"I say it doesn't matter." The scattering of the mp3s into how the purposes of the keys seize my heart into how I wish to depart. She had torn me from myself onto the shelf that holds a soul. I can't, and mustn't, enroll in the herbal arts. Some hearts are forever.

"I cannot fear the ground. This place that we exist in..." as I hear the sweetest sound.

I know that I can't go searching for Natalie like I wished to. I also know that the decades of time are minor compared to the millennia of Orvieto. I thought she was there. I was wrong. The fumbling and bumbling *dell'ape* says there are signs that shred the path into the shoulic math. I think Aristotle was right though. There are some truths lingering in the world.

Anyhow... I clear the veil of Lisa's allusion in the conclusions of how we know I may fuse some lines into my own wish to have a heart that doesn't just wish. There are many that we'll provide for, though I also know the doors to the future I must open, and not just for myself. There are some who also need to know that my love's still alive. Thank You for the reminder tonight.

Sip a deep drink into how we link. There's a bit of how I sit so often think in the chair putting the words to the page. I've told her quite a few 'stupid' things, yet the wings hold us up to find the sky a place that guides our heart. Though we may share a soul, there's also the control of my mind that assures the bodies don't hit the floor. There are some secrets I'll shed, yet, though, believing that some truths shouldn't be told or misled.

I know that truth is a super-high value I hold; yet there too is the value of keeping people's secrets safe. There's a difference between lying, being honest, and knowing what the facts are. I may not be able to know when those three things are or aren't true, yet True, it may just be you to know that there still is a life in the future for us two.

Please forgive me for the fact that I've lacked the correct ways to navigate the maze. I hope you don't have to wait much longer. I need people's help, though this Whelp reminds himself that while the shelf holds the paper folds, the bold's choices must be trusted in the spin of us into kin.

Thank you for letting me do what I do, and for some like Michael J. Fox too for reminding me that his Tracy too knew that changes have been made for our future; a future where your own heart may have spoken and betrayed my true feelings. Maybe you are the secret I must keep to assuring we guide the night into your voice to protect and project me into sleep. I still don't know. The sands sleep reap that which we keep.

Grazie mia amicia piccola… vi amo, anche se non ti conosco ancora.

CHAPTER EIGHT – Buckle Up Koyich

(This chapter was me convincing myself to contribute more of my creative earnings to the Seed Fund)

Hardcopies too, Rob? How's that been going? I've sold a few of those and I do keep some money from those. The small gains and gladness from actually selling a book personally is a pretty cool thing! There's a great feeling of knowing someone's okay to give me money for my work. I don't know if I'll budge on the hardcopy sales. A book sold gives $5 to the Seed Fund per copy with the rest to cover costs. I like that a lot and think to stick to that agreement.

For online sales, though? When this chapter was started, the commitment was 80% of online sales to go to the Seed Fund. Diana says she thinks there's an underlying fear by waffling and talking about these percentages so much. There is! I'm afraid *I* won't have enough money to live. I have a rational want to earn my own income; and an income greater than my own current levels. I want to have more than enough for myself too!

Okay, what if I give 100% of all *Fountains* earnings to the Seed Fund? What about the other books? *Shared Node*? The others I'm forming? *Shared Node* (the rhyme book) hasn't been marketed yet, though then I've been thinking about weaseling sales money from that book for myself. I'm really not clear with this. How could I tell people that some books go to Seed and some don't?

If the Fountains are 100% Seed, then we may more easily describe their monetary purpose; to provide. Without even 20% to myself, then I can actually market and push them wholly as a Seed Fund income source. I've been mutzed up with this %'s dilemma for the past four weeks regarding the percentages. The argument is that if I get *some* proceeds, I also may be paid for my work. I also really don't know that if books'll sell if we do allocate 100% of the earnings to the Seed Fund. I just want to know and assure I'm making the right choice for the right reasons.

What are the reasons why 100% is the best bet? 100% means that we'll have more money for sharing. If there's utter success with funding Full Seed how could my own fear of lack even exist? I feel like a weasel even thinking a small percentage could go to myself. My materialistic side still wants a car and I forget not of Glass House ideas, yet I've no rational way of understanding how I afford to build that home for my family. I don't have much income right now, and a car seems like a distant idea at this point too.

I'm really afraid that I'm wasting all of my thoughts, ideas, and energy, as the books aren't yet selling. If 100% is given, then where shall my own income come from? Patreon is an idea, though the issue again is my lack of faith. We did get our first patron though! A trusted cousin pledged $5/month! If I just commit and make an agreement, then my revised declaration may be formed and signed.

Okay, I'll try that. Bit by bit, I'll state my commitments based on the values of truth, providing, and self-reliance.

Since I don't want to rely on other people like my parents to support me AND I want to have a self-derived income that isn't governmental, I must form a way of earning a personal income. I can't work full time, and I know that my days of a standard job being paid minimum wage are a thing I've passed also. I want to earn my own income. How may I do that?

Do I earn honour and generosity for myself through Patreon? Do people believe in me and my work? If the book earnings go solely to the Seed Fund, my work is create to earn grace, love, and blessings from others who'll support? My wish and hope for an assured guarantee of prosperity, though, hasn't yet arrived. I don't want to make bargaining pleas and proclamations, so let's approach this differently.

If I was to earn zero money from books, would I still write them? Yes. I also want to have a way to purchase personal copies so I can share them. I know too because of my ethics, creative freedom, and personal integrity I must abide by what I commit to. Must this be an all or nothing thing? If I commit to doing so, then yes.

What of the other books? If Patreon earns me enough, then what about using the other books for Glass House ideas? Would people allow me to do that? One position is that anything anyone earns can be used to do whatever they want with it. I also want to urge myself to remember some other motivations or gains for forming a 100% Seed pledge.

If 100% Seed, does that give people a different reason to buy the books? If they are actually read, will readers help with additional sales? If we share my ideas, it mustn't be just for myself. I know I'd like to write the books with a purpose, though repent I've partly been writing for an income. *Finding Natalie* was not released for money, so that may be a sign dredged up to recover.

What if I restate my primary objectives, both personal and organizational? To provide. To learn. To develop. To share the truth with tact. To keep myself alive and be there when my parents are more than 80 year old. To earn and cultivate love. To keep our peace. To assist unity. To be respectful. Also, to honour my commitments and make positive forward development.

If we sell copies of the Fountains, they must be used properly and actually bring value to others and not just myself. I've said quite a few times that money's not the only worth, and that's true. I know that and still am stubbornly hooked up to a fear-based lack mentality.

I also know fairness is a value I hold. Recently, I've thought that it's not fair that other people have to have jobs and work or are homeless and have no income. I've had a home to live in, enough resources to smoke even, and all doing so without having to work a job I hate. I work, just my work's not the standard form of an hourly job.

In *Fields of Formation*'s chapter five I wrote: "Hired by Earth as a Contialitic Shoulsman June 15th, 2017, even if I'm terrified it's true." I guess that means I'm past my three month probation period at this point. Robert... Just buckle up and commit!

Okay... 100% online book and music earnings go to the Seed Fund. Personal copies are my own personal income with $5 per copy to Seed. Patreon is the channel where people can pledge to help me with my own living income.

I do, though, want to keep a security blanket for myself and my own dreams. I'm afraid of giving away too much. Since the books are my own work and creation, there's the fact I can theoretically do anything I want with the earnings. What I'd like to do, is put a hedge. I'd like to keep 49% of brick and mortar *bookstore* sales to build my own dreams.

As of when this was written, my books were not in bookstores, though I know that's part of the next bit of my work. Even if I feel a twinge of guilt, I hope you may forgive me for wishing my dreams come to fruition also. If I do achieve an income far greater than I currently imagine, then I also may give more in the future.

The Seed Fund focuses first locally. The list made for Full Seed is tended to until all are provided for. We can now market the books online for Chilliwack until Full Seed is reached; a seemingly irrational goal, yet audacious enough to work toward. I also now can move forward in peace.

Lil' Wayne called in through the stereo just then reminding me of some things. The facts come from how I know the plow is what I must tend with; for more than just some who I've yet to know as a friend. We tend forward and outward. I ask you to share a divinity told by those who mould the records fold into the mix. I just caught something there, and I do pair it up. I want to tip my cup and let it overflow into the things I add to you and yo.

The music too holds a commitment that my music earnings go to the Seed Fund. I now rely only on Patreon and personal sales for support. Alex K, you stepped up by being the first patron! Thank you! There's a weird feeling I know of how I need to start at the bottom and reset. If I refuse to climb the ladder to the top, I can still just drop the lines into signs of spines, and confuse to stop the lines.

Without purpose, things could go off direction. There's a need, sometimes, to stop and become conscious of what we're doing and why. If this chapter was meant to be used to convince me to allocate 100%, and the choice was made to do so, then why continue with this?

For those that have been patient with me and have allowed me the grace to create, thank you! For those that have believed in me and my dreams, I also am grateful you've allowed me grace! When I'm allowed to create for the sake of creation itself, and not needing to think of money, it's a lot easier. I know that some people think that an easy life is a lazy or unearned one, and there's a layer of that that I intuit. If we can, though, find the ease to give others a life where they need not thirst for money or resources, we also can form some pretty monumental things.

I do have a fear of releasing 100% to Seed as my irrationality then thinks that if all the earnings go to Seed, then there's no need for me. That might be true if what sells is only that I've made up to now. What about that I create in the future? The hope is that there's also worth in my work yet formed. I recall the other three books I started and now my wish and want isn't so much money, yet rather that the books come to fruition. I must craft them to be valuable for what they are and not only for what they earn. Sometimes a money or profit focus erodes quality. That may happen when people are competing to cut costs to earn more or rush production.

Now I get to hone my craft? Hmm… What dare shall my focus be then? What ideas do we fuse into the mix? If I'm not earning money from my work, then what's the lure for me to search for sales? My dream girl was the initial lure, though that one was chewed off the line and spit out. The Glass House is an objective and, yes, still is a vision. If I'm not working to earn that, though, how shall it manifest? If I'm not plotting and planning marketing schemes, how will the books sell? Does my wish to push for sales wane? That's an honest concern.

As my books are used for the purpose of providing, I don't need to have my own twinge of negativity for pushing sales for *my own* benefit. I have an honest fear of myself, though, being greedy. Does this hinge the start of a non-profit organization that's represented by individual artists? Artists that provide their works to provide for others and then receive support through patronship? We can do that. I guess my branch of Seed work is under the banner Introversial. I thought Introversial was to be a company name, yet it seems that it's now just Rob and his full spectrum of work. Hmm...

Okay. There's an odd pause here as I type this. If I'm to write and/or record, and it's not for my own money, then how does that change what I write? I know it does, yet again. It takes time for some decisions to settle in.

There are benefits to being a Seed provider, and I do wonder how we can gather others to work for the Seed Fund. This may now find my shift from trying to earn money, to earning people's hearts and then turn into helping us work to find solutions. From the book *Built to Last*, the ideas of core purpose and core values guided this. The core purpose: to provide. Core values? Those depend on the individual.

Introversial is what I do with my work for the Seed Fund, our communities, and my own creative process. I have my own prerogatives and we note I do have my own selfish intents and interests. I set aside the previous plots and plans, and now may restart and restructure. I guide my Introversial work.

Some people may assume that I don't like work and that's why I don't have a job. I don't have a job because I've found in work environments what I emotionally, mentally, and metaphysically felt and thought wasn't tolerable. For some a job's definitely not worth the hate, angst, or even money. I think there's a misconception of myself and some others on PWD too. For myself, I don't think many people value or appreciate the fact that I've spent so many late nights working on projects, organizing files, designing online content or sites. There's an investment made in connections, communications, and heart.

I understand how some people may have a strong animosity toward me for not being in the workforce. I also think that I put in additional work with the creative projects. I know for the book *Fragments of Intent* that there's a lot of work to be done to make the book available in bookstores. I need to get the ISBN registration, form the sales sheet, and actually contact the stores to carry the book. I also must trust my ulterior motives still benefit others. Money's ruined a great deal of my own ethical behaviour, yet it motivats myself to cause some great peripheral benefits.

I hope you too know when you feel certain feelings shown as a confirmation by God, the Universe, or your own ethical compass. Intuition, when heeded, can assure that the right choice is made. There is, when felt, an edge of excitement, a slowing of energy, and a confidence and release of other pressures. These feelings allow me to ease out of one moment of time and peacefully into the next. Be sure to find the things that put you at this type of ease.

Hold on... pause... take a breath... trust in Gabby's book title; *The Universe Has Your Back*. Draw long, slow, and deeply in this moment before thrusting yourself back into the fray of what you must do in life. Purpose need not always be a push. Sometimes it's enjoyable to relish and revel in the fact that, even if only once in a while, you know you've made the vital and needed choice and allowed yourself and others a positive future.

For those that buy the books online, you are helping. For each copy of *Fragments of Intent* or *Committed to the Process* sold online through Amazon, the royalty of just over $5USD goes to a person who may not have access to some basic needs.

The steps of how we expand outwards from our local communities are tracked in the Fountains books. As of now, the Seed Fund is providing gift cards to local grocery stores (and also, yes, some Starbucks cards) to people who are below the poverty line. The objective on a super audacious scale are to assure that *all* people have a home, food, water, and sanitation. Extended benefits of Seed recipients may be transportation and clothing with a longer term idea to scale money into funding education and supporting other charities too.

My commitment:

    100% online book earnings → The Seed Fund

    100% online music earnings → The Seed Fund

    $5 per personal hardcopy → The Seed Fund

    100% Patreon = My earnings.

51% of bookstore earnings → The Seed Fund

49% of bookstore earnings → My own dreams

Adding that hedge of 49% for myself has me, now, wondering if I'm being greedy. I know I'm neurotic. Maybe there's value in that too?

For now, though, one of the first step's been made; the commitment. I finally have passed the moment of time, and yes, still with a bit of fear. To commit part of my creative earnings for those who need support stimulates the feelings of excitement and fear. I've also put myself up and out into the world as and Introversial artist/author exposed to the world.

Please put your faith into your work and process too. I can't assure or tell you what is *your* right or correct choice or path is. That's something you'll need to come to an agreement with within your own being. I know there *is* an explicit freedom once a commitment is made. I hope we'll be okay many years after the point of these choices and appreciate them for what they've become.

CHAPTER NINE – Potting Soil

There's a delicate boundary between playing in the garden and getting run in the mud. I'm not clear at this moment which I'm doing. I intuitively know there must be more than I can do than just write, and I have an idea I've overwatered. Potentially, worse yet, I've over caffeinated.

I've been told that seeds need time to grow. This applies to other parts of life too. There may be the wish for radical sprouting and germination, yet a McDonald's advertisement tips into my mind about how Joe was wondering why his flowers weren't growing. What was needed was time, the chance for the flowers to take their natural course of time to bloom. This is true for other things as I tell myself to be patient.

I can't expect things to magically happen overnight. I blurred the previous chapter into this one by writing during the same period of late night wakefulness. I may need to rethink that idea. A pause to roll and light a smoke then had me thinking to report some secular repentance, though I'm not clear about the value or wisdom of doing so. I think about how running full through the night has its own high and there's also the idea of avoidance. The idea of pushing my limits and putting in effort and work also finds that I'm terrified of going to bed when there are precious moments of wakefulness to be had. When writing, I just heard my alarm clock's music. That means it's been 24 hours of wakefulness since I was last called from my bed.

Why would I sleep when I can still do things!? Why would I quit the day and submit to sleep when, clearly, I'm too sketched out from coffee to even think of a restful sleep? This pattern of staying up all night and writing isn't adding to my faith that I'm going to succeed and form valuable works. "Fatigue makes cowards of us all" – Vince Lombardi. My repentance is staunched from the obvious wounds of my lack of character. Is this a flow of time and ideas, or just a leak in a boat that's sinking like an elephant in a canoe?

Sploosh!!! Into the drink!

Okay, if fatigue makes me a coward, and I know I'm a coward from a sushi lunch a few days ago, let's use this chapter to shred away some of my own insecurities. Let's peel away some layers of shoulic flesh from my rotten core. There's a strong argument that revealing one's weaknesses isn't a good thing, yet there may be additional worth in deeper inner exploration.

Let me take the position and argument that all of my books are an entire waste of time. If the initial reason for writing was to meet Natalie, I've cowered from seeking her. I've allowed myself to fall into my own pathetic pattern of not following my own heart and instead have done what other people projected was 'best' for me; which is to not focus on her. I sacrificed a responsible life by not preparing for a vocation or profession, and I now am unemployed. It's been one year since I put the first book online, and my entire royalties since that point are $42.70 which haven't yet been collected. That means that one year of creative work has resulted in $0 of royalty payments total.

Consider too the results of my social life and connections with friends. I've not tended my own garden of life to include even five visitors in the past three months. A few months ago I said I wanted to have focus sessions at my home and, as of today, there are zero planned visits to my home. Of the friends or people that have called me on my phone, there are, though a few more than I thought. This realization calls a strange idea to explore.

What happens when we think we have nothing or lack, and then really analyze it? It's the opposite of searching for abundance and finding where we don't have it. A weird thought right now is linked to the saying 'count your blessings'. As I focus on searching for where I'm lacking, I actually find things that I have. I make some assessments of my attitudes, resources, and situation here from this idea of searching for lack to find prosperity.

If I think about my lack of money, I did have a large deposit on September 11th. My money pattern has been being tapped out and near overdraft almost always. Though I'm often maxed out in overdraft (-$750), my current focus on lack of money finds that I'm not at that limit right now. I note also that my bills are all paid up right now. I have $125 available, $80 in my Freedom Fund, and another deposit's made within 24 hours. Money is usually the first resource that I'm aware of when it comes to lack, and right now I have some.

Next, onto another resource. I've often had a lack of smokes. If I assess my tobacco situation, I have a near full pouch and a full tin to cover me for the next 10-12 days. More than usual. It's often been the case that I wonder when and where the next $30 or $60 comes from to buy a pouch or tin (3-7 days smokes). With my current tobacco situation, I know I won't need to spend money on cigarettes for at least until October (again, September 19th was the day I wrote this section).

Food is another thing I've had a lack of sometimes. There have been times where I'm literally at the point of relying on peanut butter and the last few slices of bread. More than some others have, though having food is a rational want. Last night I made tacos!? Thank you! I even have coffee! This is good and, yes, I'm grateful.

This attempt to focus on where I'm lacking actually found me to be glad, appreciative, and aware of having access to excess. A conversation with a friend a few days ago found me telling her some things. I told her how my having groceries is an excess that I fear jealousy for. I see how some people don't have a home, meanwhile, I'm one who's got a home and food.

It can be said that because I'm grateful and thankful to have what I have *and* that I'm okay to sacrifice from my own access to others sometimes. This is because I do have more than I need. The disparity between me having things, and others not having things, seems unfair as I'm not working a standard job. My belief is that it's just and right to share and provide for others. I like fairness and it sometimes seems unfair that I have what I have when others don't.

When I see some strangers behaving in ways that I think negative or unlikable, I also know I get a bit judgmental. When I see negative behaviour from some people, I sometimes have a near instant awareness of where their life is lacking in goodness. It's not that I want them to have negative things either, I just also have a weird belief that their choice of how to behave have caused or resulted in those things. Even if from my own projected belief, I see the causational results linked to one of my Mom's statements when growing up: "Behaviours have consequences."

I see some who have been treated unfairly and don't like that. The classic saying or belief that "life's not fair" is one I'm sure is embedded in many people's worldviews. I don't like unfairness and think that often it's been the case the scales are tipped in my favour, and not from my own doing. The fact that I have amazing parents is a blessing that can be chalked up to luck. The fact that I was born a white male also has been an accusation that people have put upon me. I know too that I'm so exceptionally fortunate to be in a city and country where I have access to taps in my kitchen and bathroom that bring water. I'm humbly and dearly blessed by these things. This gladness causes me to wish that others have these things too.

If I'm so fortunate to have the life I live, then how do we form a way for others to have their basic needs and also extended wants provided for? In the discussion where I was trying to assure my friend I have excess, she was telling me I don't. Another friend's been upset about corporations and high-level earners and says they are greedy and not helping those in need. I think of some wealthy people that *have* given a great deal of their wealth away and acknowledge that they do hold the power of giving. Bill Gates would be accused of greed by some, while I don't see that so much.

The weird statement and objective I've made for myself: "to earn like the 1% so that I can give away 99%." As we should know, for now, I'm not earning even above the poverty line. My math and faith is audacious, though, and increases greatly. For now, I know where I am. I also know what needs to be done. That isn't so much a set of tasks, yet rather instilling correct action, intent, and commitments that allows an ultra-prosperous future to unfold. Additionally, I also know I need to level up and learn to adult a lot before I'm granted the capacity to tend that high level of responsibility.

Bit by bit.

Grain by grain.

Seed by seed.

Multiply!

Remember to pause, Robert. A memory of Concord Place in Vancouver is one where my hands typing on the computer seemed to be one, my Mom, and the other, my Grandfather. How far past psychosis have I come? Two and a half months ago I couldn't even comprehend. I felt like I was over-immersed into life and would not be able to cope with the days and nights, let alone hold a job. Now I'm talking huge ideas again that're far past my current experience.

Slow down. Breathe. Reset.

This is where I still am one to pause for a cigarette. My guilt is then felt by the fact of myself being heavily blessed when others deserve far more than they've yet been granted. I wish not to be wasteful. I know I'm in excess. That excess, even if not understood by others, makes me feel unbalanced when there are people who don't have a place to sleep, access to running water, or dare even, food or bathroom. I want there to be a balance. If I'm to be a conduit to earn so that we can share and help others find their needs to be met, then that's a win/win. They get their homes, their food, their water, their transportation and basic income. Perchance as we find those things provided, we also help some people find hopes, goals, wishes, knowledge, and dreams.

There have been some concerns others have shared about the Seed Fund. Some believe (and I agree) that education and life skills should be gained and provided too. There's a concern about what people do when all their expenses are covered. What do people do with their time? Do people use their resources for alcohol, tobacco, or drugs? Who will we provide for at the start when we can't support everyone immediately? If we house all the homeless people in Chilliwack, would other people move to the town to reap the benefits of Seed? How are people's actual quality of life change if they are fully covered? To the value of fairness, what about those who'ill be working jobs to support themselves when many others don't and won't have that need? These are ideas and questions to ask and answer. I know that I can't perform the work of Full Seed on my own. My books aren't even a predictable income for even one person's Full Seed ($13.4k per year). Even if using 100% of the earnings, how do we provide that first person their own home let alone the entire 300 others locally? With the big shiny wishful goal of providing *all* people with food, shelter, and water, 300 people are less than one-millionth of the total people on Earth who don't have clean water and sanitation! This isn't something that can be provided for by only one kid and his books earnings. It'll include many people, organizations, logistic wonders, and devoted humans to gather in a united cause for basic humanity. It's a worthwhile objective.

I don't think it's fair that I have so much even if I'm shamefully glad to have such. Some could argue that people who have a spouse, kids, and a mortgage need to take care of them and stay focused on earning for that core unit. I agree. I note I'm at a level of abundance that I feel guilty for having because so many others don't and if the book sales, up to when this was written, haven't yet earned big money big prizes, that's okay too. If they do, it'll be best to use the earnings wisely to help others who've not had the fortunate blessings that I've often had.

There's the agreement I have that throwing money at issues can't fully resolve them. That isn't the correct path. There also are some who think that people try to take as much for free as they can. There could be some people that have too much time on their hands and cause mischief due to boredom. There's the case that some people might just watch Netflix or sleep all day if they didn't have to be at work. There also are some in desperate need that have no other source of support.

There are the people that are grateful for anything given to them, even a hello. There are people that go far out of their way to help others, even at their own cost when they have little themselves. There are people that want to teach how to thrive so that we also live a loved life. There also are people that defend tooth and nail when some other people are afraid of getting involved in a violent situation.

There are people that want to improve the quality of life for others and raise what the average standard of acceptability is. There are people actively pool together their hearts, minds, bodies, spirits, souls, and resources to strengthen and bolster the lives of other individuals; those who may not otherwise have a wish, want, or even imagination that they'll live another day.

There's much for us to work for. We need not be on someone's payroll to make a contribution to our communities. We may need to suspend our own judgments, and even intuition, to find out what the truths are so that we may nurture and foster the seeds of forgiveness. If we do want to thrive and have more than enough, then is gratefulness, appreciation, and gladness enough thanks to the world for allowing it to be so? For some that may not be enough. Each person is different in their wants and expectations and what I consider excess for myself might be laughable for another. Then again, if I'm allowed access to excess and share my excess with others, would that be something that does improve another's life?

For those that are in financial lack, it's likely you won't read these pages yet. There are many of the people that benefit from these ideas that don't have access to luxury items like books or a computer. Some people might not like books and computers to be considered luxury items as for some people, books and computers are a vital need. What happens as we shift people from viewing food, water, shelter, and sanitation as a dream to something they are given full access to? What happens to their mindsets then? How many shackles are torn from our community's members when they're allowed to lift their fears and be granted a life they too are safe, happy, warm, and thankful within?

There's love out there. Some of it just hasn't sprouted yet. There are some angels that have been dragged through the mud and denied yet a glimpse of compassion. There also are some that should come down to Earth and make a visit to their soul. Some humans also recall others that have tipped the scales and their drinks to quench the fires of consumption.

Baldly, I also guess that if you've read this far into the book there are some dangling ideas that help reassess the view of when enough is enough. I may go overboard with some things, yet please don't forget that others need a life-saving device too. The waters aren't always safe; there are sharks, and dolphins aren't always the kindest animals as they are presumed. I won't infuse further metaphors into this chapter. Just be known that if you've read this book, this is part of my 'work' and there's still much that each of us shall do.

CHAPTER TEN – Some Delicate Accusations

Of me? Or, of others? Let me get my coffee brewed and let you know. Actually, for an idea for this chapter, let's just use the word 'you' and absolutely make some accusations of specific person some may not know.

You've been an amazing friend. You've been a loyal supporter of many people, shops, and other friends. You've hidden my mind into the world in ways the days need not call the Maze to grip the plays. You've kept my tears wept in a flask of rhyme that shares the dime. You've loved me as a friend, even when you may not want to interact with me. You've kept the salty flavors of some things under wings without drinking the blood. You also remind me that there are many other people that I don't know that call me a bud.

I think you know how fragmented my mind and thoughts are, even when fluid and held on an mp3 or completely unknown to even my own self. You also aren't the one I think of now. They've guided and directed me differently, and I seem to intuit the plot and plan that stems both from my lack of trust and devotion. She's told me some things that're clearly not okay with me and my own ethics, yet I also know some accusations are as clear the moment of then, as you were clear to the moment of now.

I could accuse another of sharing their own repentance to me and charge them with being completely honest. I could accuse them of being a pretty rad and amazing person also and make the claim that they'll find much in our community that we've yet to understand. You are helping us both. I also could accuse a fourth person of being almost entirely unknown to my mind and awareness, even though a fifth node is You. The effect of capitalizing a letter drags in an entire slew of ideas without slaying those few with an allusion to Blue. Who is who I sometimes can't tell her too.

Another completely different person should know their world is also a bubble that's cleaned from the outside. It's not just so that others can peer in and observe, though also that they need to clearly look from within, and also step out of the bubbles of others; with permission and kindness. We must not disrupt the other's inner and outer forms and not be so permissive.

I've accused many a person about MFBing; a thing that's deplorable and invasive behaviour. Some may accuse me that it's a secret want, yet I clearly am baffled that anyone would think I'd like that. Some people sneak up and 'poke' and I think them pretty offensive terms about them doing so to anyone with any level of thought or action. There are some things that I instinctively know won't ever be a 'love' action for me. Some people try to insight my hate and anger by diddling. That said, I too have been accused of being negative and invasive.

What about accusing myself of some things? I've definitely not tended the Seed Fund effectively with my actions. I've not been pushing for earnings from online sales. I've been far too accepting and passive. I've not been one to properly show care and appreciation for too many people. I've not given to some people when I feel resentment, spite, or have feared my own lack. I've been too pushy with some people while overly lax with others. I know I've not adulted well and have been exceptionally unhealthy with my cigarettes, coffee, and staying up late. I think also that I've been a bit too accepting of some things.

I could make some generalized accusations of people, though those generalizations could bundle some others who aren't performing such actions. With that idea lingering, what of making some bold accusations about others if they aren't true? Some people could be falsely accused and not have the truth spoken about them. People may be tainted by people believing falsities. This is where our own beliefs may not be based on truth or fact. When claims are made based on untruth, lies and deceit may be spread. We must be careful about proclaiming false belief as slander, even if based on the accuser fully believing the truth they hold.

I hope you found a flaw in that last statement. A false belief in the truth. Two people stand across the pond. In the middle of the pond is a frog. One person could say "There's a frog looking at me from the center of the pond." The other person on the opposite side of the pond: "There's a frog sticking its butt in my face from the middle of the pond." Both are true if the frog extends its ass and eyes outwards from the pond to both of those people. My advice, go have KFC and remember that I'm not a frog. (On edit I also add that it's not a Sub-Zero or Shang Tsung thing. I don't keep my eyes on my enemies, I tend to watch my friends and sometimes have to watch out for 'friends'.)

There are many people and jokes that linger in the world we live in. It's the same planet, the same time of now, yet with the fact that each person is so exclusively held in their own body and frame of reference, there's going to be a lot of missed ideas, contacts, context, and perceptions. I wanted to write this chapter as an acknowledgment of some friends in Chilliwack, though then limited the idea twice. First, I limited the idea by fearing that if I started mentioning names, that I'd miss mentioning people, and two, I thought also that if these books reach a mass audience, that the chapter would not be relevant to other readers who would not recognize or know the names of who I write about.

This is the first time in my writing where I've encountered consciously a thing I have with my spoken voice. When I speak, sometimes, I find that I have more than one thing I want to say, yet only one mouth to say it. In this case, I had two things I wanted to type at the same time, and only one series of text could be formed. It's not as simple as pausing to choose which word to use, it's rather that there are two ideas that had started to form in the sequence that branched.

Do you think we each only have one path of life? Like, every event that's happened up to now is one linear series of experiences that we've not looped in or deviated from to reach this moment of time? It goes to the idea of how time is linear. There are ways we can manipulate how things are perceived (rewind on VHS (Ha! Elder point!)), or even adjusting the speed of audio recordings, yet our experience of life has almost always been a one-way directional flow.

I love time. Not the "I'm going to jail to serve time" type of time. I've had fears of others wishing to do some time to do harm to me. I mean 'time' rather by the notion of the passing and inverting of moments. I like how our own memories call back to the past and can be in our awareness, though our waking lives are almost always a one-way path. We tend not to start our days by going to bed and then waking up into sleep. My timelines are all strewn about from staying up really late (5:53 AM PST when I wrote this) though if I keep on writing, it's not all of a sudden going to be 5:52 AM. That moment's already happened and isn't ever going to repeat itself again in immediately perceivable reality.

Even if I could capture the memory of how I felt, the position of my thoughts, the exact oscillation of the air conditioner I hear, and the distance of time since I made the first accusation in this chapter, are all a memory and fragment of time that's never going to happen again. We have the words I wrote as fragments of what happened, as though they were etched in stone.

The actual real-life immediacy of the moment of then can't be re-experienced. That's when I have moments of déjà vu where I know I've *already* lived the experience is the closest to a purely shouled (fused) awareness of perception. Clearly put, we may psychically predict, foresee, or dream of future moments and find ourselves pass through them, though we can't rewind back into time to live that first perception.

Anyhow… What're the accusations? For me, it too doesn't matter what the personal accusations of myself are by some if those accusations don't reach you. What others accuse me of that I don't know (when I've not heard of their accusations) leaves me no way for me to confirm or denounce them even if they question a core truth of who I am. I've made many accusations of people that, even if true, should not have been made. This is where even if *not* slander, my own belief is that I'd like to withhold potentially negative opinions about some to not defame them. I also believe and value truth, though I too honour people secrets and private information. A kind bit of advice tonight from another that is if we don't want to share a truth, just to say we don't want to say so instead of lying about it.

That's another accusation I could make. I believe that a lot's been kept secret, shielded, and hidden from me. Yes, I could maybe more often ask what the truth is. When I don't know what the truth is and secrets are kept from me, it sometimes results in me not trusting fully. Even if there's no animosity or negative intent, when I think secrets are being kept, it can tweak my insecurities and paranoia of people. I also don't like how there are some that may have ultra-negative intent yet speak love and good to me, and when I don't fully believe them adjust my own responses. Don't worry, it's not you.

Dare though, yes, I mention some names in truth and secret. I then think of the secret code words and names and of not wanting to divulge identities, even to the ultra-few who do know them. There are some things I'd like to keep hidden. I sometimes don't want to hide who I am, yet sometimes want to hide who and what I know. If I'm to turn into glad-wrap (I may suffocate some, I'm often found in a roll, and the initial idea of being transparent) I also should remember some need a tinfoil hat. I dare then mention an initial node and the jokes that we made stemmed from the Misty. One thing I've filtered out of myself is a sometimes rude and vulgar sense of humour.

Is that the premise of a filter? That we catch some of the bad parts of ourselves so that they're either a) discarded, b) kept safe from the rest of the mix, or c) to be saved for later to throw at a person for a shared shred of experience. I think of how through time I've filtered out some of my own impurities, yet think that there are accusations and beliefs about me from my past that people think are still an issue. Then the wonder of how much of myself should I reveal, and the question, again, who's going to read this anyways!? Certainly not a person who is already dead. OR, what if the people that have died *are* still able to perceive through ourselves or their ghostly perception?

That's a really key thing. There's so much that we as humans don't know about the points of time that we've not experienced yet from the past or the future before birth or after death. Even when we catch ourselves in full awareness of the present we can be obsessively self-focused and centered when in our own perceptions. When we read, we get to take in a series of thought from a person and take in what they formed for us. When you read, though, remember that most people don't write as fast as you read. There also are the pauses between sentences, or, as it's been with me, even breaking for days between paragraphs. Add in the inceptive edits and restructure you can't perceive. When we read, it's all downloading what another put up and out seeming to be one fluid stream even if sourced from fragments of time.

Is there also safety in reading a book compared to hearing another speak? If we don't like what we're reading, it's pretty easy just to stop reading. (If you've read this far… THANK YOU!!!) It's not so difficult to just 'turn off' a book. If a real-life person is talking though, we can't just close them like a book. This makes me think of how violence is a thing of control. A person doesn't like what they're 'reading' (the person) they can then close the book on them (drop them). It's difficult to stop a person that's in our thoughts or metaphysically interacting with us because those things aren't physical. We can't as easily stop or pause what we perceive of them.

This is where some people would potentially be upset about not being able to control me. If my thoughts are all wild and out there, or if a person hears or sees me and doesn't like how I behave, then there could be the wish that I'm gone so the input stops. Bringing the book metaphor back in, what though if people love and adore the book (or in this case ourselves as people) and we *were* dropped by another. If there was no book to be read and people loved it, how can a life be easily stored, shared, or recorded? People need to be kept alive so that they may create more experiences and write more chapters with and for the people that they love and love them.

I'm an introverted person in the way that I source a lot of my thoughts from myself. I also know I like some people a lot and love interacting with groups of people. I like groups and crowds because of the random interactions and not just reading a predictable person like a preconceived book. My like and love of good, safe, random interactions is a super/amazing/ultra-high value and one that I sometimes try to pass onto other people with my own self. I want to be an interesting person to entertain, earn some love and luck, and also be kept around for another few decades because people like, love, and want me to be around in the live version and not need to read the book. I accuse you of being one of those people if I have, now, gone back to the initial person I accused in this chapter. Thank you Jeskai!!!

And Jund!?!? I dare not call you out by name, yet she knows your family name. I also think I've been a bit too pushy with book sales and sharing. I get gimmicky and think of marketing tactics. I start plotting and planning for the future and make promises that I've yet to fulfill. I've also labeled some people with the Magic codes while neglecting to include others. I'm guilty sometimes of latent care that's not yet been verified as truth. Some others do want to be a friend. I also note that I'm overly money focused sometimes and that I feel guilty for wanting to have a car and build a home in the future. I've not yet created books worthy of people investing their money and time into buying and reading them.

I also could accuse many of ruse and the clues that the dues I use are to fuse the blues with white and share the black right of speaking intonation into sight. I could accuse Dave as one to save and hold with the electoral fold of how some have told me they think it's from the Devil when it's really another person changing, evolving, and moving up to a certain level. I could accuse the curtains of remaining open since June other than once when the sun got too bright, and not because I stopped watching internet girls in the night. I could allude a rude notion of her dripping like a potion into the ocean of devotion trying to seal me like a notion to tend that I'm really too one who'd love to cuddle and not just find a fuck friend to befuddle.

Dave was right, though. I did use to swear a lot. I also used to lie a lot. I used to steal things. I also can accuse myself of being one to not conscribe to a life of hate just so that I could have money. I seem to think I also don't do some things just to find a mate. I note that I can, and maybe shall, dwell within my artistic freedom and creative integrity without slurring, vulgarity, or heralding contempt for me. There are some who may get jealous of who we are, what we do, or even what we have, yet I also invite others to keep a keen eye toward the future to assure we won't need to make a movie from the book.

There are things that I believe are the truth, even when I don't like those truths. I also hope that some of my intuitions of what is the case, don't manifest as fact. People that are right, good, noble, and even true bridge, bond, connect, and mesh in gladness. The chains of disparity allow a just resolution to evolve. There are many things that people could, can, or have accused me of, yet the forces of above and below (and of love) keep the toes in the warm water and out of the socks to assure that none are found trying to shatter a Mox.

CHAPTER ELEVEN – Scattered to the Winds

There's a dangerous boundary between working at a glacial pace, and freezing solid. There's also a fear of things expanding too quickly. I've had a belief and intuition of some things being for drastic expansion, yet deem them unsafe and a potential threat. Foundationally, there must be supports in place to assure that the whole project doesn't crash and go sideways.

Turn that into a different notion. What of deep trust, and whimsical fancy? I know I tainted the words by the use of the adjectives 'deep' and 'whimsical'. Deep usually is profound and can be considered monumental and solid. The whimsical notion is like the poetic flowers we were talking about in English class. The transient rose that may show or speak love, yet be also clouded with its proclamation of impending death. I prefer solid and sure things, yet some say that we must take on risks to reap a reward. I think this has its limitations.

Some people posit that we should be active, working, and busy. I barely ever have moments of boredom, and a rare few people attempt to intercept me from working or living when I'd prefer them not to interrupt. Then too, a random message from a loved AND trusted friend amd a super quick "Hi! Hello? Are you okay? Yes? Okay, carry on." can be far more loved and appreciated than an hour-long chat trap. When I feel trapped and constricted by people or situations, I turn into a reactive person that wishes to distance myself by great amounts of time.

When I'm reactive and trying to regain my own space and attitude, it's difficult to feel appreciation and love for some. When one is smothered, they generally aren't wanting to reach out and praise the one who's smothering them, even if it's a loved one. Take note of that. Just like the idea of overwatering seeds, we also should be careful not to drown out a relationship or friendship. I think I put a bit much water toward a dearly liked and loved friend today, with a slight and subtle idea she wanted a drink. I should remember, she's not my glass to drink.

I also fear, of the glacial pace, that my own craft and work isn't moving mountains, let alone being anywhere useful for others. I seem to think it doesn't matter what I think or say or do. I need to let the natural course of time occur to let us learn if these books are worthwhile and valuable. When there's no one in my space when I write or read, it's not easy to comprehend the vital feel and warmth of a female friend. I know I appreciate some guys I know, though the physical contact of a gal is a near-mythic thing for my own self. I best not get too thirsty for some things.

Throwing away concerns of a conspiracy is helpful. If I don't think of the idea of me being played like a riddle, rook, or pawn, then I also remind myself of some I love like my father Ron. Although we meet less than once a year in person, he is one of the people that I love and trust the most. My Mom and he separated when I was in grade seven, and though we've lived across an ocean for a long while, I'm happy to know he too knows, shares, and teaches me.

My Mom, I love her a bunch too. In another book, I wrote about the triangle of love/trust/appreciation and it's clear even cryptically now. There are some people I don't trust, yet know they are valuable and appreciated in my life. The love part for some isn't so easy, especially when I show my love sometimes through gifts and physical touch. I'm not one to have the words "I love you" stolen from my mouth in English easily. I like it a lot when I say those words and actually mean them. It takes a lot of appreciation, space, and trust to allow myself to say that sometimes.

Though what of the wishes: "Love and luck"? I say that a lot to some, and also write so at the end of some messages. My wish for there to be love isn't so much that *I'm* loved more, though rather that *I* learn how to truly love others. There are some people that say "I love you" often. My own doubt clouds my ability to utter the words "I love you" sometimes as I know I must believe and feel it truly, and it must *not* be coerced.

Is eternity too slow? Are there variations in the textbooks that share the looks into True that remind us there was a knot where two said "I do"? The vast violet hue cannot construe there are many few lies and deceits they delicately placed for us to view on the streets.

That's a question, though. How long is forever? It seems like years since I shoveled snow in the winter. That was literally the previous winter. The way I've been living since the first book in 2016 seems like I've ensnared many ideas and thoughts onto pages that have yet to be read. Some online mentors say it takes years for success to develop. Am I too impatient about not achieving publishing success after a mere year and a bit? It's weird too, because I seem to catch the winds of fate casting the smell of fertile soil heeding there may be some gravity gathering the ideas and works together.

The star fields are bright. They've taken millions and billions of years to form according to many astronomers. This idea of Earth is one that's theoretically coalesced five billion years ago. Am I tripping out over the span of five seasons? Be patient Rob! If we've only now entered autumn, that means too you should not forget what you planted in the spring! Think also about the fact of what you gather to plant for next year's harvest!

Seeds, they need time to grow.

And it seems (continuing a few days later) so do I.

I shut my eyes at this point of the chapter. I went inwards to the fact that there are some who know we come from a point of my own self-obsessive nature. The fact is, now, that I too know we're still decades away from being there in the same room. I don't know that my heart's grown exponentially for some that assure I must come from a point of love and near nothing else. I thank some key people like Arlinn and Gideon right now as two of the most subsonically influential people in my mind when I typed this.

I know I overcommit. I've souled myself to the walls of life with the fact that I know I shan't retract my devotion to some and the causes I pursue. There are some things I wish you help us renew, yet there too are some that find the kind thread round about the loom and assure we resume. The correct plume selects the tonects to not fume at the throat.

Sergio and the goat. Scott would remind the idea that there are some other people named the same that aim for peace like I had told Sarah. I called her Diamond Sprite today and noted later that I had double noted. This calls my own penance for the fact that I want so many people to receive authentic and true love from me that aren't just one focal nodal point of imagined life; rather a REAL love that's for a multitude.

I know I can never be you.

I opened my eyes again and see the words I put one after the next onto the screen. They seem to coddle my own lies and abuse. I've not told some of the ideas that she and, dare I say, I, aren't ones that we'll ever chase. This applies to many 'she's, even though I know that there are shackles and chains of my obsessive and proclamatic heart. The shackles are removed so that we prove I'm not for only one. I can't even claim yet that my own son is reminded there are still books to write. His Mom is one that I seem to cleave to and from my heart with a rite. I rely then solely on the fact that she'll claim herself as mine. With my own acceptance as to whom she is finds that life seems to wish me to free the key.

I'm exhausted. Decades have been spent, shattered, and wasted by my own lack of knowing how to respect and honour one that I know. My prison and prism-like nature cascades across the world. I still don't know. I've typed that a lot in these books, that one line "I still don't know" and it tappers my own innards. I don't like how much I've thought and yearned and pined for that spirit or idea of Natalie, when I know the real one is never going to be good for me. I know instinctively that I'm still obsessed, and though I've strayed so far away from the intent of *Finding Natalie*, I know that I may never find her. I know too, she should, and probably shouldn't, ever find me.

God is the key. I'm me. Two entirely different people and ideas. I've been vacant in my ability to actually share and show care for some. I know that my knowing of likeness and love is, like myself, exceptionally selfish. I like and love some people because of how *I* feel when I'm aware they are there. There could be the argument of people being valuable to us for other reasons, though then that's not a true like or love either. Liking someone because of what we gain from them, even if just a super rad and positive feeling, isn't appreciating the other person for who they are.

It's nice to be appreciated or valued. It's even better when we're treated with love, kindness, or affection because the other person actually loves us. I think my own expositions of thought haven't even yet brought me to my own understanding of how to love, and I still wish not to assert my position.

Maybe it's the case that my purpose is to find ways of showing and guiding others how to love so that the world improves as a place of good and kindness. It may mean that I must be isolated and set apart from the majority of other people that *do* know how to like and love. I'm inclined to think that I've learned how to value people, though I still don't know how love is how I treat and respect that person in action from our seeds of appreciation.

Io sono un piu troppo pazzo.

The realms of the spirit should be held from me. They are far too powerful for me to handle. There are times when I get home from a day or night out and then I'm brought back to my own home where there's silence and no pet, friend, or person. I don't know how I'd respond if there was an actual live human or cat to interact with when I get home. It's not so easy.

I sometimes hear the tones of voice of people in my mind. These allusions to people that matter and affect me in different ways while my mind tries to navigate. I've pushed away so many thoughts from my mind that when a kind and loving soul makes the risk to reach out to me, my own fear hides me away again. She may never read this. Have I squandered the resources of my being to have so many wistful notions that I just don't know any other idea as to what *real* love is?

Even with Felicia, she's one I like a lot. I also think I'm a creep for even thinking of being close to her. The embarrassing fact of not having a girlfriend for the past many years has left me thinking that I may have diffused any understanding of how to love a woman with any decency. I don't want a fuck buddy. It also is the case that I don't know what it's like to just snuggle with a gal that I do like and love. I've denied myself the own basic human need of a lovestone.

I was told the other day about how someone admired my optimism. I don't feel that way with my love life. Inversely, I also don't want to go out and about a lure in all sorts of attention with a deceptive premise. My own nature would accept physical contact as an idea or wish from gals, yet when I get close and personal, I feel like I've acted inappropriately. I used to have a huge issue with impulsive internet girls, and now that I don't do that, I wonder am I actually doing the right thing for the right reasons. Am I still based on a misguided belief (or rather idea) that it helps me be a good or decent person. I don't think that I know.

I know thar to lust on Internet girls was a True Lovestone betrayal. I also see it as a habit that was ethical to stop. I also could say that it's a manipulation to find real girls, yet I don't think that'll find me a real girlfriend either. If I want a 'real' girlfriend, then why don't I go out and actually approach gals and then abysmally try to form a new relationship? I don't want to have finally given up on the arbitrary notion that I haven't 'found' the one that called for my life even if she does or doesn't know who I am. Paradox… You seem aptly named right now, even when my own won faith is severely lacking the truth.

Poetic, right? *A Distant Glimmer*? Am I committed to the process, or just obsessively pushing for something that I'm afraid of? I don't think she'd like me. I don't think I really know who the real version of her is. I got hooked up on an imagined girl that's yet to tell the words to my face that she has never even thought of me, let alone flattered by how I comprehend she's more than the world understands. There are realms of the soul and spirit that have tainted, clouded, and abused my own sanity by understanding my own heart. I'm a pawn to paw and prod and plod to God asking the bare question "Why am I here?"

If I'm on this planet for any reason that I yet know, other than a substantial series of graces, positive betrayals, and manipulation from those I've yet to believe in, I still think I can't just declare a purpose and then fulfill it. I wish, hope, and pray that I'm not the one they wish to put up as a savior claimed known by the world. I'm, still, just a kid who wants to know where his family and home is. I live in an apartment, I have many luxuries and basic supplies, and I too have the damned blasted entrapments of a life I never wish to love, leave, or lose. I let my typographical error stand as using a V not and S when I know I'm too tired of thinking about one when almost everything in my perceived reality (including my own mind) believes I should be eternally alone to create for the rest of life.

Even if everyone drinks from the same fountain, that fountain knows that it's made of stone. It's used by people that know what it's like to drink, yet don't know what it's like to be one themselves. Is it that also that fountains provide for many, yet can't go to visit the other fountains? Some may go from fountain to fountain catching the universal gifts that are shared by them, yet never understand that some humans too wish to be born of flesh.

A spirit can only call my heart for so long. She's become almost vacant from my belief. Other stones have seemed alluring to behold and the lack of love I seem to emit and project is too clear. Yet once in a while, I know that it's being projected outwards like a jet around the center of the galaxy; pressing outwards with high intensity illuminating the other stars in the binary system that seems to be falling inwards. Imploding in upon the realms of sleep to again be teleported back to wakefulness wondering so many things, yet not clearly enough how my own muddle may find escape velocity.

As a separate side note about my work and creative process, the book *Fragments of Intent* was to be accepted by Ingram. Once accepted to Ingram as a wholesaler, I'll be able to market the books to bookstores to carry copies of the work. My faith in the success and worth of *The First Three Fountains* is near nil. I'll market and promote the book to bookstores for sales to finance my own future wants such as the Glass House, though you should know I now hold little faith those books sell. Even if my work holds novelty in some people's imagination, even with this book, I still didn't believe that I'll find your distant glimmer, Aeris.

Celest and Paradox. I can't imagine you yet. Even if another thinks I'm optimistic and worthy, I sometimes don't think that. I see myself as having the potential to create amazing works, though my faith in there being enough support for what I form to actually provide as negligible also. I write for our future, yet our future includes a great many more than just ourselves, even as I yet often feel as one.

For those that read this book; I assure you that even though I feel overinvolved and separate from those that do like or love me, I can't tell you how I'll make amends for the fact that I shattered the stone. I've discarded my hopes, my goals, my wishes, and my dreams, and then scrambled to hold onto the basic gladness that I'm alive. I know that I can't guarantee what my future is, though it's worth knowing that at least there are some rare shards that *Fragments of Intent* have scattered like seeds to the wind.

Shards of my Soul. That seems right. It's not that I want to shatter the mirror, though that kid that I see in it does tell me some things. There's work to do. Some people say that music, books, and other art are an extension of our souls. When we harmonize them and gather the components, it may clearly show who we are and who it is that forms what we perceive.

Thank You explicitly for letting me falter and flounder through this creative journey and process. I promise many things, yet tomorrow isn't something I can predict. Though we may have different guiding motives, I must remember to enjoy the expositions of my being as something to help provide.

Yet still, I call forth the whims and wishes of above and below to tow along the raft of my craft. Though some have laughed at me, my goals, my wishes, and my dreams, there are teaming waters that are brought forward. We started with the idea of yesterday into faith, yet perchance I need to sit in the boat alone to understand the pain of the rain to let the fortitude of sanity remain.

ACKNOWLEDGMENTS

Thank You (capitalized) and the friends, family, and communities that have shaped me and my work. For the fact that we are all on this planet is pretty miraculous. I thank the forces of life and death for allowing me to persist and move onward with our work, alive.

My Mother, Father, and my Stepparents have been vital in helping me create. I thank them for the support, guidance, and grace to allow me many parts of the life that I live.

I thank you, the readers, for reading what I have written. If it was not for the fact that people actually read, process, and share my books, I'm not clear on what the results of our work would be.

I also put thanks out to those that have guided me indirectly through wish, prayer, and affiliation even if we haven't met in locative 'real' life. There are many forces on Earth that help keep the balance, and I pray each the full elements and intents of PLU8R. It's a word I use that stems beyond just Peace, Love, Unity, and Respect using the '8', yet it's crucial to my own understanding and wishes of and for life.

For the fact that the first six Fountains are complete, I'm glad, exhausted, and not ready to quit. Although I've yet to see or understand the consequences of forming these works, I give a wish and prayer of thanks out to the Universe and God for them to do with them as they wish.

It starts with a seed
Floating in the wind
We see them land
Take root

.

Thank You!

Made in the USA
Columbia, SC
02 December 2017